Penguin Education

Sale of Goods and Hi
Second Edition

R. Lowe

Foundations of Law

Advisory Board
I. H. Jacob
S. B. Marsh
Neil Merritt
Harry Street
K. W. Wedderburn

R. Lowe

Sale of Goods and Hire-Purchase

Second Edition

Penguin Books

Penguin Books Ltd, Harmondsworth,
Middlesex, England
Penguin Books Inc, 7110 Ambassador Road,
Baltimore, Md 21207, USA
Penguin Books Australia Ltd,
Ringwood, Victoria, Australia

First published 1968
Second edition 1972
Copyright © R. Lowe 1968, 1972

Made and printed in Great Britain by
C. Nicholls & Company Ltd
Set in Monotype Times

Contents

Preface to Second Edition

This edition takes into account the various changes which have taken place since the publication of the first edition in 1968. These changes are not very far-reaching, but major changes may well be on the way. The Law Commission has recommended amendments to the Sale of Goods Act, and in particular the right of parties to exclude the terms implied by the Act. At the time of going to press the Bill promised in the 1971 Queen's Speech has not appeared. I have, however, dealt with the Law Commission's proposals (which are likely to form the basis of new legislation) at the end of chapter 5. Much more far-reaching is the Crowther Report on Consumer Credit which proposes a complete re-shaping of the law relating to credit transactions in general and consumer credit transactions in particular. It is quite likely that legislation will be forthcoming in a year or so; accordingly I have added a chapter (chapter 17) to deal with the Crowther proposals.

I would like to thank my friend Professor R. M. Goode of Queen Mary College, University of London, for reading the proofs and making a number of very valuable suggestions. I would also like to thank the publishers for preparing the index.

The law is stated as at 12 June 1972.

Part One
Sale of Goods

1 Introduction

'The bag of coal contained a detonator.'
'The underpants were made with too much sulphite.'
'There were worms in the pork chops.'
'The dealer said, "It's a good little bus – I'd stake my life on it."'
'There was a snail in the ginger beer.'

These dramatic illustrations are taken from actual cases involving the sale of goods. There is no doubt that the sale of goods is by far the most important of all commercial contracts. Millions of these contracts are made each day – in supermarkets, shops, market places, restaurants, pubs, business houses and private homes. They may be made face-to-face or by telephone, telegram, telex or letter. Fortunately, only a very small proportion of these contracts gives rise to problems like those set out at the beginning of this chapter. The great majority gives rise to no problems: the seller delivers the correct goods at the correct time and place, and the buyer pays the price. Nevertheless, it is important to have a sound knowledge of the law relating to sale of goods in order to know what the obligations of each party are, and also to know what remedies are available if either the seller or the buyer fails to perform his obligations.

The law relating to sale of goods has been developed over many hundreds of years, and over the years one can see different social attitudes reflected in the decided cases. In the eighteenth and early nineteenth centuries, for example, the emphasis was on letting the parties make whatever arrangements they pleased, with a minimum of interference from the law. This was reflected in the doctrine of *caveat emptor* which means 'let the buyer beware'. Under this doctrine it was for the buyer to satisfy himself that the goods were merchantable and fit for his purpose. Gradually, however, the mood changed and cases were decided which showed that a seller who was a dealer in the goods did incur certain liabilities if they were faulty.

The law developed as part of the common law – it was built up as the result of cases decided in the courts. Now one problem which gets larger as the years go by is that of finding out what the law is on any given point. In a case-law system, the law is buried in law reports going back for hundreds of years, so that even a lawyer may have great difficulty in making sure that he has not overlooked a relevant case. For instance, in *Tucker* v. *Farm and General Investment Trust Ltd* (1966), the Court of Appeal was asked to decide this question: If an owner of livestock lets it out on hire-purchase, who owns the offspring? In deciding that the offspring belonged to the hirer, the court based its decision on a case decided as long ago as 1586! The task of having to fish out the answer from all these reports is clearly inconvenient, time-consuming and inefficient. Accordingly, when the law has become fairly settled, it is sometimes 'codified' – i.e. it is set out in a single Act of Parliament. In the case of sale of goods, codification took place at the end of the last century, and the Sale of Goods Act 1893, is the basis of the modern law of sale of goods. Two observations can be made about this Act:

1. When it was passed, the case law was in a somewhat unsatisfactory state, largely as the result of the gradual change from 'let the buyer beware' to the principle of consumer protection. The draftsman of the Act, Sir Mackenzie Chalmers, sought to reproduce the case law exactly as he found it, and accordingly the Act is not as good as it might have been had it been passed some twenty or thirty years later, when the case law might have been less confusing and contradictory.

2. The Act does not contain the whole of the law. In the first place the Act expressly provides in section 61 that the common

law rules shall continue to apply unless they are inconsistent with the express provisions of the Act. Secondly, the Act is now more than seventy years old, and some of the more modern types of contract, such as hire-purchase and export sales, have developed independently of the Act. Thirdly, there is a large amount of case law illustrating the operation of the Act in particular circumstances. Fourthly, the Act itself has been amended from time to time (for examples of this see pages 19, 46, 62). Finally, it may sometimes be necessary to refer back to the pre-1893 case law. Although the whole object of a codifying Act is to avoid the need for this, a reference to earlier cases may be justified where the Act is ambiguous or doubtful, or if it is sought to show that particular words had acquired a particular technical meaning. These rules were laid down by Lord Herschell in *Bank of England* v. *Vagliano Bros* (1891), and although his words related to a different codifying Act, they can be taken to be of general application.

One further point of vital importance must be stressed at the very beginning. The Act was passed at a time when the concepts of 'freedom of contract' and 'sanctity of contract' had an almost divine ring about them, and dominated legal thought. Accordingly, the Act (unlike the Hire-Purchase Act 1965) does not set out to make a contract for the parties. It is for them to make their own bargain, and the Act merely lays down what is to happen where a matter is not covered by express agreement. Section 55 reads:

Where any right, duty or liability would arise under a contract of sale by implication of law, it may be negatived or varied by express agreement or by the course of dealing between the parties or by usage, if the usage be such as to bind both parties to the contract.

The freedom given by this section has been extensively used (and sometimes abused) by draftsmen of exemption clauses, with the result that a buyer receiving defective and even dangerous goods has sometimes found himself without a remedy because of a small-print exemption clause excluding the various conditions implied by the Act. This subject has recently received much attention from judges, writers, consumer associations and the Law Commission. The Commission has recently recommended the banning of exemption clauses in consumer sales and it seems that amending legislation is not very far away. A brief summary of the Law Commission's views is set out on page 90.

2 The Contract of Sale

In this part of the book any reference to 'the Act' is to the Sale of Goods Act 1893, and any reference to a section is to that section of the Act.

Definitions

A Contract of Sale is defined in section 1(1) as:

a contract whereby the seller transfers or agrees to transfer the property in goods to the buyer for a money consideration called the price. There may be a contract of sale between one part owner and another.

What is property? It is vital to grasp at the outset that 'property' is used in the Act to mean 'ownership' and is quite distinct from physical possession. It is the transfer of ownership that is all-important, and we shall see later that a seller who transfers physical possession but fails to transfer ownership will usually have to refund the entire purchase price, even though the buyer has used the goods for a considerable time.

Sale and agreement to sell. Section 1(3) makes it clear that the term 'contract of sale' covers two distinct transactions, namely a 'sale' and an 'agreement to sell'. It reads as follows:

where under a contract of sale the property in the goods is transferred from the seller to the buyer the contract is called a sale; but where the transfer of property is to take place at a future time or subject to some condition thereafter to be fulfilled, the contract is called an agreement to sell.

The distinction between 'sale' and 'agreement to sell' is an important one because (for example) the risk of accidental loss will generally be on the buyer in the case of a sale and on the seller in the case of an agreement to sell. The detailed rules relating to passing of property are considered in the next chapter.

Conditional contracts. Section 1(2) states that a contract of sale may be absolute or conditional, and section 5(2) provides that there may be a contract for the sale of goods, the acquisition of which by the seller depends on a contingency which may or may not happen. Thus if a seller agreed to sell '200 tons of potatoes to be grown on Blackdown Farm', and the crop failed to mature owing to a drought, the contract might be construed as 'conditional' on the maturing of the crop, so that neither party would have any rights under the contract if the crop failed. Alternatively, such a contract might be treated as frustrated, so that the Law Reform (Frustrated Contracts) Act 1943, would govern the rights of the parties (*Howell* v. *Coupland* (1876) as explained in *re Wait* (1927)).

This type of conditional contract must be sharply distinguished from a 'conditional sale agreement' (see p. 165).

What are goods? Section 62, which is the definition section, defines goods in the following way:

'Goods' include all chattels personal other than things in action and money. . . . The term includes emblements, industrial growing crops and things attached to or forming part of the land which are agreed to be severed before sale or under the contract of sale.

In English law, property can be broadly classified as follows:

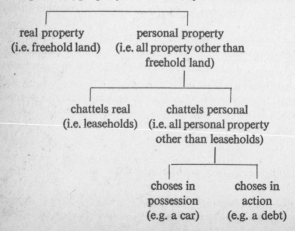

The term 'chose in action' refers to property which cannot be reduced into physical possession and which requires legal action if it is wrongly withheld. Examples include cheques, shares, theatre tickets, rights under an insurance policy and debts. If real property, chattels real, and choses in action are eliminated, we are left with choses in possession, and it is this type of property which the Act defines as 'goods'.

Money. The reason why money is excluded from the definition of goods is that, in the words of Channell J. 'when current coins of the realm have passed *bona fide* from hand to hand as currency and as money they are considered, for all purposes of property in them, not to be identifiable' (*Moss* v. *Hancock* (1899)). If, however, a specific coin were transferred as such (e.g. to a collector), it is thought that the contract would be one for the sale of goods.

Produce of the soil. The term 'emblements' is a very old one and may be defined as vegetable produce which matures once a year. In order to encourage good farming, a tenant who had sown one of these crops was allowed to reap it, even though his tenancy of the land had come to an end before the crop matured. 'Industrial growing crops' has a similar meaning, but its meaning may be slightly wider so as to include crops not maturing within the year. All these crops are now within the definition of 'goods'. Finally, the term 'things forming part of the land' includes such items as grass, trees and fruit on trees, but not the soil itself. In *Morgan* v. *Russell* (1909) a seller agreed to sell some slag lying on a piece of land, but when the buyer came to take delivery, the slag was claimed by someone else. The buyer sued the seller for damages for non-delivery under section 51 of the Act, but the court found as a fact that the slag had merged with the soil and no longer had separate identifiable existence. Consequently, the slag was not 'goods' at all, and the action failed.

Existing and future goods. Section 5 provides that the contract may relate to existing goods owned or possessed by the seller, or to goods to be manufactured or acquired by the seller after the making of the contract. The latter type of goods are called 'future goods' and a sale of such goods takes effect as an agreement to sell them (section 5(3)).

Formation of the contract

The general law of contract governs the formation of a contract for the sale of goods, and the provisions of the Act are largely declaratory of the common law. Thus:

1. There must be offer and acceptance

It will be recalled that an offer must be distinguished from an invitation to treat. The seller who puts an attractive new tape recorder into his shop window does so to attract custom; he is not legally bound to sell it if a customer comes in and wants to buy it. Similarly, when a customer picks up an article from the shelf and goes to the cash desk to pay, it seems that no contract is concluded until payment has been made (*Lacis* v. *Cashmarts* (1969)). If, therefore, the article were a bottle which burst before the customer reached the cash desk, the customer could not claim damages for breach of contract since at that time no contract had been made. He might, however, have an action for negligence against the shopkeeper or the manufacturer, but only if negligence and damage could be proved.

2. There must be an intention to create legal relations

This is generally inferred from the surrounding circumstances but it can be excluded if the transaction is expressed as 'binding in honour only' (*Rose and Frank Co.* v. *J. R. Crompton & Bros Ltd* (1925)).

3. The contract need not be in any particular form

Section 3 reads:

Subject to the provisions of this Act, and of any statute in that behalf, a contract of sale may be made in writing . . . or by word of mouth or may be implied from the conduct of the parties.

Provided that nothing in this section shall affect the law relating to corporations.

Three points deserve brief mention. First, the words 'subject to the provisions of this Act' refer to section 4. This section, which required certain formalities where the price was £10 or more, has been repealed by the Law Reform (Enforcement of Contracts) Act 1954. Secondly, the words 'and of any statute in that behalf' indicate that, under certain other Acts, formalities are required. An important modern example is the Hire-Purchase Act 1965, under which certain conditional-sale and credit-sale agreements must be in writing (see pp. 165–6). Finally, the concluding words have lost their importance since the effect of the Companies Act 1948, and the Corporate Bodies Contracts Act 1960, is to enable corporations to make a contract in the same way as private persons.

4. *The parties must have capacity to contract*

Section 2, which again is largely declaratory, provides that:

Capacity to buy and sell is regulated by the general law concerning capacity to contract, and to transfer or acquire property.

Provided that where necessaries are sold and delivered to [a minor] or to a person who by reason of mental incapacity or drunkenness is incompetent to contract, he must pay a reasonable price therefor.

Necessaries in this section means goods suitable to the condition in life of such [minor] or other person and to his actual requirements at the time of the sale and delivery.

The law relating to minors' contracts has been described as 'absurdly technical' (Latey Committee on Age of Majority, Cmnd 3342, at p. 71), and there is no doubt that the present law, which was clearly designed for the minor's protection, can be used by unscrupulous minors to avoid their just obligations. In the sale of goods field, the position depends on whether or not the goods are 'necessaries'. If they are not necessaries, the Infants Relief Act 1874, firmly declares the contract to be 'absolutely void'; but despite the uncompromising sound of these words, it probably means only that the contract cannot be enforced against the minor. If the goods are necessaries and they are actually delivered to the minor, we have just seen that he must pay a reasonable price. Since a tradesman is on risk if the goods do not turn out to be necessaries, it is not surprising that few tradesmen will grant credit to a minor unless an adult enters into a contract of guarantee or indemnity. From the tradesmen's point of view, an indemnity is clearly preferable in view of the decision of Oliver J. in *Coutts and Co.* v. *Browne-Lecky* (1947) that where the main contract was void a guarantee of the minor's obligations under that 'contract' was also void.

Fortunately the anomalies and injustices discussed in the previous paragraph have lost much of their practical importance; the age of majority has recently been reduced from twenty-one to eighteen (Family Law Reform Act 1969) and accordingly a person is only a 'minor' if he is under eighteen.

5. There must be consideration

We have already seen that it must be in money. A contract can, however, be one of sale, even though the consideration is partly goods or partly money, or even the alternative of goods or money (*Dawson (Clapham) Ltd* v. *Dutfield* (1936)). Thus, in the common case where a new car is sold and an old car is taken in part-exchange, the transfer of the new car will clearly be a contract of sale; it is not certain whether the transfer of the old car could be so treated, since there is no money consideration for it.

The price can be fixed (1) by the contract itself (this is the usual case); or (2) by course of dealing; or (3) in a manner laid down by the contract (e.g. valuation). These fairly obvious points are to be found in section 8(1). Section 8(2) goes on to provide that, if the price is not fixed in one of these ways, the buyer must pay 'a reasonable price', reasonableness being a question of fact depending on the circumstances of each particular case. It seems that section 8(2) will apply only where the contract itself is silent as to the price. If it provides that the goods are to be sold at 'a price to be agreed', the negotiations and documents must be carefully examined to see whether the parties have clearly intended to bind themselves by their contract, or whether they are still negotiating. In the former case, the courts may well seek to give effect to a commercial document by implying a term that a reasonable price is to be paid (*Foley* v. *Classique Coaches Ltd* (1934)). In the latter case there is no contract at all (*May and Butcher* v. *The King* (1934)).

It may sometimes occur that S agrees to sell goods to B and they agree that the price shall be fixed by the valuation of a third party. If for some reason the third party cannot or does not make the valuation, the contract is avoided (section 9). This means that S and B must be restored to their previous position and neither of them has any rights under the contract. Section 9, however, modifies this general position in two cases. After stating the general rule, the section reads as follows:

1. . . . provided that if the goods or any part thereof have been delivered to and appropriated by the buyer he must pay a reasonable price therefor.

2. Where such a third party is prevented from making the valuation by the fault of the seller or buyer, the party not in fault may maintain an action for damages against the party in fault.

These words are self-explanatory.

Contract of sale distinguished from other transactions

Having analysed the nature and the essential elements of a contract of sale, it may be useful to round off this chapter by distinguishing this contract from other similar contracts.

Contract of exchange

A contract of exchange is one where there is no money consideration. Thus if X transfers his film projector to Y in return for Y's tape recorder, the Sale of Goods Act would not apply.

Contract of hire-purchase

For reasons which will be explained later, the contract of hire-purchase has developed in a strange and artificial way.

The essence of the contract today is a hiring coupled with an *option* to purchase. Until the option is exercised, the hirer is not a *buyer* as defined by section 62 of the Act and accordingly the Act does not apply to hire-purchase. (The case of *Felston Tile Co. Ltd* v. *Winget Ltd* (1936) appears to have overlooked this point and is almost certainly wrongly decided.)

Contract for work and labour

Whenever A agrees to produce a chattel for B, there is an element of sale, and an element of work and labour. How should the contract be classified? After earlier doubts, it now seems clear that the courts will examine the contract as a whole to decide whether the substance of the contract was the production of a chattel for sale, or the skill of the workmen in producing it. In the former case, it will be classified as sale of goods. Examples include the manufacture of a ship's propeller (*Cammell Laird* v. *Manganese Brass Co.* (1934)), the making of a 900-guinea fur coat with fur supplied by the furrier (*Marcel Furriers Ltd* v. *Tapper* (1953)), and the painting of pictures ordered in bulk by a dealer (*Isaacs* v. *Hardy* (1884)). In the latter case, the contract will be a contract for work and labour. Examples include the painting of a portrait for 250 guineas (*Robinson* v. *Graves* (1935)), and the repair of a car, even though new parts were supplied (*Stewart* v. *Reavell's Garage* (1952)). In *Samuels* v. *Davis* (1943) the Court of Appeal had to consider the distressing case of a set of false teeth which did not fit. They held it was unnecessary to decide whether this was sale of goods or work and labour, since there was an implied term in either case that the denture should be reasonably fit for its purpose.

Formerly, the distinction was often of vital importance, since section 4 required formalities in the case of sale of goods, whereas no formalities were required for work and labour contracts. Now that section 4 has been repealed, the distinction has lost much of its importance.

Self-tuition test 1

1. How did the law relating to sale of goods develop, and where is the modern law to be found?

2. What is the meaning of the word 'property' in the Sale of Goods Act?

3. How is a 'sale' distinguished from an 'agreement to sell'?

4. Are the following items 'goods':
   (a) money.
   (b) a cheque.
   (c) a crop of wheat growing in a field.
   (d) trees?

5. A customer goes into a shop and asks for a television set shown in the shop window as available for sale at £60. The shopkeeper says that the label was a mistake and that the true price is £80. The customer insists on having it for £60. What is the legal position?

6. What special rules (if any) apply where the buyer of goods is a minor?

7. What is the effect of an arrangement between S and B that S will supply all petrol which B may require for the next two years at a price to be agreed from time to time?

8. X agrees to sell 100 tons of corn to Y at a price to be fixed by the valuation of Z, who dies before he can start the valuation. What is the position? What would be the position if Z had not died but X had prevented Z from making the valuation?

9. How is a contract of exchange distinguished from a contract for the sale of goods?

10. How is a contract for work and labour distinguished from a contract for the sale of goods, and why has the distinction lost much of its importance?

For answers, see p. 178.

3 Passing of the Property and Risk

We saw in the last chapter that the transfer of property (ownership) from seller to buyer was the central feature of the contract of sale of goods. In this chapter it is proposed to examine the precise moment when the property passes and the reasons why this is important. It must be emphasized that 'property' is an abstract concept and is quite distinct from physical possession. Thus, a buyer may have (a) property *and* possession (e.g. X buys a car and takes delivery), or (b) property without possession (X buys a car and agrees to take delivery in a week's time), or (c) possession without property (X takes away his new car after agreeing that no property will pass to him until his cheque has been cleared).

Why is the passing of property important? In the first place, we shall see that, as a general rule, the risk of accidental loss or damage passes with the property (see section 20, p. 34). Secondly, the buyer's right to claim the goods on the seller's bankruptcy will generally depend on whether or not the property had passed to the buyer. Thirdly, once the property has passed, the seller can sue the buyer for the price (see section 49, p. 110). Finally, the passing of the property as between seller and buyer is important where the goods have been resold to a third party, because a resale by the owner will always pass a good title to the third party, whereas a resale by a non-owner will pass title only if the sale comes within one of the rules considered in the next chapter.

Classification of goods

We saw in the last chapter that goods could be either existing or future, and that a sale of future goods operated as an agreement to sell them. Another and much more important distinction is that between specific, ascertained, and unascertained goods. Only the first of these terms is defined in the Act.

Specific goods are defined by section 62 as 'goods identified and agreed upon at the time a contract of sale is made'. Thus, if S shows B his supercharged Bentley and B agrees to buy it, that is a sale of specific goods.

Unascertained goods can be either purely generic goods (e.g. '100 bottles of beer' or 'a Morris car') or goods forming part of a larger consignment (e.g. '20 tons of wheat from the consignment of 50 tons on board S.S. *London*').

Ascertained goods probably means goods which are identified and agreed upon *after* the making of the contract (*re Wait* (1927)). Thus, if a car dealer agreed to sell 'a Morris 1100 car', this would be initially a contract for unascertained goods, if at the time of the contract no particular car was agreed upon. If, a few days later, the dealer obtained such a car from the manufacturers and the buyer agreed to take it under his contract, the goods would then become 'ascertained'.

The importance of this classification can be seen by examining the case of *re Wait*.

B bought '1000 tons of wheat on board S.S. *Challenger*'. He re-sold 500 tons to C who paid by cheque. When the ship arrived B was bankrupt. Nothing had been done to separate C's 500 tons from the bulk. Accordingly, no property had passed to C (see section 16 below). C therefore applied for specific performance of the contract to deliver 500 tons to him. By section 52 this can only be ordered if the goods are 'specific or ascertained'. As they were at all times unascertained, the action failed. The result was that C was merely an unsecured creditor in the bankruptcy of B.

Passing of property in specific goods

In the case of specific or ascertained goods the crucial factor is the intention of the parties because, by section 17, the property is transferred from seller to buyer when the parties intend it to be transferred. By section 17(2):

For the purpose of ascertaining the intention of the parties regard shall be had to the terms of the contract, the conduct of the parties and the circumstances of the case.

Thus, in an export sale, the retention of the bill of lading by the seller is a strong indication that the seller has retained the property in the goods (see *Cheetham & Co. Ltd* v. *Thornham Spinning Co. Ltd* (1964) and see also section 19, pp. 31–2).

Usually, however, the contract is completely silent on the question of intention, and here the first four rules of section 18 become all-important. The opening words of section 18 must not, however, be overlooked:

Unless a different intention appears the following are rules for ascertaining the intention of the parties as to the time at which the property in the goods is to pass to the buyer.

By far the most important of these four rules is the first one It reads:

Rule 1 Where there is an unconditional contract for the sale of specific goods in a deliverable state, *the property in the goods passes to the buyer when the contract is made*, and it is immaterial whether the time of payment or the time of delivery, or both, be postponed. [Italics supplied.]

The significance of this rule can be seen from an example:

X goes to Y's furniture store and agrees to buy a suite of furniture for £100. It is agreed that the furniture is to be delivered and paid for in three weeks' time when X's new house will be ready. Just before the expiry of the three weeks, Y's storeroom and all the contents are destroyed by fire for which Y is in no way to blame. *Result*: (1) By section 18 rule 1, the property has passed to X. (2) By section 20 the risk has also passed to X and, accordingly, (3) X must still pay the full £100 to Y.

It must be emphasized that this rule is subject to a contrary intention. In *re Anchor Line (Henderson Bros) Ltd* (1937):

The sellers agreed to sell a crane to the buyers. The contract referred to a 'deferred purchase price' of £6000 and the buyers agreed to pay annual sums by way of 'depreciation'. The Court of Appeal held that the buyers would never have agreed to pay a sum for depreciation of their own goods, and that accordingly it must have been the intention of the parties that the property was to remain in the sellers until the price had been paid.

Whether there is a contrary intention or not will of course depend on the facts of each case; but it is interesting to note the remarks of Diplock L. J. in a recent case that 'in modern times very little is needed to give rise to the inference that the property in specific goods is to pass only on delivery or payment' (*R. V. Ward Ltd* v. *Bignall* (1967)). A contrary intention will not, however, over-ride rule 1 unless it is present *at the time of the contract*. In *Dennant* v. *Skinner* (1948):

A fraudulent person called King went to an auction and bid for a Standard car. He was the highest bidder and the car was knocked down to him. He went into the auctioneer's showroom, described himself as the son of a well-known garage proprietor, and asked whether he could take the car away and pay by cheque. The auctioneer agreed, on condition that King signed a form stating that his cheque would be cleared and that 'the ownership of the vehicle will not pass to me' until the cheque had been cleared. King signed the form, took the car away and sold it to B. When the cheque was dishonoured, the auctioneer tried to recover the car from B. Hallett, J. held that: (1) the property had already passed to King under section 18 rule 1 as soon as the hammer fell; (2) consequently the form signed by King was ineffective, and accordingly (3) King was owner of the car when he sold it to B and B had acquired a good title.

Presumably a statement in the auction particulars that 'no ownership shall pass until payment in cash' would oust section 18, rule 1.

The next two rules of section 18 are concerned with cases where the seller has to do something to the goods:

Rule 2 Where there is a contract for the sale of specific goods and the seller is bound to do something to the goods, for the purpose of putting them into a deliverable state, the property does not pass until such thing be done and the buyer has notice thereof.

Rule 3 Where there is a contract for the sale of goods in a deliverable state but the seller is bound to weigh, measure, test or do some other act or thing with reference to the goods for the purpose of ascertaining the price, the property does not pass until such act or thing be done and the buyer has notice thereof.

Section 62(4) states that goods are in a deliverable state when they are in such a state that the buyer would under the contract be bound to take delivery of them. Thus:

S agrees to sell a specific consignment of peaches, and to pack them into boxes each containing 30 tins. As the buyer is not bound to take them until they have been packed by the seller, they are not in a 'deliverable state' at the time of the contract and, accordingly, rule 2, and *not* rule 1, will apply.

Rule 3 requires no comment, except to emphasize that if the weighing, etc., is to be done by the buyer or a third party, the matter will be governed by rule 1 and not by rule 3 (*Turley* v. *Bates* (1863)).

Rule 4 deals with a fairly common commercial transaction – the delivery of goods to a prospective buyer 'on approval' or on 'sale or return'. It provides that in such a case property passes to the buyer:

(a) When he signifies his approval or acceptance to the seller or does any other act adopting the transaction.
(b) If he does not signify his approval or acceptance to the seller but retains the goods without giving notice of rejection, then if a time has been fixed for the return of the goods, on the expiration of such time, and, if no time has been fixed, on the expiration of a reasonable time. What is a reasonable time is a question of fact.

This type of transaction is fairly common in the jewellery trade, and there have been several reported cases where a retail jeweller has received jewellery 'on approval' from a manufacturer and has then pledged it with a pawnbroker. It is clear from *Kirkham* v. *Attenborough* (1897) and from *London Jewellers Ltd* v. *Attenborough* (1934) that such pledging will be an act 'adopting the transaction' within rule 4(a) and this will pass the property. The way for the manufacturer to avoid this result is to stipulate that 'no property shall pass until payment has been received'. Since the contract specifies a 'contrary intention' there is no room for section 18 at all and the pledging of the goods will not pass the property (*Weiner* v. *Gill* (1906)).

What happens if the goods are damaged during the approval

period? If the damage is due to the fault of the buyer, he will clearly be liable, but if it is purely accidental, the risk will remain with the seller since the property will not have passed. Thus in *Elphick* v. *Barnes* (1880) a horse which was out on approval died during the approval period, and it was held that the seller could not sue for the price. If, however, the buyer allows a reasonable time to elapse without intimating rejection, the property will pass to him and he cannot defeat an action for the price by claiming that the goods were accidentally damaged (*Poole* v. *Smith's Car Sales* (*Balham*) *Ltd* (1962)).

Finally, what happens if the goods are seized by a sheriff during the approval period? This is what happened in *re Ferrier* (1944):

An antique dealer gave some antiques to Mrs Ferrier on seven days sale or return. After only two days, a sheriff acting on behalf of one of Mrs Ferrier's creditors entered her premises and seized some goods there, including the antiques. She took no further action during the seven day period. Subsequently the dealer claimed them from the sheriff. It was held that (1) Mrs Ferrier had not 'retained' the antiques for seven days within rule 4(b) and accordingly (2) they still belonged to the dealer who was entitled to recover them from the sheriff.

If the goods were stolen during the approval period, the principle of *re Ferrier* would presumably apply, and the buyer would not be liable for the price, although he would be liable to pay damages if the theft was due to his negligence.

The genuine 'sale or return' contract must be distinguished from the situation where a seller sends goods which the 'buyer' has not ordered at all. The Sale of Goods Act does not deal with such a transaction and in certain circumstances it takes effect as a gift of the goods (see Unsolicited Goods and Services Act 1971).

Passing of property in unascertained goods

It will be recalled that goods are unascertained if they have no separate identity at the time of the contract. The key provision here is section 16, which reads:

where there is a contract for the sale of unascertained goods no property in the goods is transferred to the buyer unless and until the goods are ascertained.

An interesting attempt to exclude this provision was made in *McDougall* v. *Aeromarine of Emsworth Ltd* (1958), where S agreed to build a pleasure yacht for B and the contract provided that the first instalment was to be paid by B on the signing of the contract, whereupon the yacht and all materials used in its construction were to become 'the absolute property of the buyer'. Diplock J. (as he then was) held that, despite the clause, no property could pass to the buyer, because the materials were not physically in existence at that time.

In practice, the passing of property in unascertained goods is frequently governed by section 18, rule 5, although this rule, like the others, only applies unless a different intention appears. Rule 5 reads as follows:

1. Where there is a sale of unascertained or future goods by description, and goods of that description and in a deliverable state are unconditionally appropriated to the contract, either by the seller with the assent of the buyer, or by the buyer with the assent of the seller, the property in the goods thereupon passes to the buyer. Such assent may be express or implied, and may be given either before or after the appropriation is made.

2. Where, in pursuance of the contract, the seller delivers the goods to the buyer or to a carrier or other bailee ... for the purpose of transmission to the buyer and does not reserve the right of disposal, he is deemed to have unconditionally appropriated the goods to the contract.

Thus, in order to pass the property there must be (a) unconditional appropriation by one party and (b) assent by the other party. The meaning of 'unconditional appropriation' was considered by Pearson J. (as he then was) in *Carlos Federspiel & Co.* v. *Twigg & Co. Ltd* (1957), and in the course of his judgment he said this:

A mere setting apart or selection by the seller of the goods which he expects to use in performance of the contract is not enough .... To constitute an appropriation of the goods to the contract, the parties must have had ... an intention to attach the contract irrevocably to those goods, so that those goods and no others are the subject of the sale and become the property of the buyer.

Rule 5(2), which deals with delivery to a carrier, must be read subject to section 16. This was decided in the case of *Healy* v. *Howlett* (1917), where the facts were as follows:

B ordered twenty boxes of fish from S. S consigned 190 boxes by rail, and directed the railway to set aside twenty for the buyer's contract. At the same time S sent B an invoice stating that the fish was carried at buyer's 'sole risk'. Before the twenty boxes had been set aside, the fish went bad. It was held that: (1) the invoice formed no part of the contract, because the contract had been made before the invoice was sent; (2) at the time of the deterioration the goods were still unascertained; (3) consequently neither the property nor the risk had passed to the buyer, and he could reject the fish.

The buyer's assent to the appropriation can be (and often is) inferred from the surrounding circumstances. If, for example, the buyer orders goods by post, it may well be (although the point is unsettled) that he assents in advance to the seller's subsequent appropriation. The case of *Pignatoro* v. *Gilroy* (1919) provides another illustration of implied assent. In that case:

S sold to B 140 bags of rice and sent B a delivery order for 125 bags. He also told B that the remaining fifteen bags were available for collection at S's warehouse and asked B to take them away. B delayed for a month and when he finally arrived at the warehouse he was told that the bags had been stolen a very short time previously. It was held that (1) by his silence, B had impliedly assented to S's appropriation and consequently (2) the property and risk had passed to B, who was liable to pay the price.

The provisions of rule 5 have little or no relevance in the field of export sales, because the circumstances of the case will usually show a different intention (see chapter 10).

Reservation of right of disposal

It should be clear by now that a seller can always stipulate when the property is to pass, and he can (for example) insist that no property shall pass until he has been paid. Section 19 begins by confirming that this is so, and then goes on to specify two cases where an intention to retain the property can be inferred. The section reads as follows:

1. Where there is a contract for the sale of specific goods or where goods are subsequently appropriated to the contract, the seller may, by the terms of the contract or appropriation, reserve the right of disposal of the goods until certain conditions are fulfilled. In such case, notwithstanding delivery of goods to the buyer or to a carrier or other bailee ... for transmission to the buyer, the property in the goods does not pass to the buyer until the conditions imposed by the seller are fulfilled.

2. Where goods are shipped, and by the bill of lading the goods are deliverable to the order of the seller or his agent, the seller is prima facie deemed to reserve the right of disposal.

3. Where the seller of goods draws on the buyer for the price, and transmits the bill of exchange and bill of lading to the buyer together to secure acceptance or payment of the bill of exchange, the buyer is bound to return the bill of lading if he does not honour the bill of exchange, and if he wrongfully retains the bill of lading the property in the goods does not pass to him.

Bill of lading

In an export sale, the key document is the bill of lading which is a document signed by the master of the ship acknowledging that he has received the goods on board. While the goods are on board, the bill of lading represents the goods, so that ownership of the goods can be transferred by transferring the bill of lading. Clearly, if this vital document is made out to the order of the seller, it is very strong evidence that he still retains the property.

Bill of exchange

For many centuries, a bill of exchange was used to finance trade. It is essentially a document where one person (the drawer) orders another person (the drawee) to pay a sum of money either to the drawer himself or to a third person (the payee). Now if Smith in England sold goods to Brown in New York and Brown wanted time to pay, a bill of exchange was used to enable Smith to obtain his money and Brown to obtain credit at the same time. What happened was that Smith drew a bill of exchange 'on' (i.e. addressed to) Brown, thus:

1/10/71   35 Mincing Lane

90 days after date pay to my order £1000 (one thousand pounds)

To B. Brown   S. Smith
    53 West 23rd Street
    New York

This was sent to Brown with the bill of lading. If Brown agreed with the order he would write his name on the bill of exchange, thus:

'Accepted B. Brown'

The bill was then returned to Smith and Smith could raise money on the bill by selling ('negotiating') it to someone else, for example a bank. When the ninety days had expired the bank would go to Brown for payment. In the meantime Brown would have got the goods off the ship and he would probably have re-sold them to put himself in funds to pay the bill of exchange.

This scheme (which is less common now than formerly because of the introduction of a system of direct finance known as bankers' commercial credits) would clearly break down if Brown merely kept the bill of lading and refused to honour the bill of exchange. Accordingly, by section 19(3), no property passes to the buyer in such a case, although we shall see later that if the buyer obtains the bill of lading and then transfers it to a transferee who takes in good faith, the property will pass to the transferee (p. 51).

The risk

We have seen that one of the main consequences of the passing of property is that the risk of accidental loss or damage passes at the same time. By section 20:

Unless otherwise agreed, the goods remain at the seller's risk until the property therein be transferred to the buyer, but when the property therein is transferred to the buyer the goods are at the buyer's risk, whether delivery has been made or not.

A number of examples of the operation of this section have already been given (see, for example, the furniture example, p. 26; *Healy* v. *Howlett*, p. 31; *Pignatoro* v. *Gilroy*, p. 31).

The opening words 'unless otherwise agreed' should by now be familiar. Thus, in *Bevington* v. *Dale* (1902) furs were delivered on approval and were stolen during the approval period. The sellers proved that there was a well-established custom in the fur trade that goods out on approval should be at the buyer's risk. Accordingly, the buyer was liable to pay the price. Again, in *Sterns Ltd* v. *Vickers Ltd* (1923):

S agreed to sell to B 120,000 gallons of spirit out of 200,000 in a tank on the premises of a third party. S gave B a delivery order which was not acted on for some time and, in the meantime, the spirit deteriorated. It was held that even though the property might not have passed (because the goods were still unascertained), the parties had intended the risk to pass (and it had passed) to the buyer as soon as the delivery order was handed to him.

The general rule of section 20 is qualified by two provisos. The first one states that:

Where delivery has been delayed through the fault of either buyer or seller the goods are at the risk of the party in fault as regards any loss which might not have occurred but for such fault.

Thus if, in the example on p. 26, Y had agreed to deliver the furniture on 1 May and had wrongfully failed to do so, and Y's store had been burnt down on 3 May, the proviso would operate to throw the loss on to Y. The proviso was applied in *Demby Hamilton* v. *Barden* (1944) where S agreed to sell thirty tons of crushed apple to B, and B wrongly failed to give delivery instructions, as a result of which the juice went bad. It was held that the loss fell on B.

The second proviso is straightforward. It reads:

Nothing in this section shall affect the duties or liabilities of either seller or buyer as a bailee ... of the goods of the other party.

Thus if S, having sold a car to B, agreed to look after it until B wanted it, S would become a 'bailee' of the car for B, and would be liable to B if the car was damaged as the result of S's negligence.

The perishing of the goods

Before leaving the question of risk, it may be useful to group together a number of provisions dealing with the 'perishing' of the goods. It seems that goods can be said to 'perish' if they no longer exist in a commercial sense. Thus, in *Asfar* v. *Blundell* (1896) a consignment of dates became impregnated with sewage when the ship carrying them sank. Although the dates were recovered it was held that, in a commercial sense, they had ceased to be dates. Clearly the term 'perish' also covers physical destruction. Whether it also covers theft is less certain. Can a car be said to have 'perished' merely because at the time of sale it had been stolen from the seller's garage? This is an unsettled point.

What is the position if the goods perish? Clearly, the seller will be liable if he is in breach of one of his duties under the Act, as, for example, the duty under section 14 to supply merchantable goods, or the duty under section 32 to make a reasonable contract of carriage. Apart from these cases, the position depends on (a) whether the goods are specific or unascertained and (b) the precise moment at which they perish.

Perishing of specific goods

1. *Before contract*. Section 6 provides that if specific goods have perished, without the seller's knowledge, when the contract was made, the contract is void. Thus, if X agreed to sell Y a specific consignment of wheat on board a ship and, unknown to X, that ship and all its cargo had perished when the con-

tract was made, the contract would be void, so that X could not sue Y for the price, and Y could not sue X for damages for non-delivery. The position would, of course, be different if there were an express or implied promise by X that the wheat had not perished. In this case there would be a contrary agreement under section 55 ousting section 6, and X would be liable for breach of his undertaking. In any event, section 6 does not apply in the case of a sale of goods which have never existed at all. This is what happened in the case of *McRae* v. *Commonwealth Disposals Commission* (1951) where S agreed to sell to B a specific ship-wrecked oil tanker which had never existed at all. It was held that S was liable to B because he had impliedly warranted (i.e. promised) that the tanker did exist.

What is the position where only part of the goods have perished? In *Barrow Lane and Ballard* v. *Phillips* (1929) a seller agreed to sell a specific consignment of '700 bags of Chinese nuts' and, unknown to him, 109 of them had disappeared when the contract was made. It was held that section 6 applied and that the contract was void. If the contract had been severable (e.g. 'to be delivered by seven instalments of 100 bags, each to be separately paid for'), it is possible that the position might have been different.

2. *After contract*. Section 7 provides that:

Where there is an agreement to sell specific goods and subsequently the goods, without any fault on the part of the seller or buyer, perish before the risk passes to the buyer, the agreement is thereby avoided.

This provision is of limited practical importance. It only applies where, on a sale of specific goods, the risk does not pass immediately to the buyer. Usually, of course, the combined effect of section 18 rule 1 and section 20 is to pass the risk immediately the contract is made. If, however, a case comes within section 18 rules 2 or 3, section 7 could apply. If, for example, the seller agreed to do some work on the goods to put them into a deliverable state, and the goods perished before the buyer had been notified that the work was completed, section 7 would apply and neither party would have any rights under the contract.

3. *After risk has passed.* If the goods perish after the risk has passed to the buyer, the buyer bears the loss.

Perishing of unascertained goods

It will be recalled from the definitions given at the beginning of this chapter that unascertained goods may be either (a) purely generic or (b) part of a larger consignment. In the former case the position is clear. If X agrees to sell to Y '100 bottles of 1949 port' he must perform his contract. If it should happen that the warehouse of X's usual supplier has been destroyed, that is unfortunate for X – he must find 100 bottles from somewhere else or pay damages to Y for non-delivery.

If, however, the goods are agreed to come from a specified source ('100 bottles of 1949 port from the stock now in my cellar') and if, unknown to the seller, the entire stock had perished when the contract was made, the contract would clearly be void – not under section 6 but under general common law rules preserved by the Act. If the entire stock perished after the contract was made but before the risk had passed to the buyer, the contract would be frustrated and the Law Reform (Frustrated Contracts) Act 1943, would govern the rights of the parties (see *Howell* v. *Coupland*, p. 16).

It will be recalled that a contract will be treated as frustrated if performance has been rendered impossible, or totally different, by reason of some external event not contemplated by the contract. If the 1943 Act does apply, the general position is that moneys paid are repayable and that moneys payable cease to be payable. Nevertheless, certain adjustments can be made where a party has incurred expenditure, or has received a benefit, under the contract.

Self-tuition test 2

1. What are (a) specific goods? (b) ascertained goods? (c) unascertained goods? (d) future goods?

2. Why is it important to decide whether or not property has passed to the buyer?

3. X buys a car from Y, and Y agrees to deliver it to X's premises in ten days' time. On whom will the loss fall if (a) the car is damaged two days after the agreement is made or (b) the car is damaged on Y's premises two weeks after the agreement is made?

4. When are goods in a 'deliverable state'?

5. X sells ten specified bags of flour to Y at a price of £10 per ton and it is agreed that Y will weigh the bags at his warehouse. He does so and finds that they weigh twenty-five tons but, before he has time to inform X of this, the entire consignment is destroyed. What is the legal position?

6. Goods are delivered by X to Y on seven days 'sale or return'. After four days, Y pledges them with Z. Does the property pass?

7. (a) When does the property pass in unascertained goods? (b) What is the position where a bulk consignment of ten boxes is handed to a road haulier for delivery to various buyers, each of whom has ordered two boxes?

8. Give two examples of cases where a seller is deemed to have reserved the right of disposal.

9. When do goods perish?

10. X sells ten live chickens to Y. He owns exactly that number but, unknown to either X or Y, four of them were killed before the contract was made. What is the legal position?

For answers see p. 180.

4 Transfer of Title by a Non-Owner

In the previous chapter we saw how property was transferred from seller to buyer. What happens if the seller does not own the goods at all? Here the law finds itself in a quandary. Should it protect property rights, so that the innocent purchaser gets nothing? Or should it protect commercial transactions, so that the original owner (who may have been tricked into parting with the goods) will find that he has lost them forever? This is the problem discussed in this chapter, and we shall see that there is a general rule protecting ownership, followed by a large number of exceptions protecting commercial transactions.

Nemo dat rule

There is an old Latin maxim *nemo dat quod non habet*, which means 'a person cannot give what he has not got'. This maxim must be the starting point for any discussion of this topic. Section 21(1) provides that:

Subject to the provisions of this Act, where goods are sold by a person who is not the owner thereof, and who does not sell them under the authority or with the consent of the owner, the buyer acquires no better title to the goods than the seller had, unless the owner of the goods is by his conduct precluded from denying the seller's authority to sell.

This section, then, starts by re-affirming the basic principle of ownership, so that if X sells to Y goods belonging to Z, no title passes to Y unless (a) Z authorizes X to sell or (b) Z is precluded by his conduct from denying X's right to sell.

Exceptions to the nemo dat *rule*. There are altogether ten exceptions to the basic rule, namely:

1. Estoppel.
2. Agency.
3. Disposition by a mercantile agent.
4. Sale under an order of the court.
5. Sale under a common law or statutory power.
6. Sale in market overt.
7. Sale under a voidable title.
8. Disposition by a seller in possession.
9. Disposition by a buyer in possession.
10. Disposition of motor vehicles by hire-purchasers.

These exceptions bite fairly deeply into the general 'protection of property' principle, although in the opinion of a recent Law Reform Committee they do not go far enough. The basic problem is often a very old one – which of two entirely innocent persons shall suffer loss as the result of the fraud of a third? A suggestion by Lord Devlin that the loss should be apportioned between them was considered by the Law Reform Committee, but in their Twelfth Report (Cmnd 2958) they rejected the idea as impracticable.

We can now examine the ten exceptions in a little more detail.

Estoppel

The word 'estoppel' is a highly technical term used in the law of evidence. If A by his conduct makes B believe that a certain fact is true, and if this causes B to alter his position, A will be precluded (i.e. 'estopped') from saying that the fact is untrue. Thus, in *Eastern Distributors* v. *Goldring* (1957)

M, a mobile greengrocer, owned a Bedford van. He went to see a car dealer C, with a view to buying a Chrysler owned by C, but he did not have the money to buy it outright. C suggested a rather complicated scheme whereby (1) M was to sign forms showing that C owned both vehicles and that M wanted them both on hire-purchase (2) C would show these forms to a finance company who would then buy both vehicles from C and (3) the finance company would let M have both vehicles on hire-purchase. M signed the forms, and C took them to a finance company who rejected the proposal for the Chrysler but accepted the one for the Bedford.

Clearly, as far as M was concerned, this knocked the whole scheme on the head, but C went on to sell the Bedford by itself to the finance company. The Court of Appeal held that (1) by signing the forms M had represented that C had the right to sell the Bedford, and the finance company had altered their position in reliance on the representation; (2) consequently M was 'precluded' (i.e. estopped) from denying this and accordingly (3) when C sold the Bedford to the finance company they acquired a good title under section 21.

The facts of this case were very special, and it must be emphasized that the mere transfer of possession will not usually give rise to an estoppel. Thus if the owner of a car lends it to a friend and the friend wrongly sells it, the owner will not be 'estopped' from setting up his ownership and recovering the car from the purchaser. What is the position if a car dealer allows a prospective customer to take the car and its registration book away? This is what happened in *Central Newbury Car Auctions Ltd* v. *Unity Finance Ltd* (1957) where the customer turned out to be a rogue. Many people would feel that the dealer was extremely careless, but a majority of the Court of Appeal (Lord Denning dissenting) held that he was still entitled to assert his ownership and recover the car from an innocent buyer who had bought it from the rogue.

Agency

If X appoints Y as his agent to sell X's goods to Z, any sale by Y in accordance with his instructions will clearly pass title to Z, both under the general law and under the express provisions of section 21. If Y exceeded his instructions in some way, no title would pass to Z, unless Y had what is called 'apparent authority' which was acted on by Z. The rules for apparent authority are the same as for 'estoppel' which was discussed above, and a particular example of apparent authority can be seen in the case of dispositions by a mercantile agent, which are discussed below.

Dispositions by a mercantile agent

Let us suppose that the owner of a car hands it to X, together with the ignition key and registration book, because X has told the owner that he has a buyer for the car (which is untrue). The owner tells X not to sell for less than £400, but X sells the car to Y for £250 and disappears with the proceeds. Does Y get title? The answer depends on the status of X. If X is a private individual it seems that Y gets no title, because X has neither actual nor apparent authority to sell the car for £250 (*Heap* v. *Motorists' Advisory Agency Ltd* (1923)). If, however, X is a professional selling agent (e.g. a car dealer) then the delivery of the car to X would create the impression that he had full authority to sell. This is the principle behind section 2 of the Factors Act 1889, and under that section Y would acquire a good title if he took in good faith and if X sold in the ordinary course of business.

Section 2 is concerned with dispositions by a 'mercantile agent' and by section 1 this means 'a mercantile agent having in the ordinary course of business as such agent authority to either sell goods or to consign goods for the purpose of sale, or to buy goods, or to raise money on the security of goods'. This definition includes such agents as factors and brokers, but it does not include a mere clerk or servant. A person can be a 'mercantile agent' even though he has only one customer (*Lowther* v. *Harris* (1927)) and apparently even if he acts only on one isolated occasion, provided that he does so in a commercial capacity (*Budberg* v. *Jerwood and Ward* (1934)).

Section 2(1) protects a purchaser from such an agent by providing that:

Where a mercantile agent is, with the consent of the owner, in possession of goods or of the documents of title to goods, any sale, pledge or other disposition of the goods made by him when acting in the ordinary course of business of a mercantile agent, shall, subject to the provisions of this Act, be as valid as if he were expressly authorized by the owner of the goods to make the same; provided that the person taking under the disposition acts in good faith and has not at the time of the disposition notice that the person making the disposition has not authority to make the same.

Various problems have arisen under this subsection. First, it has been held that the agent must receive possession *as* a mercantile agent, so that if a car is delivered *for repair* to a person who also happens to be a mercantile agent, a sale by him would not pass title (*Cole* v. *North Western Bank* (1875)). Secondly, what happens if the owner's consent was obtained by fraud or by a trick? After earlier doubts it is now clear that, with one possible exception, the fraud or trick will not prevent a buyer acquiring title (*Pearson* v. *Rose & Young* (1951)). The exception is that of an owner who is tricked into parting with possession by a trick relating to the agent's identity. It was suggested in *Folkes* v. *King* (1923) that this might nullify consent altogether so that the section would not apply. The distinction between 'consent obtained by a trick' and 'no consent' is clearly a very fine one, and is somewhat similar to the distinction between voidable contracts and void contracts (see p. 47). Finally, what is the precise significance of a car registration book? In *Pearson* v. *Rose & Young* the owner of a car took it to a garage and asked the dealer to obtain offers. He never intended to hand over the registration book, but by mistake he left it with the dealer, who sold the car with the book to an innocent buyer. The Court of Appeal held that the owner's consent must extend to the book as well as to the car; as the owner had never consented to the dealer having the book, the sale by him must be treated as the sale of a car without its registration book, and this would not be a sale in the ordinary course of business. Consequently, the buyer did not get a good title. It seems from the case of *Stadium Finance Ltd* v. *Robbins* (1962) that the owner's consent must also extend to the ignition key. If, however, the car is a brand new one, it seems that the absence of the log book is not necessarily fatal (*Astley Industrial Trust* v. *Miller* (1968)).

Section 2 also protects a buyer where the agent is in possession of documents of title. This term is defined as including:

any bill of lading, dock warrant, warehouse-keeper's certificate, and warrant or order for the delivery of goods and any other document used in the ordinary course of business as proof of the possession or control of goods.

The definition in the Sale of Goods Act is in identical terms. It is important to note that, according to the decided cases, a motor-car registration book is *not* a document of title, although it is the best evidence of title (see e.g. *Central Newbury Car Auctions Ltd* v. *Unity Finance Ltd* (1957)).

Sale under an order of the court

This requires no particular comment. There are certain rules of court which authorize a court to order a sale of goods which are the subject matter of legal proceedings.

Sale under a common law or statutory power

Both at common law and by statute there are a number of cases whereby a non-owner is entitled to sell and such a sale will pass a good title. Thus at common law a person who has made a contract with the owner of goods (for example, a carrier) may be able to sell those goods as an agent of necessity if (a) there is an emergency, and (b) it is impracticable for him to communicate with the owner, and (c) he acts in good faith for the owner's benefit. Statutory powers of sale can be exercised by various persons including

(a) An unpaid innkeeper (Inkeepers Act 1878).
(b) An unpaid bailee who has done work on goods (Disposal of Uncollected Goods Act 1952).
(c) An unpaid seller of goods (section 48, p. 108).

Sale in market overt

By section 22:

Where goods are sold in market overt, according to the usage of the market, the buyer acquires a good title to the goods, provided he buys them in good faith and without notice of any defect or want of title on the part of the seller.

The protection of a buyer in 'market overt' is very old – it goes back to the sixteenth century when the market place was the usual place of business. A 'market overt' has been defined as any 'open, public and legally constituted market' (*Lee* v. *Bayes* (1856)), whether established by Public Act of Parliament, or charter, or merely by long use. There is also a well-established custom in the City of London that the public part of every shop there is 'market overt'. Thus if a shopkeeper in such a shop sells stolen goods, the buyer acquires title; if he had bought the goods in another shop outside the boundaries of the City he would not have done so. This is one of the many anomalies thrown up by market overt. Another anomaly is that, as a result of the Laws in Wales Act 1542, market overt has never applied to Wales.

The conditions which must be satisfied if the buyer is to acquire title are straightforward and reflect the more leisurely trading conditions of earlier days. Thus, the sale must be public and open, it must take place between sunrise and sunset, and the goods themselves (not merely a sample) must be on display in the market. So far as shops are concerned, the sale must take place in the public part of the shop (*Hargreaves* v. *Spink* (1892)) and the sale must be *by* the shopkeeper and not *to* him (*Ardath Tobacco Co.* v. *Ocker* (1931)). It is also necessary that the goods should be of a kind which are normally dealt with in that market, and the sale must take place in a way which is usual in that market. This point was illustrated by the only modern reported case on market overt – *Bishopsgate Motor Finance Co.* v. *Transport Brakes Ltd* (1949). In that case, X had a car on hire-purchase, and he had no right to sell it. He took it to a car market in Maidstone, tried unsuccessfully to sell it there by public auction, and then sold it there privately to Y. The Court of Appeal held that (1) the market was market overt for cars, having been set up by a statute passed in 1823; (2) a private sale was quite usual there; (3) Y had acquired title.

The final requirement is that the buyer must take in good faith and without notice of the fact that the seller had no right to sell. It is interesting to note the suggestion made by Lord Denning in the Bishopsgate case that if a car was sold without its registration book a buyer might find it difficult to prove good faith, since he should have been put on inquiry as to why it was not there.

We have seen that, as a result of the market overt rules, an entirely innocent owner of goods may lose them forever if, for example, they are stolen from him and then sold in market overt. To encourage him to find and prosecute the thief, section 24 provided that if the thief was convicted of larceny the property in the goods re-vested in the original owner, despite any intermediate dealing with them, whether by sale in market overt or otherwise. This section has been repealed by the Theft Act 1968; the result is that a title acquired in market overt will not be upset by conviction of the thief.

The Law Reform Committee were agreed that the ancient rules relating to market overt were capricious, but they were not agreed about what should be done. Thirteen of the fourteen members urged that market overt should be replaced by a general provision protecting an innocent buyer who buys by retail at trade premises or by public auction. The fourteenth member, Lord Donovan (a judge of the House of Lords) felt that this would facilitate the sale of stolen property. In giving his reasons, he drew attention to a Parliamentary answer stating that in 1964 the value of stolen property was £14 million in London and three times that amount elsewhere, and that in London only one-seventh was recovered. He also quoted from the evidence of Lloyd's Underwriters who felt that the 'injured innocence' of the buyer was 'all too often tinged with lurking doubts which he had successfully stifled when the transaction took place.' Lord Donovan felt that, in the circumstances, the best thing to do was simply to abolish market overt and to put nothing in its place. This difference of opinion highlights once again the difficulty of reconciling the two conflicting principles of protecting property and protecting commercial transactions.

Sale under a voidable title

We have already seen a number of cases in which an owner was tricked into parting with his goods. The rules on this topic are highly technical and they have recently been severely criticized. If X is induced by a trick to make a contract with Y, the contract may be completely void because of X's mistake, or it may be 'voidable' by reason of the trick. The term 'voidable' means that the contract is fully binding until X takes steps to have it set aside. In practice, it is often immensely difficult to decide whether a contract is 'void' or 'voidable', but the distinction is often a vital one because, strange though it may seem, the rights of an innocent buyer will depend on it. Section 23 reads:

Where the seller of goods has a voidable title thereto, but his title has not been avoided at the time of the sale, the buyer acquires a good title to the goods, provided he buys them in good faith and without notice of the seller's defect of title.

In *Phillips* v. *Brooks* (1919)

A rogue went into a jeweller's shop and selected a valuable ring. He said to the shopkeeper 'I am Sir George Bullough' (which was untrue). The shopkeeper knew that name, checked the address which the rogue gave, and allowed the rogue to take the ring away in return for a cheque which was dishonoured. The rogue pledged the ring with a firm from whom the shopkeeper sought to recover it. It was held that (1) the shopkeeper had intended to deal with the rogue, although his intention was induced by the fraud; (2) accordingly the rogue acquired a voidable title to the ring and the pledge by him was valid.

On the other hand, in *Ingram* v. *Little* (1961)

Three old ladies owned a Renault Dauphine car. They wanted to sell it for cash. A rogue appeared, described himself as 'P. G. M. Hutchinson' and said that he had substantial business interests. The ladies checked his name and address in a telephone directory and, believing him to be Hutchinson, sold the car to him in return for a cheque which was dishonoured. They then brought an action to recover the car from an innocent buyer who had bought it from the rogue. A majority of the Court of Appeal (Lord Devlin dissenting) held that (1) the offer for sale was made to Hutchinson and could not be accepted by anyone else; (2) consequently the 'contract' with the rogue was completely void and he acquired no title at all; (3) the ladies were entitled to recover the car from the innocent buyer.

The Law Reform Committee felt that this very narrow distinction between void and voidable contracts was far from satisfactory, and they recommended that in all such cases the contract should be voidable (so that an innocent buyer would be protected). So far this recommendation has not been acted upon by Parliament, but the recent case of *Lewis* v. *Averay*

(1971) gets very near to achieving the result desired by the Committee. The facts of that case were similar to those in *Phillips* v. *Brooks* and the Court of Appeal had no difficulty in holding that the original contract was voidable not void. The judgments make it clear that this will be the normal result and that *Ingram* v. *Little* can be treated as a case turning on very special facts.

Even if the original contract is voidable for fraud, the owner can sometimes preserve his ownership if he can set the contract aside before the buyer has sold the goods to a third party. Here a practical problem arises: since the innocent party will almost certainly not know the whereabouts of the rogue, how can he set about avoiding the contract? In the case of *Car and Universal Finance Co. Ltd* v. *Caldwell* (1965) the original owner went to the police and to the A.A. as soon as the rogue's cheque was dishonoured, and he asked the police and the A.A. to help him to get the car back. It was held by the Court of Appeal that by his conduct he had avoided his contract with the rogue. The important point brought out in this case was that in the case of a fraudulent buyer, who is unlikely to be too precise about his whereabouts, the original contract can be avoided without giving notice to him. The practical result of this was, however, severely cut down by a later case (*Newtons of Wembley Ltd* v. *Williams*) which shows that, even after the avoidance of the original contract, the rogue may still be able to pass a good title under another section of the Act (see p. 50).

Disposition by a seller in possession

We have seen that a contract of sale may be complete and valid even though the goods are still in the seller's physical possession. It may often happen that a buyer may leave the goods with the seller for some time. What happens if the seller sells those same goods to another buyer, or pledges them with an innocent pledgee? Clearly if the goods still belong to the seller, he can sell or pledge them and pass a good title. Suppose, however, that at the time of the second sale the goods belong to the first buyer. Does he lose them to the second buyer? Very often the answer is yes, because section 8 of the Factors Act 1889 (and also section 25(1) of the Sale of Goods Act 1893) protects an innocent transferee. The transferee will be protected if:

1. S sells goods to B and remains in possession of the goods or documents of title to goods; and

2. S then transfers the goods or documents under a sale, pledge, or other disposition; and

3. the transferee takes in good faith and without notice of the previous sale.

Viewed diagrammatically the section operates as follows:

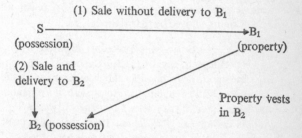

(1) Sale without delivery to B_1

S —————————————————————→B_1
(possession)   (property)

(2) Sale and
delivery to B_2

Property vests
in B_2

B_2 (possession)

The transferee will not get a good title merely by buying the goods; he must also take *delivery* of the goods themselves or the documents of title from the seller. Accordingly, in the case of *Nicholson* v. *Harper* (1895), a warehouseman stored some wine on behalf of X. X sold the wine to Y and later executed a document whereby he pledged the wine to the warehouseman in return for a loan. At the time of the pledge the wine no longer belonged to X, so that he had no right to pledge it; further, section 8 could not apply because there had been no delivery from X to the warehouseman; accordingly, the pledge gave the warehouseman no rights at all.

The moral is that a buyer who leaves his goods with the seller runs the risk of losing them. He will, of course, have an action against the seller for depriving him of his goods.

Disposition by a buyer in possession

The next problem is the exact counterpart of the previous one: does a seller who retains the property run the risk of losing it if he lets the buyer have possession? The answer again is yes, because section 9 of the Factors Act 1889, and section 25(2) of the Sale of Goods Act 1893, protect an innocent transferee from the buyer. The transferee may be protected if:

1. B buys or agrees to buy goods from S.

2. B obtains possession of the goods or documents of title with S's consent (and this includes consent obtained by fraud).

3. B then transfers the goods or documents to a transferee under a sale, pledge, or other disposition.

4. the transferee takes in good faith (i.e. honestly) and without notice of any rights enjoyed by the original seller.

This is not quite all, because these sections do not say simply 'the transferee will get a good title'. They use much more cumbersome language by providing that the transfer made by the buyer shall take effect as though the buyer were 'a mercantile agent in possession with the owner's consent'. It was held in *Newtons of Wembley Ltd* v. *Williams* (1964) that, as a result of this curious wording, the transferee will only get a good title if the original buyer acted in the ordinary course of business of a mercantile agent. This apparently means that the second sale must take place at business premises and during business hours. This decision cuts down appreciably the protection given to an innocent buyer. In fact, many earlier cases, in which this point was never raised at all, may well turn out to have been wrongly decided.

Three other points on section 9 and 25(2) are worthy of note:

1. These sections only apply if the original buyer had either bought or 'agreed to buy'. They do not apply if he merely had an option to do so. This is why the modern hire-purchase agreement takes the form of a hiring with an option to purchase. If the hirer disposes of the goods to an innocent trans-

feree before the property has passed to him, sections 9 and 25(2) cannot protect the transferee because the hirer had never 'agreed' to buy (*Helby* v. *Matthews* (1895); see also p. 166).

2. These sections can override section 19(3). Where a buyer wrongly keeps a bill of lading, it will be recalled that no property passes to him (see pp. 32–3). Even so, he is still a buyer who has obtained a document of title with the seller's consent. If this document is transferred to an innocent transferee, the property will pass to him and the original seller will be left with an action against the buyer (*Cahn* v. *Pocketts Bristol Channel Steam Packet Co.* (1879)).

3. The Newton case shows that these sections can apply even where the original buyer had a voidable title which had been avoided before he sold to the transferee. We saw when discussing section 23 that the original owner, by going to the police, could thereby avoid the contract. Nevertheless, if the rogue originally got possession of the goods with the owner's consent, it seems that the withdrawal of that consent will not stop an innocent transferee acquiring title under section 9 or 25(2).

Disposition of motor vehicles by hire-purchasers

We have just seen that the modern hire-purchase agreement was designed to prevent the hirer from passing a good title to a third party. Until 1965, this was indeed the position, unless the sale by him took place in market overt. Some concern was felt at the number of innocent buyers of motor-cars who subsequently discovered that it was the subject-matter of an unexpired hire-purchase agreement. The government proposed a new system of licensing cards which the hirer would take instead of the registration book, but the finance companies rejected the scheme for administrative reasons. Instead, with the finance companies' consent, the government brought in new proposals which passed into law as sections 27–9 (Part III) of the Hire-Purchase Act 1964, and which added yet another exception to the *nemo dat* rule. These provisions only apply to motor vehicles that are let out under a hire-purchase agreement or which are agreed to be sold under a conditional sale agreement. The Act makes a new departure by distinguishing between a 'trade or finance' purchaser and a 'private' purchaser. The position is that if the hirer disposes of the vehicle to a private purchaser taking in good faith and without notice of the hire-purchase agreement, the original owner's title will vest in the private purchaser, although the hirer himself will remain liable to the owner for breach of contract and for the tort of converting the vehicle to his own use.

If, on the other hand, the hirer disposes of the vehicle to a trade or finance purchaser, no title will pass. Clearly, however, such a trade purchaser usually buys the vehicle with a view to re-sale, and accordingly the Act goes on to provide that, if further dispositions take place, the first private purchaser will be protected and will acquire title if he buys in good faith and without notice. The trade or finance purchaser remains liable to the owner for the tort of conversion.

The Act defines 'trade purchaser' as a person who carries on a business of buying motor vehicles for re-sale, while a 'finance purchaser' is a person who provides finance by buying motor vehicles and then letting them out under hire-purchase or conditional-sale agreements. Any other purchaser is a private purchaser. The term 'private purchaser' is much wider than 'private person', so that, for example, a large public company can be a private purchaser if it is not a finance company and is not a motor dealer.

The reason why Parliament has singled out trade and finance purchasers is the fact that such purchasers can find out more easily than other purchasers whether the car which they are buying is held on hire-purchase. The finance companies operate a voluntary registration scheme through a company called H.P. Information Ltd. The essence of the scheme is a register of cars held under subsisting hire-purchase agreements. Finance companies and motor dealers have access to this register and will frequently consult it before buying a vehicle. The scheme is not widely known by the general public, but inquiries can be made through the motoring associations or through the Citizens' Advice Bureaux.

Self-tuition test 3

1. What is the *nemo dat* rule?

2. What are the ten exceptions to the *nemo dat* rule?

3. What is estoppel, and what is its importance in relation to the transfer of title to goods?

4. What is the position where an agent sells his principal's goods without the principal's authority?

5. Arthur owns an old Bentley car and takes it to Sharp, a car dealer, with instructions to obtain offers for sale. Nothing is said about the registration book but, after Arthur has gone, Sharp finds the book on the floor of the car. He sells the car to Jack and disappears. Does Jack get title?

6. A borrows B's camera, takes it to a London shop owned by C, and sells it to C. A day later, C sells it to D. B has now managed to trace the camera and claims that it still belongs to him. Is he correct?

7. X sells a radio to Y and it is agreed that Y will collect it from X in three days' time. When Y comes to collect the radio, he finds that X has sold it to Z (together with all his other stock) and has gone out of business. To whom does the radio belong?

8. Fred hires a motor scooter from Hiracar Ltd, and after paying one instalment he sells it to John. Can the company recover the scooter from John?

9. Charles agrees to sell a second-hand car to a man who describes himself as Blinkarn, a reputable car dealer well known to Charles. His true name is Blinkiron, and he is a worthless rogue. He takes the car and pays Charles by cheque. As soon as the cheque is dishonoured, Charles goes to the police and asks them to find the car. On the following day, the rogue sells the car to Tom, and two days later the police find it in Tom's possession. Tom claims that the car is his. Is he correct?

10. Albert agrees to take a lorry on hire-purchase from the Never-Never Finance Company. After paying two instalments

he sells it to Crash Ltd who run a car breakdown service. Six months later, Crash Ltd, having no further use for the lorry, sell it to Alf, a car dealer, in part-exchange for another vehicle. To whom does the lorry belong?

For answers, see p. 182.

5 Terms of the Contract

The essential obligation of a contract for the sale of goods is the transfer of property. But there are many other obligations as well, and many problems may arise if these obligations are not performed. A car described as a 1959 model may turn out to be a 1956 model; it may be totally unroadworthy or unfit for the buyer's particular purpose; it may not go at all. A seller may sell a quantity of cloth by sample, and he may supply goods not corresponding to the sample or goods which are unmerchantable. This type of problem is dealt with in this chapter.

When a seller is trying to clinch a sale he is likely to make a number of statements relating to the goods. Some of these may be untrue, and the question then arises as to whether the buyer has a remedy. Statements made by a seller can be divided into three groups:

1. Trader's Puff.
2. Representation.
3. Contractual Term.

Trader's puff

It has been the practice of traders for centuries to praise their goods in glowing terms. Thus, a seller offering a new sports car may say 'she is a beauty', or a new product may be described as 'the best on the market'. In general, this type of talk does not give rise to legal liability.

Representation

A representation differs from trader's puff because it is a statement of fact which can be verified. Thus a person selling an expensive camera might state that it was ideal for indoor photography. If in fact this was totally untrue, the buyer would be anxious to get his money back, or at least to get some form of compensation. The precise nature of his remedies depends on whether the statement is a 'representation' or a 'contractual term'. The former expression is used to refer to a statement which brings about a contract but is not itself a term of the contract, because the person making the statement does not warrant it to be true. Thus in the case of *Oscar Chess Ltd* v. *Williams* (1957) a private person trading-in his Morris car was asked its age. He had no personal knowledge, and so he looked at the registration book and told the dealer that it was a 1948 model. The part-exchange allowance was calculated on that basis. It turned out to be a 1939 model, although of course neither party knew this at the time of the sale. The Court of Appeal held that the owner of the Morris was not guaranteeing the truth of the date appearing in the registration book. He had merely made a 'representation' and (as the law then stood) the dealer had no remedy against him.

It is important to remember that the person making the statement in this case was a private person. If he had been a dealer with specialist knowledge (so that he could have found out the true position) the statement might well have been classified as a 'contractual term', i.e. a statement which the maker warranted to be true. This is what happened in *Dick Bentley Ltd* v. *Smith* (1965) where, in answer to an inquiry for a Bentley car, the dealer informed the prospective buyer that he had a model which had done 20,000 miles with its present engine. He did not know (but presumably could have found out) that the engine had in fact done 100,000 miles. It was held that he was liable to the buyer for damages for breach of contract.

Remedies for misrepresentation

If a buyer makes a contract as the result of a misrepresentation, what are his rights when he finds out the true facts? This can be an important matter when (for example) goods are foisted on to a gullible housewife by an aggressive (and perhaps over-aggressive) doorstep salesman. The legal rights of the buyer can be summarized as follows:

1. If the statement was fraudulent (if the seller knew that what he said was untrue, or if he was quite indifferent as to whether it was true or not), the buyer can set the contract aside and recover his price; he can also bring an action for monetary compensation or 'damages' if he has suffered further loss.

2. If the statement was innocent (as, for example, the representation in the *Oscar Chess* case that the Morris was a 1948 model) the rights of the injured party have recently been strengthened by the Misrepresentations Act 1967. Before that Act was passed, the only remedy was 'rescission' (i.e. setting aside the contract), but this remedy was severely limited, and was not available where there had been unreasonable delay, nor where the contract had been affirmed, nor where an innocent third party had acquired rights under the contract. There was no general power to award damages. If, for example, the buyer of a car was told that it did fifty miles to the gallon, and if he subsequently found that this figure was much too high, he might well have found himself without any remedy, unless the seller was fraudulent, or unless the seller had made a contractual promise. It might have been too late for the buyer to rescind, and damages for innocent misrepresentation were not available. Now, however, section 2(1) of the Misrepresentation Act gives the innocent party a right to sue for damages, unless the maker of the statement had reasonable grounds to believe, and did believe, that the statement was true.

Apart from this important new right to damages the innocent party still has the right to have the contract set aside, although we have seen that this right is somewhat limited. Formerly, it was generally thought that a contract could not be set aside for innocent misrepresentation after it had been completed by the transfer of the property to the buyer. This was clearly most inconvenient, since it might be a considerable time before the true facts came to light. Section 1 of the 1967 Act now provides that the completion of the contract will not destroy the right of rescission. If, therefore, a housewife buys curtain material, and the seller states that it will not run, or fade, or shrink, she can send the material back if it starts fading almost as soon as the curtains are put up.

There may, of course, be cases where the setting aside of the contract will cause considerable hardship to the party who made the statement as, for example, where the goods have lost most, or all of their value, or if the cost of dismantling the goods and taking them back would be enormous. To cover such a case, section 2(2) provides that where one party has a right of rescission, the court may in its discretion refuse rescission and award damages instead, if the granting of rescission would be unjust to the other party.

Thus, the present law can be summarized as follows:

1. *Fraudulent misrepresentation*: rescission and damages under the general law.

2. *Negligent misrepresentation*: damages under section 2(1) and rescission under the general law (subject to the court's discretion under section 2(2) to refuse rescission and award damages instead).

3. *Innocent misrepresentation*: rescission (or discretionary damages) as in (2) above, but no damages as of right.

One final point – and a possible pointer to the future – is contained in section 3. It provides that any clause excluding liability, or remedies, for misrepresentation shall be void unless the court considers it to be fair and reasonable. There has, as yet, been no reported case in the operation of section 3, but clearly the courts are more likely to uphold such a clause in the case of a contract between two businessmen of equal standing than in the case of a 'contract' between a huge commercial organization and an individual consumer. This section is causing headaches outside the field of sale of goods (e.g. in the case of glossy brochures prepared by travel agents), and it has also led to re-writing of auction catalogues.

Contractual terms
Conditions and warranties

We have seen that a statement is a contractual term if the person making it expressly or impliedly warrants it to be true, i.e. if he assumes responsibility for its truth. Contractual terms may be 'express' (i.e. those expressly set out in the contract), or 'implied' (i.e. implied by law). By far the most important of the implied terms are those implied by sections 12–15 of the Sale of Goods Act, in so far as they have not been excluded by agreement.

The Act divides contractual terms into 'conditions' and 'warranties'. The term 'condition' is nowhere defined in the Act, but it is clearly a vital term, because by section 11(1)(a) the breach of a condition usually enables the buyer to treat the contract as at an end. We shall see that the major implied terms relating to the description, quality and fitness of the goods, and the seller's right to sell them are classified as 'conditions'. On the other hand, a 'warranty' is a much less important term. It is defined by section 62 as:

an agreement with reference to goods ... collateral to the main purpose of such contract, the breach of which gives rise to a right to damages but not to a right to reject the goods and treat the contract as repudiated.

It may often be a difficult matter to decide whether a term is a condition or a warranty, the key factor being the importance of the term. Section 11(1)(b) reads:

Whether a stipulation in a contract of sale is a condition ... or a warranty ... depends in each case on the construction of the contract. A stipulation may be a condition even though called a warranty in the contract.

As an illustration of the problem, let us consider a time clause. Section 10(1) reads as follows:

Unless a different intention appears from the terms of the contract, stipulations as to time of payment are not deemed to be of the essence of a contract of sale. Whether any other stipulation as to time is of the essence of the contract or not depends on the terms of the contract.

The Act draws a distinction between a time for payment clause and other time clauses. As regards time for payment, the idea behind section 10 is that a seller is unlikely to be seriously prejudiced by a few days' delay in payment and, accordingly, such delay will not normally entitle him to treat the contract as repudiated and to re-sell to someone else. If he wishes to make time for payment a condition of the contract, he should insert a clause giving him a right to re-sell in the event of the buyer's default. Such a right of re-sale is, in any event, implied where the goods are perishable (see section 48(3)) and even if time for payment is not of the essence it can be made of the essence by giving the buyer reasonable notice of intention to re-sell unless the price is paid (*Ward Ltd* v. *Bignall* (1967)). As regards other time clauses, these are frequently construed as vital terms, i.e. conditions. In commercial transactions, the time for shipment and delivery are clearly vital for the buyer because of such matters as sub-sales and market fluctuations. It has even been held that a buyer may be able to reject goods which have been shipped too early rather than too late. In *Bowes* v. *Shand* (1877) the sellers agreed to ship a quantity of rice during March and April. In fact, most of it was shipped during February. The House of Lords held that the seller had broken a condition of the contract by supplying the goods in February, and accordingly the buyer was entitled to reject them.

Time for delivery may be of the essence (i.e. a condition) even though the buyer buys for his own use and not to re-sell. In the case of *MacDougall* v. *Aeromarine of Emsworth Ltd* (1958):

S agreed to build and deliver a pleasure yacht to B. Delivery was to be on 1 May but the contract stated that 'owing to the effect of delays and shortages such delivery cannot be guaranteed'. The yacht had not been delivered on 19 September, by which time the season was almost over. The buyer treated the contract as repudiated. Diplock J. held that (1) on the true construction of the contract, the sellers were bound to deliver within a reasonable time, and this was a condition and not merely a warranty; (2) on the facts of the case, a reasonable time had elapsed; (3) consequently the buyer was justified in treating the contract as at an end.

We have already seen that where time was not of the essence, it can be made of the essence by giving reasonable notice. What happens if time was of the essence but a breach of the time clause has been waived? The problem arose in *Rickards Ltd* v. *Oppenheim* (1950), where a contract for a Rolls Royce body to be built on to the chassis of a car provided for delivery by 20 March. That day came, but the car did not; the buyer ignored the breach and went on pressing for delivery. Eventually he wrote to the sellers informing them that he would not take the car unless it was delivered within a further four weeks. It was finally tendered to him three months later. He refused it and it was held that his refusal was justified because he had again made time of the essence by giving his four-week notice.

Remedies

The remedy for a breach of warranty is an action for damages representing the buyer's actual loss. If, on the other hand, the seller breaks a condition, the buyer usually has an option:

1. He can treat the contract as repudiated by the seller's breach, reject the goods (or refuse to take them), and ask for the return of his money (or refuse to pay it). This is the effect of section 11(1)(b). Further, although the Act does not expressly say so, there is no doubt that if he suffers additional damage, he can claim this from the seller. If the buyer were to buy a gleaming new washing machine, subject to a condition that it was fit for the buyer's purpose, and if the machine was so bad that it ruined all the clothes when it was used for the first time, the buyer could return the machine and he could also claim, as damages, the price which he had paid and compensation for the clothes.

2. He may treat the breach as though it were a breach of warranty, i.e. he may keep the goods and merely claim damages from the seller.

There is, however, one case where the right of rejection is not available to the buyer. Section 11(1)(c) reads:

Where a contract of sale is not severable, and the buyer has accepted the goods or part thereof ... the breach of any condition to be fulfilled by the seller can only be treated as a breach of warranty, and not as a ground for rejecting the goods and treating the contract as repudiated, unless there be a term, express or implied, to that effect.

Until recently, there was a far more drastic restriction on rejection, although little was heard of it in the decided cases. There was another limb of section 11(1)(c) which provided that specific goods could not be rejected for breach of condition once the property in the goods had passed to the buyer. If we remember that, in the case of specific goods, the property usually passes as soon as the contract is made, it will be apparent that under this provision the right of rejection was completely non-existent, because as soon as the contract was made, the property passed and the right of rejection disappeared. If it is realized that in the case of many manufactured goods the defects do not become apparent until much later, the injustice of the restriction on rejection was obvious. The Tenth Report of the Law Reform Committee recommended its abolition and, by section 4(1) of the Misrepresentation Act 1967, this has been done. This leaves only one case where rejection is not available – the case where the contract is not severable and the buyer has accepted the goods or part thereof.

It is interesting to note that the Act contains no mention at all of what usually happens in practice – namely, the repair or replacement of the faulty goods by the seller. The Act apparently gives a buyer no right to have the goods repaired or replaced, although the so-called 'guarantee' which the buyer receives (see p. 87) usually gives him such a right.

What contracts are severable? Although the Act does not expressly deal with the point, it seems clear that a contract is only 'severable' if it is capable of being split up in some way, as where a seller agrees to deliver the goods by instalments and it is agreed that each instalment is to be separately paid for. In this type of case, the acceptance of an instalment will not prevent a buyer from rejecting a later one for breach of condition. The rights of the parties are dealt with by section 31(2) which reads as follows:

Where there is a contract for the sale of goods to be delivered by stated instalments, which are to be separately paid for, and the seller makes defective deliveries in respect of one or more instalments, or the buyer neglects or refuses to take delivery of or pay for one or more instalments, it is a question in each case depending on the terms of the contract and the circumstances of the case, whether the breach of contract is a repudiation of the whole contract or whether it is a severable breach giving rise to a claim for compensation but not to a right to treat the whole contract as repudiated.

If, therefore, one or more instalments are defective this may be a repudiation of the entire contract, or merely a severable breach, and the matter turns primarily on the size of the breach and the likelihood of its repetition (*Maple Flock Co. Ltd* v. *Universal Furniture Products* (*Wembley*) *Ltd* (1934)). In that case, a contract for the sale of rag flock was subject to a condition that the flock did not contain more than 30 parts of chlorine. Fifteen instalments were duly delivered and paid for, and were perfectly satisfactory, but a sample taken from the sixteenth instalment showed that it contained too much chlorine. The buyers claimed that they were entitled to cancel their order and that they were not bound to take any further instalments. It was held, however, that the breach relating to the sixteenth instalment was an isolated occurrence and did not amount to a repudiation of the entire contract. Consequently, the buyers remained liable to take and pay for the remaining instalments. On the other hand, in *Munro* v. *Meyer* (1930), a buyer who had ordered a large quantity of bonemeal found that all the instalments he had received (almost half of the contractual amount) had been adulterated by the manufacturers with cocoa husks. It was also likely that future instalments would be similarly defective. The buyer succeeded in obtaining a declaration that he was no longer bound to take any further instalments.

In both of these cases the contract provided that delivery was to be by instalments and that these were to be separately paid for. The contracts were therefore 'severable', and section 11(1)(c) did not apply. What is the position where a seller merely has an *option* to deliver by separate instalments? It is clear from the case of *Rosenthal & Sons Ltd* v. *Esmail* (1965) that such a contract will only be severable if the seller, in fact, exercises his option. If he sends all the goods together, even though he ships them under two separate bills of lading, the contract is not severable. Consequently section 11(1)(c) will apply, and if the buyer 'accepts' any part of the goods he cannot reject the remainder on the grounds that they are un-merchantable.

When does a buyer accept the goods? The question of acceptance is dealt with by sections 34 and 35. Section 34, which is largely self-explanatory, reads as follows:

1. Where goods are delivered to the buyer, which he has not previously examined, he is not deemed to have accepted them unless and until he has had a reasonable opportunity of examining them for the purpose of ascertaining whether they are in conformity with the contract.
2. Unless otherwise agreed, when the seller tenders delivery of goods to the buyer, he is bound, on request, to afford the buyer a reasonable opportunity of examining the goods for the purpose of ascertaining whether they are in conformity with the contract.

This is reasonable enough. The buyer may well be seeing the goods themselves for the first time and the mere fact that the buyer physically takes delivery from, e.g., a ship, train, or lorry, will not prevent him from examining them and then rejecting them if they do not conform with the contract.

It is now necessary to turn to section 35 which specifies three cases where a buyer is deemed to have accepted the goods. As originally drafted, it read:

The buyer is deemed to have accepted the goods when he intimates to the seller that he has accepted them, or when the goods have been delivered to him and he does any act inconsistent with the ownership of the seller, or when, after the lapse of a reasonable time, he retains the goods without intimating to the seller that he has rejected them.

What is the relationship between section 34 and section 35? Clearly, if the buyer allows a reasonable time to elapse he will be held to have accepted the goods, because during that time he would normally have had reasonable opportunity for examination. Similarly, if the buyer chooses to inform the seller that he has accepted the goods, this will indicate either that the buyer has examined the goods and found them satisfactory, or that he has waived his rights of examination. This leaves one question: what happens if the buyer does some act inconsistent with the seller's ownership *before* he has had a reasonable opportunity of examination? In *Hardy Ltd* v. *Hillerns & Fowler* (1923) and in *Ruben Ltd* v. *Faire Bros Ltd* (1949) the buyer re-sold the goods, and had them delivered to the sub-purchaser before he (the buyer) had had a reasonable opportunity of examination. In both cases it was held that section 35 prevailed over section 34, and that the buyer had accordingly 'accepted' the goods. The result was that it was too late for him to reject the goods for breach of condition. Although these cases have been criticized, it is perfectly possible to argue that they were correct, since the buyer's conduct showed an intention to waive his rights of examination. As time went on, however, the principle established by these two cases became inconvenient, since a great many goods were sold in sealed containers and it was clearly within the contemplation of the parties that the buyer would re-sell the goods unopened. It was largely to cover this type of case that section 4(2) of the Misrepresentation Act 1967, was passed. This section provides in effect, that an act inconsistent with the seller's ownership (for example, delivery to a sub-buyer) shall *not* be an act of acceptance unless and until the buyer has had a reasonable opportunity of examination. Section 35 must now be read by adding the words 'except where section 34 of this Act otherwise provides' before the words 'when the goods have been delivered'. Thus:

S sells goods to B, and B re-sells to B2. The goods are delivered by S to B and by B to B2. B2 rejects for breach of condition. If B has not had a reasonable opportunity for examination, he can also reject.

Implied terms

We now turn to some of the most important provisions of the Act – the implied conditions and warranties contained in sections 12–15. At the end of this section, the subject of exemption clauses will be dealt with, and it is important to bear in mind throughout this section that the implied terms laid down by the Act can be (and often are) negatived or varied by agreement. Possible reforms are examined on page 88.

Title. Section 12 states that:

unless the circumstances of the contract are such as to show a different intention, there is

1. An implied condition on the part of the seller that in the case of a sale he has a right to sell the goods, and that in the case of an agreement to sell he will have a right to sell the goods at the time when the property is to pass.

2. An implied warranty that the buyer shall have and enjoy quiet possession of the goods.

3. An implied warranty that the goods shall be free from any charge or encumbrance in favour of any third party, not declared or known to the buyer before or at the time when the contract is made.

The condition that the buyer has a right to sell is clearly a vital term, since the passing of the property is the central feature of the contract.

If the seller has no right to sell, the buyer may find himself in a strong position. In *Rowland* v. *Divall* (1923) the following facts occurred:

The defendant sold a car to the plaintiff who used it for four months. Unknown to either party the car was stolen property and the police took it away from the buyer. He sued the seller to recover the price which he had paid. The seller argued that (a) an allowance should be made for the four months' use and (b) by using the car for four months the buyer had 'accepted' the car within section 11(1)(c), so that he was compelled to treat the breach of condition as a breach of warranty and could not recover the full price. Both arguments failed. The Court of Appeal held that (a) the buyer had paid for the property in the goods and he had not received it; (b) the four months' use was irrelevant; (c) as the buyer had not received the property in the goods there was nothing for him to 'accept'; (d) accordingly, the buyer was entitled to recover the full price which he had paid.

What happens if a seller has no right to sell at the time of the sale but removes the defect later? This is what happened in the case of *Butterworth* v. *Kingsway Motors* (1954), where the buyer again found himself in a strong position. In that case:

A hire-purchase finance company let a car to A on hire-purchase. A had no right to sell but, in breach of his contract, he sold it to B. It then passed through several hands and finally D sold it to P for £1175. P used the car for some eleven months and at the end of that period (when the value of the car had dropped to £800) he received a letter from the finance company informing him of the hire-purchase agreement and demanding payment of the outstanding balance. He immediately wrote to D and claimed the return of his full £1175. A week later, A made the final payment under the hire-purchase agreement and the title then passed to A and through him it passed down the line to the other buyers. It was held, however, that as soon as P had given notice of rejection to D he had a vested right to the return of his money and nothing done by D afterwards could deprive him of this right.

If, of course, D had perfected P's title before P rejected, it seems pretty clear that P would not have got all his money back, since he would have got the property in the goods (even though he got it rather late). He would, of course, have had a claim for damages. It should also be noted that if these facts were to happen again, the result might be very different, because the very first buyer would probably get the property in the goods from the hirer under the special rules protecting private purchasers contained in the Hire-Purchase Act 1964 (see pp. 51–2).

It is also interesting to notice that a seller may be in breach of the 'right to sell' condition in section 12(1) even though he can and does pass the property in the goods. This is what happened in *Niblett* v. *Confectioners Materials Co.* (1921) where foreign sellers of tinned milk delivered the tins bearing a wrapping which infringed a well-known trade mark. Following an objection by the owners of the trade mark, the tins were detained at the customs: the buyers had to rip off the labels, and they eventually sold the tins at a loss. It was held by the Court of Appeal that, as the owners of the trade mark could have stopped any sale, it could not be said that the sellers had a 'right' to sell. The sellers therefore were liable.

The warranties relating to quiet possession and freedom from undisclosed incumbrances clearly overlap with the basic condition relating to title. There could, however, be cases where a buyer might have a claim under 12(2) or 12(3) but not 12(1). Thus if S sold goods to B and then, after B had re-sold to B2, S himself re-sold to B3 and gave him a good title under one of the *nemo dat* exceptions, B2 would be able to sue B under section 12(2). A claim under 12(3) could arise if, for example, goods were subject to an undisclosed unpaid seller's lien or to undisclosed rights enjoyed by a sheriff acting on behalf of a judgment creditor (*Lloyds and Scottish Finance Ltd* v. *Modern Cars and Caravans Ltd* (1964)). It has also been suggested that under section 12(1) the time limit for a claim will run from the date of the contract, whereas under sections 12(2) or 12(3) it will not start to run until the buyer is dispossessed.

We have seen that if the buyer is dispossessed by the true owner, he can get his money back. Can he also recover any further sums spent by him on the goods? Much will depend on the nature of the expenditure, but in *Mason* v. *Burningham* (1949) a lady who bought a typewriter and then spent a sum of money overhauling it was held entitled to recover this sum from the seller in addition to the price when it transpired that the typewriter was stolen property.

Section 12, as we have seen, only applies where no different intention appears. It is clear from cases like *Payne* v. *Elsden* (1900) that neither an auctioneer nor a sheriff selling un-redeemed pledges gives an undertaking of title, although an auctioneer does warrant that he knows of no defect in his principal's title (*Benton* v. *Campbell Parker & Co. Ltd* (1925)). Apart from these cases, there has been some interesting discussion among writers on the question of whether the 'right to sell' condition can be excluded and, if so, whether the resulting contract can be called a contract for the sale of goods. There is, however, no case on this point (but see p. 88).

Description. Section 13 reads as follows:

Where there is a contract for the sale of goods by description, there is an implied condition that the goods shall correspond with the description; and if the sale be by sample as well as by description, it is not sufficient that the bulk of the goods corresponds with the sample if the goods do not also correspond with the description.

This condition adds very little to the law. If words are used to identify the goods, then clearly it is a term of the contract that the identification is correct. If a seller agrees to sell 'a new Singer car', 'a Constable painting', or 'foreign refined rape oil', he will clearly be in breach of contract if the goods which he supplies do not answer their description.

What, then, is a sale by description? The cases show that it covers at least three types of contract of sale, namely:

1. All agreements to sell unascertained goods (e.g. '10 dozen bottles of 1949 port').

2. A contract for the sale of specific goods where the buyer has not seen them and is relying on the description. Thus, in *Varley* v. *Whipp* (1900) a seller agreed to sell a reaping machine which he described as 'new the previous year'. The buyer had not seen it, and when it was delivered it was found to be old. It was held that he could reject it for breach of the condition of description.

3. A sale of specific goods which the buyer has seen, if the goods are sold not *as* specific goods but as goods answering a description. A remarkable recent illustration was provided by the case of *Beale* v. *Taylor* (1967). In that case the buyer read an advertisement offering for sale a 'Herald convertible 1961'. He went to look at it and saw the figure 1200 displayed on a disc at the back of the car. He bought it, but later discovered that the 'car' actually consisted of the rear half of a 1961 Herald 1200 welded to the front half of an earlier model. It was held by the Court of Appeal that, on the evidence,

the buyer had bought by reference to the description, and he was entitled to damages under section 13. Putting the matter another way, the only type of sale which is not a sale by description is a sale of a specific article sold as such, as where a buyer goes in to a dealer's showroom, sees a car and says, 'I'll have that one.' Even here it might be argued that the goods 'describe' themselves.

If a sale is by description, three points are worthy of note. In the first place, the term 'description' is extremely wide and covers such matters as ingredients, measurements, method of packing, quantity and date of shipment. As a famous judge put it in one case: 'every item in a description which constitutes a substantial ingredient in the identity of the thing sold is a condition.' On the other hand, the mere fact that the goods have a defect making them unmerchantable does not necessarily mean that the seller is in breach of section 13. It is, in each case, a question of degree. Thus, if the seller agreed to sell dates and supplied them contaminated with sewage he would almost certainly be in breach of section 13 (*Asfar* v. *Blundell*, p. 35). On the other hand, the House of Lords has recently held that 'herring-meal' could still be described as herring-meal even though it had a defect rendering it poisonous when fed to mink (*Christopher Hill* v. *Ashington Piggeries* (1971)).

Secondly, liability under section 13 is strict. In *re Moore and Landauer* (1921) buyers ordered 3100 cases of Australian peaches packed in boxes containing thirty tins. Some boxes contained only twenty-four tins, and an arbitrator found that the market value was not affected in any way. It was held, nevertheless, that the sellers were in breach of the condition of section 13 and the buyers were entitled to reject the entire consignment. Again, in *Arcos* v. *Ronaasen* (1933) buyers ordered staves ½″ thick, and most of those delivered were between ½″ and 9/16″ thick. The House of Lords held that the buyers were entitled to reject the goods because, in the words of Lord Atkin,

a ton does not mean about a ton, or a yard about a yard. Still less when you descend to minute measurements does half an inch mean about half an inch. If a seller wants a margin he must, and in my experience does, stipulate for it.

The final point about section 13 relates to exclusion. Although by section 55 any obligations arising 'under the Act' can be excluded, it is difficult to see how this can apply to the description of the goods. If a seller makes a categorical statement in the body of the contract that he is selling a '1948 Morris', and then among the small print he excludes 'all conditions', he is saying in effect, 'I agree to sell you a 1948 Morris but I am not liable if I do not sell you a 1948 Morris'. The exception clause might well be held to be ineffective as being repugnant to the main purpose of the contract. It has, however, been suggested that certain minor matters of description (for example, the measurements in the Arcos case) can be covered by a carefully drawn exemption clause. Even here, however, it would seem preferable to qualify the descriptive words themselves, rather than to give and then take away.

So far we have dealt solely with civil liability, but if the goods bear a false trade description, there may also be criminal liability under the Trade Descriptions Act 1968.

Quality and fitness. Section 14 opens with these words (which should not be overlooked):

Subject to the provisions of this Act and of any statute in that behalf, there is no implied warranty or condition as to the quality or fitness for any particular purpose of goods supplied under a contract of sale.

Although these words, embodying the old doctrine *caveat emptor* – 'let the buyer beware', have been greatly cut down by the exceptions which follow, they are still important in many cases, and particularly in all cases where the seller is not a dealer in the goods. If, therefore, A (a private person) sells his television set to B, the buyer cannot complain merely because it gives him a lot of trouble.

The basic 'buyer beware' rule is cut down by three exceptions, namely:

1. The condition of fitness (section 14(1)).

2. The condition of merchantable quality (section 14(2)).

3. Any condition or warranty which may be annexed by usage of trade (section 14(3)).

We must now examine in some detail the conditions of quality and fitness, but before doing so one point of great importance must be stressed. In a very large number of cases, a person goes to a retailer and buys goods which the retailer, in turn, has bought from a wholesaler or manufacturer. The rights available to the customer under the Sale of Goods Act are available only against the person who sold the goods to him. This means that he has no rights against the manufacturer unless he bought direct from the manufacturer or unless he can bring a claim in tort (p. 85). It follows that if a buyer buys an expensive, but unsatisfactory, car from a dealer who afterwards disappears or becomes bankrupt, the buyer may find himself without an effective remedy.

Condition of fitness. Section 14(1) imposes an implied condition that the goods are reasonably fit for the buyer's particular purpose if

1. The buyer, expressly or by implication, makes known to the seller the particular purpose for which he requires the goods.

2. He relies on the seller's skill or judgment.

3. The goods are of a description which it is in the ordinary course of the seller's business to supply (whether he is the manufacturer or not).

There is, however, a proviso that 'in the case of a contract for the sale of a specified article under its patent or other trade name, there is no implied condition as to its fitness for any particular purpose'.

Although, at first sight, it would seem that a buyer has many tough hurdles to surmount, in practice most of the points arising under section 14(1) have been resolved in his favour. From the many decided cases on this subsection, six points emerge.

1. Where the purpose is obvious (e.g. a hot-water bottle to warm up the bed, food for eating, a car for driving, a toy for playing), it is clearly unnecessary for a buyer solemnly to inform the seller of his purpose. If, however, goods are required for some particular purpose which is not obvious, the seller will not be liable unless this purpose was made known to him before the contract was concluded. This would cover, for example, a sale of raw material or material manufactured in bulk and capable of being used for a large variety of purposes in the manufacture of other articles. This point was also fatal to the buyer in the case of *Griffiths* v. *Peter Conway Ltd* (1939), where a lady who bought a tweed coat did not inform the seller that she had an unduly sensitive skin. She unfortunately contracted dermatitis from wearing the coat and she claimed damages under section 14(1). The evidence showed that the coat would not have caused this trouble if her skin had been normally sensitive, and accordingly it was held that, as she had not made her *particular* purpose known to the seller, her claim failed.

2. Reliance on the seller's skill or judgment can also be express or (more usually) implied. As Lord Wright pointed out in the leading case of *Grant* v. *Australian Knitting Mills* (1936), when a customer goes into a shop the reliance will normally be inferred from the mere fact that the buyer assumes the retailer to have selected his stock with skill and judgment. This is not, of course, an inflexible rule of law, so that, for example, if the buyer were to carry out a careful examination of the goods, this might negative reliance. It has, however, been held that partial reliance is sufficient. If, therefore, a buyer submits detailed specifications covering part of the work and relies on the seller's skill for the rest, the condition will still apply and the seller will be liable unless he can prove that the defect was outside the area of reliance (*Cammell Laird & Co. Ltd* v. *Manganese Bronze and Brass Co. Ltd* (1934) and more recently *Christopher Hill* v. *Ashington Piggeries* (1971)).

3. The condition will be implied if the goods belong to a class

in which the seller usually deals, and this is so even though the particular goods are not usually handled by the seller. In *Spencer Trading Co. Ltd* v. *Devon* (1947) the sellers, who were dealers in 'resins, gums, and other adhesive substances' received an order for glue for flypaper, a commodity which they rarely handled. It was held, nevertheless, that this glue came within the general class of goods dealt in by the sellers and, as it proved unfit for the buyer's purpose, the sellers were liable under section 14(1). A similar result was reached in the Christopher Hill case where compounders of animal food-stuffs were asked to supply a foodstuff for feeding to mink (an animal for which they had never previously compounded food).

4. The condition applies to all goods 'supplied under a contract of sale' so that it covers not only the goods themselves, but also the container in which they are supplied. It was held in *Geddling* v. *Marsh* (1920) that the condition applied even to a bottle which was to be returned – it was goods 'supplied' under a contract of sale. Presumably goods included by mistake would also be taken into account (cf. *Wilson* v. *Rickett, Cockerell & Co. Ltd*; see p. 76).

5. If the various conditions are satisfied, liability is strict. The section uses the words 'shall be reasonably fit', and if the goods are not reasonably fit for the buyer's purpose the seller will be liable even though he took all possible care and even though no amount of care would have revealed the defect. In *Frost* v. *Aylesbury Dairy Co. Ltd* (1905) a man bought milk which, unknown to him, contained typhoid germs. He and his family drank it, and his wife died. It was held that the husband (as the contracting party) could recover damages under 14(1), including funeral expenses, and the mere fact that the sellers were not negligent was no defence. It may be mentioned in passing that if Mrs Frost had been merely taken ill and had wanted to sue the sellers for her pain and suffering, she could not have sued on the contract, not being a party to it. She would have had to bring a claim in tort for negligence and, as the sellers were not negligent, the claim would have failed.

6. The trade name proviso has been generously construed in favour of the buyer. In the first place, a 'trade name' is something which has to be acquired by user, in the sense that the name must be associated in the mind of the public with the article in question. Secondly, the trade name proviso only applies when the buyer makes it clear that he is relying solely on the trade name and not on the seller's skill or judgment. In *Baldry* v. *Marshall* (1925) the prospective buyer asked the seller to recommend him a car that was both comfortable and good for touring. The seller recommended a Bugatti car, and the buyer agreed to buy one. Unfortunately it was quite unfit for his purpose. The Court of Appeal held that, since the buyer had clearly relied on the seller's skill and judgment, the 'trade name' proviso did not apply and the seller was liable. The final point to notice about the 'trade name' proviso is that even if it applies the goods must still be merchantable under the condition discussed below.

Condition of merchantable quality. This is implied by section 14(2) where:

1. Goods are sold by description.

2. The seller deals in goods of that description, whether he is the manufacturer or not.

The subsection ends with a proviso that where the buyer has examined the goods, there is no implied condition as to defects which such examination ought to have revealed. In *Thornett and Fehr* v. *Beer & Sons Ltd* (1949) a buyer of some barrels of glue made a very hasty inspection – he looked at the outside only. Had he taken the trouble to look inside the barrels, he would immediately have spotted the defect. It was held that the proviso applied, with the result that the buyer had no remedy. On the other hand, in *Wren* v. *Holt* (1903) the buyer recovered damages in respect of beer which contained arsenic. In this case, no ordinary examination would have revealed the defect.

Returning now to the main body of the subsection, it will be seen that the condition will only be implied where the sale is by description. This matter was considered earlier, in connection with section 13. A prospective customer should always ask for the article by its name, however obvious, because the condition of merchantable quality will depend on it. We have already seen that a sale under a trade name (for example, 'Coalite') is a sale by description, so that the condition will apply. The further requirement that the seller must deal in goods of 'that description' is satisfied if he deals in the general class of goods to which the contract goods belong (*Christopher Hill* v. *Ashington Piggeries* (1971)).

This subsection, like the previous one, applies to all goods 'supplied' under a contract of sale, so that it would apply to a bottle or container in which the goods were packed (*Geddling* v. *Marsh* (1920)). In the remarkable case of *Wilson* v. *Rickett, Cockerell & Co. Ltd* (1954) a lady ordered some 'Coalite' for her fire, and the goods supplied included a detonator. When an explosion occurred, the sellers put up the astonishing defence (which succeeded in the County Court) that the coal itself was satisfactory and that the detonator did not form part of the contract goods. The fallacy of this argument was demonstrated by the Court of Appeal, which pointed out that one had to look at the entirety of the goods 'supplied' under the contract. Lord Denning was emphatic; no amount of legal argument would persuade him that a consignment of coal which included a detonator was fit for burning. The sellers were liable under section 14(2) – although not under section 14(1) because the goods had been ordered under a trade name.

What is the meaning of merchantable quality, and how does this condition differ, if at all, from the condition of fitness? There have been a number of cases in which the courts have considered this problem. The Act itself is not helpful – it merely states in section 62 that the 'quality' of the goods includes their state or condition. In the case of *Niblett* v. *Confectioners Materials Co.* (the case of the tinned milk where the labels infringed the trade mark) two members of the Court of Appeal expressed the view that the sellers were liable under section 14(2) as well as under section 12(1) because the 'state or condition' of the goods included the wrapping, and the wrapping in the present case was so defective that the goods were totally unfit for the buyers' purpose – the buyers could never sell them anywhere. They were therefore unmerchantable. This case was distinguished in *Sumner Permain Ltd* v. *Webb* (1922) where buyers ordered a substance called Webbs Indian Tonic, which was manufactured by a secret process. The buyer required it for re-sale in the Argentine. The goods supplied by the sellers were perfectly useable and saleable by the buyers. Unfortunately, they contained a small percentage of salicylic acid and this infringed Argentine legislation. When the goods arrived in the Argentine, they were seized by the authorities. The buyers were unable to rely on section 14(1) because they had ordered the tonic under its trade name. So they claimed damages under section 14(2) on the grounds that the goods were unmerchantable. The Court of Appeal, consisting of the three judges who had heard the Niblett case, held that the goods were not unmerchantable. A defect making the goods unsaleable in one particular place does not make the goods unmerchantable. Presumably if the goods had been completely unsaleable *anywhere* the sellers would have been liable.

The case highlights the meaning of the word 'merchantable' and also the distinction between 'merchantable' and 'fit'. In other words, if goods can be used for several purposes they are not unmerchantable merely because they are unfit for the buyer's particular purpose. As a result of a number of house of Lords cases the rule can be stated thus: goods are merchantable if a buyer, with full knowledge of the defects, would accept the goods under his contract without a substantial abatement in the price. Thus in *Cammell Laird* v. *Manganese Bronze and Brass Co. Ltd* (1934), the sellers manufactured a ship's propeller for a particular ship owned by the buyers. The finished propeller had defects rendering it unfit for the buyers' particular ship, although it could have been used perfectly well on other ships. Having classified the contract as one for sale of goods (see p. 22), the House of Lords held that the sellers were liable under section 14(1) but *not* under section 14(2). Similarly in *Brown* v. *Craiks* (1970) buyers ordered cloth at 36.25p per yard. They did not tell the sellers that it was required for dress-making. The cloth supplied was unfit for dressmaking but perfectly saleable for industrial purposes at 30p per yard. The House of Lords held that this difference in price did not make the cloth 'unmerchantable'. The position might have been different if the cloth could only have been sold at a 'throw-away' price.

The quality of the goods must, of course, be looked at in the light of all the circumstances, and the age of the goods is clearly an important factor. In the case of *Bartlett* v. *Sidney Marcus* (1965) the Court of Appeal pointed out that a second-hand car was of merchantable quality if it was roadworthy, even though it was not as good as a new car and required some repairs. It will be recalled that this type of problem is only important where the seller is a dealer – if he is a private person the condition of merchantable quality will not be implied at all.

Three other problems have arisen all revolving around the word 'merchantable'. First, what is the legal position where a buyer gives an order for a large quantity of goods, and on delivery some prove to be merchantable while others are not? Unless the contract is severable (see p. 62) the general rule is that the buyer can reject the entire consignment unless the deviation is so small that a businessman would ignore it. Thus, in *Rapalli* v. *Take Ltd* (1958) the buyer ordered 'medium onions' and, on delivery, five or six per cent were found to be sprouting. It was held that the buyer could reject the entire consignment.

The second problem concerns goods which are subject to a defect that can be put right by a simple process. The position here is that the goods will still be classified as unmerchantable, so that the buyer can reject them, unless both parties must have contemplated that the process would be applied to the goods before they were used. In *Heil* v. *Hedges* (1951) a lady became ill as a result of eating pork chops containing tape-worms. She did not cook the chops properly; had she done so, the worms would have died. Her action for damages under section 14(2) failed, because the pork chops were delivered in such a state that they would have been merchantable had they been properly cooked, and it was reasonably to be expected that they would be so cooked. It is this last factor which distinguishes this case from cases like *Grant* v. *Australian Knitting Mills* (1936) where an unfortunate buyer became seriously ill because a pair of underpants which he bought contained too much sulphite. An argument by the sellers that the sulphite would have been removed if the pants had been washed was rejected; it was not contemplated that this new pair of pants would have to be washed before being used for the first time. The sellers were held liable.

The final point – and one on which there is surprisingly little authority – is the time during which the goods must remain merchantable. Suppose that a television set develops serious faults after a year's use. Is the seller liable? This question cannot be answered with certainty, although on principle he ought to be liable. The cases do, however, suggest that where the goods have to be sent to the buyer by land or sea (or presumably by air), the goods must remain merchantable throughout the normal journey and for a reasonable time thereafter. Thus, in the case of *Beer* v. *Walker* (1877) rabbits were sent by train from London to Brighton. They were in apparently good order when the train left London; the journey was a normal one. On arrival in Brighton, the rabbits were found to be putrid and had to be destroyed. It was held that the sellers were liable, since goods which could not withstand a normal journey could not be said to be merchantable. If, of course, the journey had been an abnormal one (as, for example, if the journey had been unduly prolonged by reason of an avalanche or a derailment) the position would have been different; in this case the normal rules as to risk (see p. 34) would have applied. It has also been suggested that the condition that the goods must remain merchantable throughout a normal journey only applies where the goods are particularly vulnerable (for example, perishable foodstuffs or potatoes which might mature or ferment) and does not apply in the case of other goods such as skins (*per* Winn J. (as he then was) in *Cordova Land Co. Ltd* v. *Victor Bros.* (1966)).

Before leaving the question of quality and fitness, it may be mentioned that conditions and warranties are also implied under certain other Acts, which are, however, limited to certain classes of goods. Examples include the Seeds Act 1920, the Fertilisers and Feeding Stuffs Act 1926, the Food and Drugs Act 1955, and the Consumer Protection Act 1961. There are also various other Acts imposing criminal liability.

Conditions implied on a sale by sample. Section 15 reads as follows:

1. A contract of sale is a contract for sale by sample where there is a term in the contract, express or implied, to that effect.

2. In the case of a contract for sale by sample
(a) There is an implied condition that the bulk shall correspond with the sample in quality.
(b) There is an implied condition that the buyer shall have a reasonable opportunity of comparing the bulk with the sample.
(c) There is an implied condition that the goods shall be free from any defect rendering them unmerchantable, which would not be apparent on reasonable examination of the sample.

In practice, the vast majority of contracts for sale by sample would also be sales by description, so that, by section 13, it is not sufficient if the goods correspond to the sample if they do not also correspond to the description. In the case of *Nichol* v. *Godts* (1854) a sale of 'foreign refined rape oil' contained a clause that the goods were 'warranted only equal to sample'. The sellers supplied a substance which could not properly be called foreign refined rape oil at all, and it was held that the words 'warranted only equal to sample' did not excuse the sellers from their over-riding duty to supply oil answering the description of 'foreign refined rape oil'.

The terms of section 15 are straightforward and only three points need be briefly noted. First, the mere fact that a sample is shown during negotiations does not make the contract a contract for sale by sample (*Gardiner* v. *Gray* (1815)). Secondly, a sale 'with all faults' may exclude the condition implied by section 15(2)(c), but the seller will not be protected if he delivers a bulk which does not correspond to the sample (*Champanhac Ltd* v. *Waller Ltd* (1948)). Finally, the words 'reasonable examination' in section 15(2)(c) mean a normal commercial examination and not, e.g. a detailed analysis in a laboratory. This was brought out by the case of *Godley* v. *Perry* (1960), where the following facts arose:

A small boy aged six went into a shop where toys were sold and asked for a toy catapult. The shopkeeper produced one and the boy bought it for sixpence. Unfortunately it broke when he used it for the first time, and he lost the sight of an eye. He sued the shop-keeper for damages under sections 14(1) and 14(2). The shopkeeper in his turn claimed damages under section 15(2)(c) from a whole-saler who had sold him two dozen of these catapults by sample. It was held that: (1) the shopkeeper was liable under section 14(1) since (a) he was a dealer in the goods and (b) the boy had impliedly made his purpose known and had relied on the shopkeeper's skill and judgment; (2) the shopkeeper was also liable under section 14(2) because, although the boy had seen the specific catapult, it was still a sale by description and the shopkeeper dealt in goods of that description; (3) the wholesaler was liable to the shopkeeper under Section 15(2)(c) because the bulk had a defect rendering it un-merchantable and this defect was not apparent on a *reasonable* examination of the sample.

Exemption clauses. We saw on p. 13 that section 55 enables any right, duty, or liability arising under the Act to be nega-tived or varied by agreement. Subject to what has been said about sections 12 and 13 (see pp. 68 and 71), there is no doubt that a clause excluding the implied conditions and warranties is valid. Nevertheless the courts have shown no great love for exemption clauses, largely because they are usually to be found in standard-form take-it-or-leave-it con-tracts. In this type of contract it is a misuse of language to talk about the customer having 'agreed' to give up his rights under the contract since (1) he has probably not read the small print anyway and (2) even if he had read it, he would have found the exemption clause wrapped up in obscure legal language which he would not have understood and (3) even if he had both read it and understood it, he would usually have been powerless to get the contract amended and (4) if he decided to take his custom elsewhere he might well find an identical set of printed conditions offered to him by every firm. Faced with this problem in the nineteenth and twentieth centuries the courts could, if they wished, have considered the clauses on their merits and, if necessary, could have declared some of them to be against the public interest and therefore of no legal effect. This has been done to some extent in the United States, but among modern English judges only Lord Denning has suggested that it might be done. His more conservative fellow judges have refused to take so radical a step, and have continued to pay lip service to 'freedom of contract' and to 'sanctity of contract'. They have, however, given help to a party faced with these clauses in a number of indirect ways. Thus, the courts have held that

1. If there is any ambiguity, the clause is construed against the party relying on it.

2. The clause is ineffective if it was introduced too late, i.e. after the contract had been concluded.

3. A party cannot shelter behind an exemption clause if he has misrepresented the effect of the clause to the other party.

The following cases relating to sale of goods illustrate the hostility of the courts towards exemption clauses:

1. In *Wallis, Son & Wells* v. *Pratt & Haynes* (1911) the House of Lords held that a clause excluding implied 'warranties' did not exclude an implied condition even though the buyer had accepted the goods and was therefore compelled by section 11(1)(c) to treat the breach as a breach of warranty.

2. In *Andrews Bros.* (*Bournemouth*) *Ltd* v. *Singer Ltd* (1934), where a buyer ordered a 'new Singer car' and received an old one, it was held that a clause excluding an 'implied' condition did not exclude an express condition. It was, indeed, suggested in this case that an express condition could be excluded, but we have already seen that this seems logically impossible, because it would enable a seller to give with one hand and take away with the other.

3. In *Couchman* v. *Hill* (1947), where the seller at a cattle market said to a prospective buyer, 'I warrant that she is unserved', it was held that this oral promise was sufficient to over-ride a printed exemption clause in the auction particulars.

Although these developments were welcome, it is clear that they did not go far enough because, since the rules laid down by the courts were largely linguistic, it was always possible that they could be outflanked by a skilful draftsman. In *L'Estrange* v. *Graucob Ltd* (1934), a lady who ran a café bought a cigarette machine. The contract was in writing and it contained a clause excluding

'any express or implied condition, statement or warranty, statutory or otherwise, not stated herein'.

The machine did not work satisfactorily, and the sellers refused to do anything about it. It was held that Miss L'Estrange had no remedy at all.

It began to look as if the draftsmen had won the day, but the courts had one more weapon left. This was the doctrine of 'fundamental breach' or 'breach of a fundamental term'. The idea behind this doctrine was that although every contract had conditions and warranties which could be excluded, every contract also had one central hard core – one basic obligation which was so fundamental that any attempt to exclude it would destroy the whole object of the contract. The seeds of the doctrine were sown as long ago as 1838, when Lord Abinger stated that a seller who contracted to sell peas and delivered beans instead was guilty of an entire non-performance of the contract rather than the breach of a particular term. This has crystallized into a general principle that, under a contract for the sale of goods, it is the seller's duty to supply the goods contracted for and not goods which are substantially different. Most of the modern illustrations are concerned with cars let out on hire-purchase. In *Karsales* (*Harrow*) *Ltd* v. *Wallis* (1956):

The hirer saw a Buick car in excellent condition; he signed a form of application for hire-purchase. A week later the 'car' was delivered outside his house. It had been towed there; tyres had been changed, the cylinder head was off and all the valves were burnt. The car would not go, and it would have cost £150 to restore it to its previous condition. The contract stated that 'no condition or warranty that the vehicle is roadworthy or as to its age, condition or fitness for any purpose is given by the owner or implied herein.' Despite the enormous width of this clause, it was held by the Court of Appeal that the owners were not protected by it, because they had committed a fundamental breach of contract.

Lord Justice Birkett went so far as to say 'a car which will not go is not a car at all', but clearly it is necessary to read this remark in the context of the very remarkable facts of that case. The Karsales case was followed in *Yeoman Credit Ltd* v. *Apps* (1962), where a car had numerous defects and could only do about three miles in one and a half hours. The Court of Appeal held that while no one defect was a fundamental breach, the overall accumulation of defects did amount to such a breach, with the result, again, that the owners could not shelter behind an exemption clause. It was followed again in *Charterhouse Credit Co.* v. *Tolly* (1963), where the 'fundamental breach' consisted of a defective rear axle. Incidentally, it should be mentioned that all these cases were decided before the Hire-Purchase Act 1964 was passed to give the hirer additional protection.

The whole doctrine of fundamental breach was recently extensively reviewed by the House of Lords in *Suisse Atlantique S.A.* v. *N.V. Rotterdamsche Kolen Centrale* (1966) – a case concerning the carriage of goods by sea. The essential point brought out in this case is that there is no rule *of law* preventing a party from contracting out of his liability for a fundamental breach; it is all a question of construction. In theory this would appear to take us back to *L'Estrange* v. *Graucob Ltd*, but in practice this is not so. If a breach is as serious as the ones in *Karsales* (*Harrow*) *Ltd* v. *Wallis*, *Yeoman Credit Ltd* v. *Apps*, and *Charterhouse Credit Co.* v. *Tolly*, it is virtually certain that any court would hold, as a matter of construction, that the parties never intended the exemption clause to cover that type of breach. Indeed, the House regarded these cases as correctly decided on their particular facts. It has even been suggested that an exemption clause will never apply if the seller tenders goods totally different from those contracted for and the buyer treats the contract as discharged (see *per* Donaldson J. in *Kenyon Ltd* v. *Baxter Hoare & Co.* (1971), citing Lord Wilberforce in *Suisse Atlantique*). In *Farnworth Finance Co. Ltd* v. *Attryde* (1970), Lord Denning M. R., while paying lip service to *Suisse Atlantique*, pointed out that normally an exemption clause should not be construed as covering a fundamental breach. The language used in this case is strikingly similar to that which was used in the earlier hire-purchase cases and which was criticized by the House of Lords in *Suisse Atlantique*. It also seems that if the breach discharges the contract altogether the seller cannot rely on a clause inserted for his protection (*Harbutts Plasticine* v. *Wayne Tank and Pump Co.* (1970)).

Duties of the manufacturer

Before leaving the buyer's rights where the goods are defective, it is necessary to say something about the liability of the manufacturer. If the customer buys direct from the manufacturer, the Sale of Goods Act will, of course, apply. Usually, however, the contract of sale is with the dealer, and the question then arises as to whether the buyer (or, for that matter, some member of the buyer's family who suffers damage) has any rights at all against the manufacturer. Until 1932, the manufacturer was only liable if he supplied inherently dangerous goods, or if he failed to give a warning of a defect of which he actually knew. Thus, in *Clarke* v. *Army and Navy Co-operative Society Ltd* (1903), a seller was held liable when he sold some tins of chlorinated lime without giving a warning that the tins were (as he knew) defective and dangerous unless opened in a particular way.

Liability, therefore, used to be very restricted but, in *Donoghue* v. *Stevenson* (1932), the position was radically altered. In that case:

A lady went to a café with a friend in Paisley and ordered a bottle of ginger beer. It was alleged that when she poured out a glass for her friend there floated out a snail in an advanced state of decomposition. The friend became ill, and since she had no contract with the café owner she sued the manufacturer in tort for negligence. By a majority of three to two the House of Lords held that if these facts could be proved the manufacturers would be liable.

Lord Atkin formulated the general principle in the following words:

The manufacturer of a product who intends it to reach the ultimate consumer in the form in which it left him without reasonable prospect of intermediate examination, and who realizes that lack of reasonable care will cause injury to the consumer's life or property, owes a legal duty to take such reasonable care.

This principle is immensely important and it has been extended beyond manufacturers to other persons doing active work on goods. Two qualifications should, however, be noted. In the first place, the principle has so far been applied only where, by reason of negligence, the goods have proved to be dangerous. There is as yet no case where a buyer has recovered damages from a manufacturer on the ground that negligence has caused him (the buyer) to spend money on repairs. Despite dicta in two recent cases (both concerned with careless statements) that there was no distinction between physical loss and financial loss, the courts have been reluctant, in other branches of the law of negligence, to award damages for negligent acts causing purely economic loss (see e.g. *Weller* v. *Foot & Mouth Research Institute* (1965) and *S.C.M.* v. *Whittall* (1970)). Secondly, the liability is based on negligence, and although the facts themselves may suggest negligence, the manufacturers can always escape liability by proving that they had in force a foolproof system, i.e. that they were not negligent. In *Daniels* v. *White & Son* (1938):

Mr Daniels bought a bottle of 'Whites Lemonade'. Unfortunately it contained some carbolic acid, with the result that both he and his wife became ill. An action was brought against both the retailer and the manufacturers. It was held that (1) the husband's action against the retailer succeeded under section 14(2) because the lemonade was not of merchantable quality; (2) the actions against the manufacturers failed, because they used a foolproof method of cleaning and filling the bottles and there was adequate supervision in their factory. Accordingly they had taken reasonable care.

Guarantees

It is very common for a 'guarantee' from the manufacturer to be supplied with the goods. This document usually contains an undertaking to replace certain defective parts within a specified time (e.g. twelve months). The precise form of guarantee varies widely, but sometimes it contains an exclusion clause, such as the following:

We cannot in any instance be held responsible for the payment of compensation for any loss or damage whatsoever, sustained through the use or purchase of this appliance.

or

The manufacturers will not be responsible for any damage caused by or arising from the use of this machine.

The word 'guarantee' clearly suggests to the buyer that he is getting certain rights. This may be so; but often, in return, he is giving away far more valuable rights which are given to him by the law, because a clause such as those quoted above will effectively exclude the manufacturer's negligence liability which was established in *Donoghue* v. *Stevenson*. The guarantee will, however, only be effective if there is a contract between manufacturer and customer. If the guarantee requires the customer to sign and return the guarantee card, a contract may well come into existence if he does so. If, however, the guarantee is merely handed to the customer, or if he chooses to ignore the guarantee, it would seem that the guarantee creates neither legally enforceable rights nor legally enforceable duties, but the customer will still have his common law rights against the manufacturer, which, as we have seen, can be far more valuable than anything offered by the so-called 'guarantee'. It is also important to remember that the guarantee is almost invariably given by the manufacturer, so that it in no way affects the buyer's Sale of Goods Act rights against the retailer, who is not a party to the guarantee.

Suggestion for reform

In a Report published in 1969 the Law Commission recommended some changes to sections 12–15 of the Act and some radical new provisions with regard to contracting out. Legislation was promised in the Queen's Speech in October 1971 but no Bill has yet appeared. When it does appear the Bill is likely to attract all-party support.

Dealing first with the sections themselves the changes to sections 12 and 13 would be slight and no changes at all are proposed to section 15 (although the new definition of 'merchantable' would be relevant under section 15(2)(c) (p. 80). The substance of section 12 is left unchanged (so that, for example, the rule in *Rowland* v. *Divall* p. 66 will still apply) but it is suggested that (a) the condition as to 'right to sell' shall apply in every case unless the seller makes it clear that he is only transferring a more limited title and (b) the warranties as to quiet possession and freedom from incumbrances shall apply in any event. The only change proposed to section 13 is a clause confirming that it applies to self-service sales.

When we turn to the implied condition of fitness we find that three changes are proposed and they can be summarized as follows:

1. Abolition of the (largely useless) trade-name proviso.

2. The need to prove reliance on the seller's skill (which is largely a formality in many cases) is to be replaced by a provision providing, in effect, that where the buyer has made his purpose known to the seller the condition will apply unless the seller can show that the buyer did not rely, or that it was not reasonable for the buyer to rely, on the seller's skill or judgment.

3. The section should apply whenever the goods are sold 'in the course of a business' even though the seller has never previously dealt in that class of goods.

The clause suggested by the Law Commission would read as follows:

Where the seller sells goods in the course of a business and the buyer, expressly or by implication, makes known to the seller any particular purpose for which the goods are bought, there is an implied condition that the goods are reasonably fit for that purpose, whether or not that is a purpose for which such goods are commonly bought, except where the circumstances show that the buyer does not rely, or that it is unreasonable for him to rely, on the seller's skill or judgment.

Turning now to the implied condition of merchantable quality the Law Commission propose that:

1. The need for the sale to be a 'sale by description' should disappear.

2. The condition should apply whenever goods are sold in the course of a business.

3. Where defects are specifically drawn to the buyer's attention before the contract is made the condition should not apply as regards those defects (compare p. 157 section 18, of the Hire Purchase Act 1965).

4. The term 'merchantable quality' should be defined in section 62 in the following way:

Goods of any kind are of merchantable quality within the meaning of this Act if they are as fit for the purpose or purposes for which goods of that kind are commonly bought as it is reasonable to expect having regard to their price, any description applied to them and all the other circumstances; and any reference in this Act to unmerchantable goods shall be construed accordingly.

The revised condition would read as follows:

Where the seller sells goods in the course of a business there is an implied condition that the goods are of merchantable quality, except that there is no such condition:
(a) as regards defects specifically drawn to the buyer's attention before the agreement contract is made; or
(b) if the buyer examines the goods before the contract is made, as regards defects which that examination ought to have revealed.

Sale by agent. What is the position if a private seller sells through an auctioneer or other person acting in the course of a business? The Law Commission propose that the conditions should apply unless the agent takes reasonable steps to notify the buyer before contract that the seller is a private seller.

Exemption clauses. A large part of the Law Commission's Report deals with the problem of exemption clauses which, as we have seen, are permitted by section 55 of the Sale of Goods Act. After receiving a great deal of evidence the Commission proposed that, in the case of a 'consumer sale', there should be a total ban on contracting out of sections 13–15 of the Act. In the case of 'business sales' there was a division of opinion as to whether or not exemption clauses should be controlled. There was, however, general agreement as to the form of control; it should follow the precedent set by section 3 of the Misrepresentation Act (p. 58) which, it will be recalled, only allows a party to rely on an exemption clause if a judge or arbitrator upholds the clause as being fair and reasonable. To assist the court the Report also suggests that certain guidelines should be laid down by Parliament, e.g. the bargaining strength of the parties and whether the buyer received any material benefit in consideration of his agreeing to the clause.

The definition of 'consumer sale' is not an easy one and problems could arise where, say, a businessman buys a car for his private use. The definition will be particularly important if exemption clauses in non-consumer sales remain completely uncontrolled. The Law Commission define a consumer sale as a sale (otherwise than by auction) by a seller in the course of a business where

(a) the goods are of a type ordinarily bought for private use or consumption; and

(b) are sold to a person who does not buy or hold himself out as buying them in the course of a business for the purposes of –
(i)   disposing of the goods by way of sale, hire or hire-purchase in the course of the buyer's business; or

(ii)   consuming or processing them in the course of that business; or

(iii) using them for providing a service which it is an object of that business to provide.

Thus in our example the sale to the businessman would still rank a consumer sale. The Law Commission also suggest a somewhat narrower definition of 'consumer sale' which could be introduced if business sales were also made subject to exemption-clause control.

Conclusion

Apart from the proposals set out above there is one other matter where reform seems desirable. The Sale of Goods Act is based on the principle that the buyer's primary rights are against the retailer (and these rights may be worthless if the retailer has gone out of business). In these days of brand names, mass advertising and sales in sealed containers, it is surely the manufacturer who should bear the prime responsibility.

Self-tuition test 4

1. What is the difference between a representation and a contractual term? Illustrate your answer with an example of each.

2. What are the remedies for misrepresentation? Can they be excluded by agreement?

3. Distinguish between a condition and a warranty.

4. In what circumstances must a breach of condition be treated as a breach of warranty?

5. When is a contract 'severable', and what are the rights of the buyer in the event of a breach of condition relating to such a contract?

6. When is time of the essence?

7. What are the remedies available to a buyer who finds, after using the goods for a year, that the seller had no right to sell?

8. What is a sale by description?

9. John goes to the showroom of Fred, a car dealer, and after looking at various models, he agrees to buy a Screetcher car. The car breaks down four times during the first month, and John wishes to know whether he has any remedies against Fred. Advise him.

10. Explain and illustrate the doctrine of fundamental breach, and indicate how the courts have recently altered the basis of the doctrine.

For answers, see p. 185.

6 Delivery, Acceptance and Payment

We have already examined most of the seller's duties – the duty to pass a good title, the duty to supply goods of the correct quality and description, and the duty to supply goods that are fit for the buyer's purpose. In this chapter, we shall examine one further basic duty – the duty of delivery. We shall also look briefly at the buyer's corresponding obligation, i.e. his duty to accept and pay for the goods.

Delivery
General rules

Sections 27 and 28 are clear and straightforward. Section 27 states that:

It is the duty of the seller to deliver the goods and of the buyer to accept and pay for them, in accordance with the terms of the contract of sale.

Further, by section 28:

Unless otherwise agreed, delivery of the goods, and payment of the price are concurrent conditions, that is to say, the seller must be ready and willing to give possession of the goods to the buyer in exchange for the price, and the buyer must be ready and willing to pay the price in exchange for possession of the goods.

It is important to grasp the basic point that the passing of property does not of itself give the buyer a right to possession. If he wants possession, he must comply with section 28 – that is to say, he must either be ready and willing to pay the price, or he must prove that the seller has agreed to allow him credit.

What is delivery?

Section 62 defines delivery as 'voluntary transfer of possession'. In other words, the legal meaning of delivery is not the same as the popular meaning, especially as we shall see shortly that, in the absence of contrary agreement, it is for the buyer to collect the goods and not for the seller to send them to the buyer.

Methods of delivery

There are five possible ways of effecting delivery. First, there is physical transfer of the goods themselves – this is the usual case. Secondly, there is the physical transfer of a document of title (e.g. bill of lading), which is of great importance in the export trade. Thirdly, there is the physical transfer of means of control. If, for example, very bulky goods are stored in a warehouse, the delivery of the key to the warehouse may well operate as delivery of the goods themselves. The fourth method, which is known as 'attornment', is dealt with by section 29(3), which reads:

Where the goods at the time of the sale are in the possession of a third person, there is no delivery by seller to buyer unless and until such third person acknowledges to the buyer that he holds the goods on his behalf; provided that nothing in this section shall affect the operation of the issue or transfer of any document of title to goods.

Attornment is important where goods owned by the seller are in the possession of a third person, such as a warehouseman. The seller will give the buyer a delivery order addressed to the warehouseman. When the warehouseman acknowledges his acceptance of the order, delivery will be complete. In the case of unascertained goods the attornment can sometimes be an 'unconditional appropriation' within section 18, rule 5(1) (p. 30) and this will pass the property and risk (*Wardar's (Import and Export) Ltd* v. *Norwood Ltd* (1968)).

The last type of delivery occurs where there is an alteration in the character of the seller's possession. This could occur if, for example, he agreed to store the goods for the buyer until the buyer should want them. The seller would then become a 'bailee' for the buyer.

Place of delivery

This is, of course, essentially a matter for agreement. In default of agreement the matter is governed by section 29(1) which provides that:

the place of delivery is the seller's place of business, if he have one, and if not, his residence: provided that, if the contract be for the sale of specific goods which to the knowledge of the parties when the contract is made are in some other place, that place is the place of delivery.

If, therefore, S sells to B a caravan and both parties know it is in a particular field, that field is the place of delivery. Apart from this, the rule laid down by section 29 is that it is the duty of the buyer to collect the goods from the seller's premises. In practice, of course, this rule is varied in virtually all export sales, and in many inland sales as well. The contract frequently requires delivery at the buyer's premises, and problems may arise if the goods are received at the buyer's premises by someone having no authority to receive them. In *Galbraith and Grant* v. *Block* (1922) it was held that a seller would not be liable in such a case if he acted reasonably in handing the goods to someone who gave the appearance of being authorized to accept delivery. This will, of course, be a question of fact in each case.

Time for delivery

Again, this is usually governed by express agreement, and it will be recalled that time for delivery is usually a vital term (i.e. condition) in a commercial contract. Section 29 has two things to say about the time for delivery. By section 29(2):

Where under the contract of sale the seller is bound to send the goods to the buyer, but no time for sending them is fixed, the seller is bound to send them within a reasonable time.

By section 29(4):

Demand or tender of delivery may be treated as ineffectual unless made at a reasonable hour. What is a reasonable hour is a question of fact.

Cost of delivery

This is essentially a matter for agreement, but section 29(5) states that:

Unless otherwise agreed, the expenses of and incidental to putting the goods into a deliverable state must be borne by the seller.

Delivery to a carrier

Frequently a seller agrees to send the goods to the buyer by land, sea, or air. In such a case section 32(1) provides that:

... delivery of the goods to a carrier, whether named by the buyer or not, for the purpose of transmission to the buyer is prima facie deemed to be a delivery of the goods to the buyer.

The effect of delivery to a carrier can be summarized as follows:

1. If the contract is for the sale of unascertained goods, the delivery to the carrier will be an 'unconditional appropriation' within section 18 rule 5(2), and this may well pass the property and risk to the buyer, unless the seller in some way reserves the right of disposal.

2. It will not affect the buyer's rights of examination and rejection.

3. The unpaid seller will lose his lien (see p. 102) but not his right of stoppage in *transitu* (see p. 104).

When the seller hands the goods to the carrier for transmission to the buyer he will have to make a contract with the carrier. The seller usually makes this contract as agent for the buyer, so that it is the buyer who will be able to sue the carrier on the contract. Section 32(2) provides that, unless otherwise agreed, the seller must

make such contract with the carrier on behalf of the buyer as may be reasonable, having regard to the nature of the goods and the other circumstances of the case. If the seller omits to do so and the goods are lost or damaged in course of transit, the buyer may decline to treat the delivery of the carrier as delivery to himself, or may hold the seller responsible in damages.

This section was applied in the case of *Young* v. *Hobson* (1949), where the seller of a fragile engine chose to send it by railway at 'owner's risk'. He could also have sent it at 'railway company's risk', and if he had done this the railway company would have stacked the engine more carefully. The engine was damaged during the journey, and it was held that the buyer could reject it because, on the facts of the case, the seller had not made a reasonable contract of carriage.

This leads naturally to the important question of what happens if the goods are damaged or deteriorate in course of transit. The position can be summarized as follows:

1. If the goods fail to withstand a normal journey, the seller may be liable under section 14 for supplying unmerchantable goods (*Beer* v. *Walker*, p. 79).

2. We have just seen that the seller may also be liable under section 32(2) if he has failed to make a reasonable contract of carriage.

3. Apart from this, the problem is essentially one of risk, so that the buyer bears the loss if the risk has passed to him, and the seller bears the loss if it has not. Two special rules relating to risk are relevant in this connection. The first is contained in section 32(3) which provides that, if goods are sent by sea and it is usual to insure them, the seller must give sufficient information to enable the buyer to insure. If he fails to do this, the goods remain at the seller's risk during the transit. This is clearly a reasonable rule which could apply if the seller shipped goods under an f.o.b. (free on board) contract and failed to give insurance particulars to the buyer. Although under an f.o.b. contract the risk normally passes to the buyer when the seller has placed the goods 'on board', this would not be so if the seller failed to comply with section 32(3).

The second special rule is contained in section 33 which reads:

Where the seller of goods agrees to deliver them at his own risk at a place other than where they are when sold, the buyer must, nevertheless, unless otherwise agreed, take any risk of deterioration in the goods necessarily incident to the course of transit.

A 'seller's risk' clause, therefore, covers such matters as accidents and excessive delays, but not natural and inevitable deterioration.

Delivery of wrong quantity

This matter is dealt with by section 30, which reads as follows:

1. Where the seller delivers to the buyer a quantity of goods less than he contracted to sell, the buyer may reject them, but if the buyer accepts the goods so delivered he must pay for them at the contract rate.

2. Where the seller delivers to the buyer a quantity of goods larger than he contracted to sell, the buyer may accept the goods included in the contract and reject the rest, or he may reject the whole. If the buyer accepts the whole of the goods so delivered he must pay for them at the contract rate.

3. Where the seller delivers to the buyer the goods which he contracted to sell mixed with goods of a different description not included in the contract, the buyer may accept the goods which are in accordance with the contract and reject the rest or he may reject the whole.

These provisions are largely self-explanatory. Quite apart from section 30, the quantity of the goods will usually form part of their description, so that a seller who delivers the wrong quantity will usually have broken the condition of description implied by section 13. Nevertheless the rights conferred by section 30 can be regarded as separate and independent; thus the right to accept part and reject part can be regarded as an exception to the general rule that this is not possible (section 11(1)(c), p. 62). It is customary in many trades for sellers to stipulate for a margin, by using such phrases as 'about' or 'little more or less'. If these words are used, the courts will have to consider whether the deviation is small enough to come within these words. In any event, if the breach is so minute that a businessman would ignore it, the courts will also do so. Thus, in *Shipton Anderson & Co.* v.

Weil Brothers (1912) a seller who agreed to sell '4500 tons, 10 per cent more or less' tendered 4950 tons and 55 lbs. It was held that this trifling breach did not prevent the seller from claiming the contract price.

Delivery by instalments

A buyer is not bound to accept delivery by instalments, unless the contract otherwise provides (section 31(1)). If an instalment is defective, the position depends upon whether or not the contract is severable. This matter was discussed in chapter 5.

Payment

It is the buyer's duty to pay for the goods in accordance with the terms of the contract. Thus, the contract is likely to regulate both the time for payment and the method of payment. In inland sales, payment is usually by cash or by cheque, and a cheque will normally take effect as conditional payment. This means that the seller cannot sue the buyer for the price unless the cheque is dishonoured. In an export sale there are other forms of payment. Thus it may be by bill of exchange or by bankers' commercial credit. The use of the bill of exchange has already been explained, when dealing with section 19 (p. 32). A bankers' commercial credit is an arrangement where a bank is instructed by the buyer to honour bills of exchange drawn by the seller, in return for the shipping documents. A seller who desires prompt payment can also take advantage of a system known as 'factoring' whereby he assigns the debt (i.e. the buyer's liability to pay the price) to a factor. The factor will pay him the price (less a commission) and will then look to the buyer for payment.

We shall deal in the next two chapters with the various remedies available to the seller if the buyer fails to pay the price in accordance with the terms of the contract.

Acceptance and rejection

We have seen that by section 28 it is the buyer's duty to accept the goods. If he fails to do this, we shall see that under section

50 the seller can sue him for damages for non-acceptance. The precise meaning of 'acceptance' and its relationship to examination were considered in chapter 5.

As regards rejection, section 36 provides that if the buyer lawfully rejects the goods (e.g. for breach of condition) he does not have to send them back to the seller. It is sufficient if he informs the seller that the goods are rejected.

Self-tuition test 5

1. Where is the place of delivery?

2. What is attornment and what is its effect?

3. What is the position where the seller delivers the goods at the buyer's premises to someone describing herself as the buyer's wife, and that person turns out to be a complete stranger who disappears with the goods?

4. What is the object and effect of a clause that the seller shall deliver '1000 tons little more or less'?

5. A agrees to sell B a consignment of 5 tons of grain, at a price of £50, delivery to be made by five equal instalments and payment to be made on delivery of the final instalment. The first instalment is satisfactory but the second is unmerchantable. What are B's rights against A?

For answers, see p. 190.

7 Rights of the Unpaid Seller against the Goods

If the buyer fails to accept and to pay for the goods, the seller can take proceedings against him. Such proceedings, however, may well be fruitless if the buyer is unable to pay. Accordingly the Act gives the unpaid seller extensive rights over the goods themselves, and these will often be far more valuable than a mere personal action against the buyer.

Who is an unpaid seller?

Section 38 reads as follows:

1. The seller of the goods is deemed to be an 'unpaid seller' within the meaning of this Act
(a) when the whole of the price has not been paid or tendered;
(b) when a bill of exchange or other negotiable instrument has been received as conditional payment, and the condition on which it was received has not been fulfilled by reason of dishonour of the instrument or otherwise.

2. In this Part of this Act the term 'seller' includes any person who is in the position of a seller, as, for instance, an agent of the seller to whom the bill of lading has been endorsed, or a consignor or agent who has himself paid, or is directly responsible for, the price.

An example of a person in the position of an unpaid seller within section 38(2) is a buying agent, such as a confirming house, who has to undertake personal liability for the price. If the principal does not reimburse the agent, the agent is in the position of an unpaid seller in relation to his principal.

Where a buyer lawfully rejects goods for breach of condition, we have just seen that he is under no duty to send the goods back to the seller. In fact, if the buyer has paid for the goods he will be well advised not to send them back until his payment has been refunded, because it was held in *J. L. Lyons and Co.* v. *May & Baker Ltd* (1923) that once he has handed them to a carrier he cannot exercise any right of stoppage if the seller should become bankrupt. In other words, a rejecting buyer is not an unpaid seller and does not have the rights enjoyed by an unpaid seller which are discussed below.

Rights

Having defined an unpaid seller, the Act then goes on to summarize his rights over the goods. These are:

1. A lien.

2. A right of stoppage *in transitu*.

3. If the goods still belong to the seller, a right of retention which is co-extensive with (1) and (2) above.

4. A right of re-sale as limited by the Act.

Lien

Sections 41 to 43 deal with the unpaid seller's lien over the goods, i.e. his right to retain possession of the goods even though the property has passed to the buyer. Section 41 reads:

1. Subject to the provisions of this Act, the unpaid seller of goods who is in possession of them is entitled to retain possession of them until payment or tender of the price in the following cases, namely:

(a) where the goods have been sold without any stipulation as to credit;

(b) where the goods have been sold on credit but the term of credit has expired;

(c) where the buyer becomes insolvent.

2. The seller may exercise his right of lien notwithstanding that he is in possession of the goods as agent or bailee for the buyer.

These provisions are basically straightforward and provide a useful weapon for an unpaid seller. Section 41(1)(a) deals with sales without credit, and it confirms the basic rule that delivery and payment are normally concurrent conditions (section 28, p. 93) If the sale is on credit and the credit term has run out, the seller will have a lien under section 41(1)(b), but this is unlikely to be of much practical importance, because in this type of case the buyer will usually have obtained possession and this will automatically destroy the seller's lien. Even if the credit term has not yet expired the unpaid seller can exercise his lien if the buyer becomes insolvent. By section 62(3):

A person is deemed to be insolvent within the meaning of this Act who either has ceased to pay his debts in the ordinary course of business, or cannot pay his debts as they become due, whether he has committed an act of bankruptcy or not.

If the buyer does go bankrupt, the unpaid seller is in a privileged position, as compared to other creditors. He is in a somewhat similar position to that of a mortgagee, in that he can keep the debtor's goods and wait to be paid off.

It seems that the lien is only available for the price of the goods and not, for example, for storage charges which the seller is compelled to pay by reason of the buyer's default.

The lien is based upon the seller's continued possession of the goods, and section 42 provides that delivery of part of the goods will not destroy the unpaid seller's lien over the remainder, unless the circumstances surrounding the part delivery show an intention to waive the lien. This problem can sometimes arise in the case of instalment contracts, and the case of *Merchant Banking Co. of London* v. *Phoenix Bessemer Steel Co.* (1877) shows that the unpaid seller has no lien over an instalment which has actually been paid for.

The unpaid seller will lose his lien in three cases specified in section 43(1), namely:

1. If he delivers the goods to a carrier or other bailee for transmission to the buyer without reserving the right of disposal.

2. If the buyer or his agent lawfully obtains possession of the goods.

3. If he waives the lien.

A seller can be said to 'waive' his lien if his conduct shows that he is no longer seeking to enforce his right of lien. This may occur if, for example, the unpaid seller accepts a cheque or bill of exchange. It may also occur if the seller does some wrongful act inconsistent with the lien, such as a wrongful sale or pledge.

We shall see in the next chapter that, side by side with his rights against the goods, the unpaid seller has certain rights against the buyer personally. If he sues the buyer for the price and obtains judgment, section 43(2) states that this will not terminate the lien unless the judgment is satisfied. When this occurs, the seller ceases to be an unpaid seller.

Stoppage *in transitu*

We have just seen that once the goods are handed to a carrier for transmission to the buyer, the unpaid seller's right of lien is normally at an end. If, however, the buyer becomes insolvent while the goods are still in transit, section 44 (which is based on mercantile custom) gives the unpaid seller a right of 'stoppage *in transitu*', and by exercising this right the seller can recover possession of the goods from the carrier. Section 46 provides that the cost of re-delivery is borne by the seller, so that if the carrier has a lien over the goods for the freight, the unpaid seller must pay this sum to the carrier before he can recover the goods. Sometimes, however, the contract of carriage goes further than this and gives the carrier a general lien over the goods for all moneys owing to him from the buyer. Despite such a clause it was held in *United States Steel Products Co.* v. *G. W. Railway* (1916) that the unpaid seller could recover the goods from the carrier after paying the carrier's charges for those particular goods.

There are hardly any modern cases dealing with stoppage *in transitu*. The reason for this is probably the development of payment by bankers' commercial credits. We have seen that under this system of finance, a bank (usually in the seller's country) honours a bill of exchange drawn by the seller, in return for the shipping documents. The seller then immediately ceases to be an unpaid seller. Accordingly, stoppage *in transitu*

has lost much of its practical importance in relation to carriage
of goods by sea.

Duration of transit

If the unpaid seller is to be able to exercise his right of stoppage it is vital that the goods should still be in transit. This
matter is dealt with in some detail in section 45. This section
underlines two basic points. In the first place, goods may be in
transit even though they are not in motion. Secondly, the
transit will usually continue until the goods come under the
buyer's control. If, therefore, the transit is interrupted by the
buyer and cannot be re-started without fresh instructions from
him, the transit will be at an end (*Reddall* v. *Union Castle Mail
Steamship Co.* (1914)). On the other hand, the mere fact that
the buyer arranges the original shipping contract does not in
itself bring the transit to an end (*ex parte Rosevear China Clay
Co.* (1879)).

Section 45 reads as follows:

1. Goods are deemed to be in course of transit from the time when
they are delivered to a carrier by land or water ... for the purpose
of transmission to the buyer, until the buyer or his agent in that
behalf takes delivery of them from such carrier.
2. If the buyer or his agent in that behalf obtains delivery of the
goods before their arrival at the appointed destination, the transit
is at an end.
3. If, after the arrival of the goods at the appointed destination, the
carrier ... acknowledges to the buyer, or his agent, that he holds
the goods on his behalf and continues in possession of them as
bailee for the buyer, or his agent, the transit is at an end and it is
immaterial that a further destination for the goods may have been
indicated by the buyer.
4. If the goods are rejected by the buyer, and the carrier ... continues in possession of them, the transit is not deemed to be at an
end, even if the seller has refused to receive them back.
5. When goods are delivered to a ship chartered by the buyer, it is
a question depending on the circumstances of the particular case
whether they are in the possession of the master as a carrier, or as
agent to the buyer.
6. Where the carrier ... wrongfully refuses to deliver the goods to

the buyer, or his agent in that behalf, the transit is deemed to be at an end.

7. Where part delivery of the goods has been made to the buyer, or his agent in that behalf, the remainder of the goods may be stopped *in transitu* unless the part delivery has been made under such circumstances as to show an agreement to give up possession of the whole of the goods.

Method of stoppage

The unpaid seller can exercise his right of stoppage either by physically re-possessing the goods or by giving notice to the carrier or to his principal (section 46). If the notice is given to the carrier's principal it will only be effective if it is given at such time and in such circumstances that the principal can, with reasonable diligence, communicate it to the agent before the ending of the transit.

Retention

The words 'lien' and 'stoppage *in transitu*' refer to rights available to the unpaid seller where the property has passed to the buyer. If the property has not yet passed, but the seller is under a duty to deliver a specific consignment or chattel to the buyer, he has a right of retention which is co-extensive with the rights of lien and stoppage. If, of course, no goods have yet been finally earmarked to the contract no problem will arise, and an unpaid seller who prepares goods for delivery to the buyer is always free to change his mind and sell them elsewhere.

Effect of a sub-sale

So far, we have been considering the question solely as between the unpaid seller and the buyer. If, however, the buyer should sub-sell or pledge the goods, the question arises as to how this affects the unpaid seller's rights. Section 47 starts by stating as a general rule that:

the unpaid seller's right of lien or retention or stoppage *in transitu* is not affected by any sale or other disposition of the goods which the buyer may have made, unless the seller has assented thereto.

In other words, a sub-sale will not of itself affect the unpaid seller's rights, even though he knows of it and even though he acts on it, as by delivering part of the goods in accordance with a delivery order issued by the buyer to a sub-purchaser (*Mordaunt* v. *British Oil and Cake Mills* (1910)). If, however, he 'assents' to the sub-sale, he loses his rights. The word 'assent' means that the unpaid seller must act in such a way as to renounce his rights. An example of assent can be seen from the case of *Mount (D.F.) Ltd* v. *Jay and Jay (Provisions) Co. Ltd* (1960), where an unpaid seller agreed that the buyer would pay the price out of the proceeds of a re-sale.

'Assent', however, is not the only case in which the unpaid seller loses his rights. Section 47 contains an important proviso to the general rule. It states that:

Where a document of title to goods has been lawfully transferred to a person as buyer or owner of the goods, and that person transfers the document to a person who takes the document in good faith and for valuable consideration, then if such last-mentioned transfer was by way of sale, the unpaid seller's right of lien or retention or stoppage *in transitu* is defeated and if [it] was by way of pledge or other disposition for value, the unpaid seller's right of lien or retention or stoppage *in transitu* can only be exercised subject to the rights of the transferee.

In other words, if S transfers a bill of lading to B and B transfers that bill to a sub-purchaser C taking in good faith, S would lose his rights of lien, retention and stoppage. If C were a pledgee, the rights of S could only be exercised after paying off C.

It will be observed that the unpaid seller will only lose his rights under section 47 if the same document passes twice – once from seller to buyer and then from buyer to sub-buyer or pledgee. If the seller were to hand a delivery order to the buyer, and if the buyer then transferred a different delivery order to the sub-buyer, the proviso to section 47 would not defeat the unpaid seller's rights. It was suggested in *Mount* v. *Jay and Jay* (above) that in such a case the rights of the unpaid seller would be lost under section 25(2), but the wording of that subsection makes it difficult to see why this should be so.

Re-sale

We come now to what is often the unpaid seller's most valuable right of all – his right of re-sale under section 48. The section begins by stating that the exercise of the right of lien and stoppage *in transitu* does not, of itself, bring the contract to an end. The section then continues:

2. Where an unpaid seller who has exercised his right of lien or stoppage *in transitu* re-sells the goods, the buyer acquires a good title thereto as against the original buyer.

3. Where the goods are of a perishable nature, or where the unpaid seller gives notice of his intention to re-sell, and the buyer does not within a reasonable time pay or tender the price, the unpaid seller may re-sell the goods and recover from the original buyer damages for any loss occasioned by his breach of contract.

4. Where the seller expressly reserves the right of re-sale in case the buyer should make default, and on the buyer making default re-sells the goods, the original contract of sale is thereby rescinded, but without prejudice to any claim the seller may have for damages.

Transfer of property. An unpaid seller can pass a good title to a second buyer is at least three cases :

1. If the property has not yet passed to the first buyer.

2. Under section 8 of the Factors Act 1889, or section 25(1) of the Sale of Goods Act 1893 (p. 50).

3. If he re-sells after exercising his lien or right of stoppage. Such a re-sale passes title under section 48(2), even though the re-sale was not justified by either section 48(3) or 48(4) and was therefore wrongful against the original buyer.

We must now consider the position between the seller and the original buyer. If the re-sale is wrongful, the seller will clearly be liable for damages to the first buyer. If, however, the re-sale was justified under section 48(3) or 48(4) the position is as follows:

1. If the unpaid seller makes a loss on the re-sale, he can sue the buyer for damages.

2. If the unpaid seller re-sells at a profit, it was formerly thought that in certain circumstances the original buyer could claim it, but it is clear from the case of *Ward* v. *Bignall* (1967) that this is not so. Whether the seller re-sells under section 48(3) or 48(4) the re-sale brings the original contract to an end, and this means that the seller will always be able to re-sell as absolute owner. If he makes a profit it will belong to him.

3. If the original buyer paid a deposit, the unpaid seller can keep it. A deposit is more than part payment of the price; it is a guarantee that the buyer will perform his part of the contract. Accordingly, if the contract is discharged by reason of the buyer's default, the seller can forfeit the deposit. If, of course, the seller sues the buyer for damages, these will be limited to the seller's actual loss and in calculating that loss any deposit paid by the buyer must be brought into account.

Self-tuition test 6

1. In what circumstances, if any, does a seller have a lien over goods which he has sold on credit? How can the lien be lost?

2. What do you understand by stoppage *in transitu*? How is it exercised, and why are there very few modern cases on it?

3. What is the position as between an unpaid seller seeking to exercise his right of stoppage *in tránsitu*, and a carrier seeking to exercise a lien because the buyer owes him freight for this consignment and a previous one?

4. S sells goods to B who re-sells them to C. Can S (who is unpaid) claim the rights of an unpaid seller as against C?

5. A seller sells goods to A and then, without A's knowledge, sells the same goods to B at a higher price. (a) Does the property pass to B? (b) Can the seller keep the profit, or does he have to account for it to A?

For answers, see p. 191.

8 Personal Remedies for Breach of the Contract

Remedies of seller

The remedies discussed in the previous chapter are sometimes known as 'real' remedies, because they can be enforced against the '*res*' or 'things' themselves, i.e. against the goods. The present section deals with two further rights which the unpaid seller has against the buyer personally.

Action for the price

Section 49 provides that where the buyer wrongfully fails to pay for the goods the seller can bring an action for the price in two cases, namely:

1. If the property has passed to the buyer.
2. If the price is payable on a day certain, whether the property has passed or not.

It will be recalled that by section 28 delivery and payment are concurrent conditions, and this means that, in the absence of contrary agreement, a seller will only be able to bring an action for the price if he is ready and willing to deliver the goods. This basic rule is subject to two exceptions. In the first place the buyer will still have to pay the price even though the goods have been accidentally destroyed, if the destruction took place after the risk had passed to him. Secondly, section 49(2) provides that if the contract stipulates for payment of the price on a specified date, the seller can bring an action for the price after that date, even though the goods have not yet been appropriated to the contract.

Two other points should be noted. In the first place, the court has a general power under the Law Reform (Miscellaneous Provisions) Act 1934, to award interest from the date on which the price became due until judgment. Secondly, a seller can link a claim for the price with a claim for damages for non-acceptance, if he has suffered damage (e.g. storage charges) by reason of the buyer's default.

Action for damages for non-acceptance

Section 50 gives the seller a general right to sue the buyer for damages for non-acceptance where the buyer wrongfully neglects or refuses to accept and pay for the goods. This remedy overlaps the previous one. We have just seen that a seller can sometimes link an action for the price with an action for damages. If the case is one where he can sue for the price under section 49, he may often have an alternative claim under section 50. Sometimes, however, the action for damages under section 50 is the only remedy available. In *Colley* v. *Overseas Exporters* (1921):

Sellers sold goods f.o.b. Liverpool. Under such a contract it is the buyer's duty to nominate an effective ship and the property passes when the seller has placed the goods on board. The sellers had the goods available at the docks and when the buyer failed to nominate a ship they sued for the price. It was held that as no property had passed and as there was no clause making the price payable on a day certain the sellers had no claim under section 49 for the price. Their only remedy was to claim damages for non-acceptance.

Before considering how damages are assessed, it may be useful to mention an additional remedy provided by section 37, which reads as follows:

Where the seller is ready and willing to deliver the goods, and requests the buyer to take delivery, and the buyer does not within a reasonable time after such request take delivery of the goods, he is liable to the seller for any loss occasioned by his neglect or refusal to take delivery, and also for a reasonable charge for the care and custody of the goods: Provided that nothing in this section shall affect the rights of the seller where the neglect or refusal of the buyer to take delivery amounts to a repudiation of the contract.

Let us now return to section 50 and see how damages for non-acceptance are assessed. In general contract law, the vital test is: was the damage foreseeable? This was laid down in the famous case of *Hadley* v. *Baxendale* (1854). The court said that a contract breaker was liable to pay for any damage which arose naturally from the breach or which was reasonably foreseeable by him from knowledge which he had at the time of the contract. The Act incorporates both limbs of the *Hadley* v. *Baxendale* formula. Section 50(2) reads:

The measure of damages is the estimated loss directly and naturally resulting, in the ordinary course of events, from the buyer's breach of contract.

Section 54 reads:

Nothing in this Act shall affect the right of the buyer or the seller to recover interest or special damages in any case where by law interest or special damages may be recoverable . . .

This section preserves the right of the innocent party to recover compensation for damage not arising naturally, if it ought to have been foreseen by the contract breaker.

If we look for a moment at damage arising naturally, the natural reaction of a seller to default by the buyer is to try to sell the goods elsewhere, and the loss (if any) made on the re-sale will be his damage. This is the principle behind section 50(3) which reads as follows:

Where there is an available market for the goods in question the measure of damages is prima facie to be ascertained by the difference between the contract price and the market or current price at the time or times when the goods ought to have been accepted, or, if no time was fixed for acceptance, then at the time of the refusal to accept.

If, for example, goods are sold for £100 with delivery on 1 May, and the buyer refuses to accept them on that date (by which time the market price has fallen to £80), the sum of £20 will prima facie represent the seller's damage under section 50(3) and this will be recoverable. It seems that such damages are recoverable even though the seller succeeds at a much later date in selling at a price above the contract price (*Campbell Mostyn* (*Provisions*) *Ltd* v. *Barnett* (1954)).

What would the position be if, at some time before 1 May,

the buyer purported to cancel his order because the market was falling and he no longer wanted the goods? The general rule is that where a party to a contract repudiates it (i.e. shows an intention no longer to be bound) the innocent party has an option – he may accept the repudiation or he may ignore it. If, in our example, the seller were to accept the cancellation, he would have to try to minimize his loss by selling the goods elsewhere. If, however, the seller chose to ignore the cancellation, he could wait until 1 May and, if the buyer then refused to take the goods, damages would be assessed by reference to the 1 May market price and not the market price at any earlier date (*Tredegar Iron Co.* v. *Hawthorn* (1902)).

Two points should be noted with regard to the 'market' rule of section 50(3). In the first place, it only applies if there is an 'available market'. This term has been much discussed in a number of cases and, although the point is not finally settled, it seems that there is an available market if there are sufficient buyers, at the appropriate level of trade, to absorb the goods. If, therefore, the defaulting buyer was a retailer, the words 'available market' refer to other retailers. It also seems from the case of *Charter* v. *Sullivan* (1957) that the 'market' test presupposes a price which fluctuates according to supply and demand, and that it is inappropriate in a case where the price is fixed in advance by the manufacturer. This particular problem is not likely to recur very often in the future, since resale price maintenance has been made unlawful by the Resale Prices Act 1964, unless the manufacturer obtains an order of the court exempting him from the provisions of the Act. The motor manufacturers have not applied for such an order.

The second point to note about section 50(3) is that it is a 'prima facie' rule only, and is readily displaced where it does not truly represent the owner's loss. If section 50(3) is discarded, the matter will be governed by the general principles found in sections 50(2) and 54. If, for example, the seller is a car dealer, and the sale goes off by reason of the buyer's default, the seller can recover damages for his loss of profit if the supply of the goods exceeds the demand (*Thompson* v. *Robinson* (*Gunmakers*) *Ltd* (1955)). This will be so even if he succeeds in re-selling that very same car at the contract price, the reason being that, by reason of the buyer's default, he has sold one car instead of two. If, however, the goods are in short supply, so that the defaulting buyer is merely replaced by the next man in the queue, the seller cannot be said to have lost a sale and his damages will usually be nominal (*Charter* v. *Sullivan* (1957)).

Remedies of buyer

In the preceding chapters we have examined the seller's duties, and in doing so we have touched upon some of the buyer's remedies, such as his right of rejection and his right to claim damages for breach of warranty. In this section it is proposed to collect all the buyer's remedies together and to discuss some of the more important ones.

Rejection

We have already examined the buyer's right to reject the goods for breach of condition. and the circumstances in which this right is lost (pp. 61–5).

Recovery of price

Section 54 preserves the buyer's common law right to recover the price where 'the consideration . . . has failed', i.e. where he has got nothing for his money. This is possible if:

1. The seller fails to deliver.
2. The seller delivers defective goods which the buyer lawfully rejects.
3. The contract is void under section 6 or is avoided under section 7.
4. The seller has no right to sell (section 12(1), p. 66).

Damages for breach of warranty

Section 53 deals with the case where a seller breaks a warranty or where a buyer elects to treat, or is compelled to treat, a breach of condition as a breach of warranty. In such a case the buyer can either sue the seller for damages for breach of warranty or he can set up the breach of warranty in diminution or extinction of the price, or he can do both. Damages are assessed under the *Hadley* v. *Baxendale* rules which we have already examined (see sections 53(2) and 54). Section 53(3) states that, where the warranty relates to quality, the damages are prima facie to be assessed by reference to the difference between the value of the goods and their value if they had answered the warranty. This prima facie rule is frequently displaced where it does not represent the buyer's actual loss. Thus, in the case of *Jackson* v. *Watson* (1909), a husband bought some poisoned salmon and his wife was poisoned by it and died. The damages included medical expenses, funeral expenses and damages for loss of the wife's society.

Damages for non-delivery

Just as a seller can claim damages under section 50 if the buyer wrongfully fails to accept, so the buyer can claim damages under section 51 if the seller wrongfully fails to deliver. The assessment of damages is again governed by the general *Hadley* v. *Baxendale* rules (see sections 51(2) and 54); and section 51(3) contains the usual 'prima facie' rule – this time it is the difference between the contract price and the market price at the time when the goods should have been delivered or, if no time was fixed, at the time of the refusal to deliver.

One problem of practical importance concerns sub-sales. If, as the result of the seller's default, the buyer loses a sub-sale or has to pay damages to his sub-buyer, is the original seller liable for such damage? In the normal course of events, the seller is not liable, presumably because the seller would normally assume that the buyer could perform his sub-contract by acquiring the goods from another source. Damages for loss of sub-contracts can, however, be recovered, if the seller knows not only that the buyer requires the goods for re-sale, but also that there are special circumstances making the prima facie measure of damages inadequate. Thus in *Patrick* v. *Russo–British Grain Export Co.* (1927), a firm of merchants ordered a large quantity of Russian wheat, and clearly they required it for re-sale. The sellers knew this *and*

they also knew that the grain could not be obtained elsewhere.
On these facts, it was held that when the sellers failed to deliver the grain, damages for loss of profit on the sub-sales
could be awarded. Another type of case where such damages
can be awarded is the case of so-called 'string-contracts',
where a seller knows that those very goods will be re-sold
several times on identical terms. This type of business is common in commodity dealings.

Damages for delayed delivery

In this case the damages are normally based on the difference
between the value of the goods when they should have been
delivered and their value at the time of actual delivery. It
seems that, in assessing their value at the time of delivery, the
courts are prepared to consider the realities of the matter and
to look at sub-sales. If, therefore, the buyer has not re-sold the
goods, the value at the time of delivery will be a question of
fact to be fought out on the evidence. If, however, the market
is falling and the buyer has succeeded in re-selling the goods at
a price above the market price, the re-sale price is treated as
the value of the goods to the buyer at the time of actual delivery (*Wertheim* v. *Chicoutimi Wood and Pulp Co.* (1911)). If,
for example, goods were worth £100 when they should have
been delivered, but only £70 when they were actually delivered,
damages are prima facie £30. If, however, the buyer has succeeded in re-selling the goods for £80, damages will be limited
to £20.

Action for specific performance

Section 52 provides that in an action for breach of contract to
deliver specific or ascertained goods, the court may, if it thinks
fit, on the application of the plaintiff, order that the contract be
performed specifically, without giving the defendant the option
of retaining the goods on payment of damages. This remedy is
an equitable one, and as such it is not available as of right but
only at the discretion of the court. It was originally developed
by the Court of Chancery to cover cases where the common
law remedy of damages was inadequate, and this principle

largely governs the availability of the decree. In a normal sale of goods, a money payment will adequately compensate the buyer, and he is unlikely to get an order for specific performance. If, however, the chattel has some special value for him (for example, a painting), specific performance could be ordered. It could also be ordered (although this is less certain) if the seller became bankrupt. At all events, the goods must be specific or ascertained (see *re Wait*, p. 25).

Action in tort

If the buyer is entitled to immediate possession of the goods and they are wrongly withheld from him by the seller or by a third party, the buyer can bring proceedings for detinue or for conversion. It seems that damages will be assessed in the same way as for non-delivery (*The Arpad* (1934)).

9 Auction Sales

The subject of auction sales is dealt with by section 58 of the Act, although like most other sections of the Act, it can be, and very often is, varied by express agreement.

Each lot a separate contract

Section 58(1) provides that where goods are put up for sale by auction in lots, each lot is, prima facie, deemed to be the subject of a separate contract of sale. In practice, the auction catalogue which sets out the lots frequently authorizes the auctioneer to consolidate several lots into one.

Contract complete on fall of hammer

Section 58(2) provides that the contract is complete when the auctioneer announces its completion by the fall of the hammer, or in other customary manner, and that until then any bidder may retract his bid. Once the hammer falls, the highest bidder becomes the buyer and the property will usually pass to him at once (*Dennant* v. *Skinner*, p. 27). There is, of course, the possibility that the auctioneer may have missed a bid, and as soon as he knocks down the goods to Mr A there will be a complaint from Mr B that he made a higher bid. This matter is almost invariably covered by a provision in the conditions of sale that

in the event of a dispute the auctioneer shall have absolute discretion to settle it or to re-offer the lot.

Terms of sale

The conditions of sale frequently contain a clause that the goods are sold 'with all faults and errors of description'. Another common clause states that 'all statements in the catalogue as to date, age, condition, or quality are statements of opinion and are not, and are not to be relied on as, statements or representations of fact'. It has already been seen that it is very doubtful whether the condition of description implied by section 13 can be excluded (see p. 71), but in this type of case the 'opinion' clause may cut down the descriptive words themselves.

Reserve price

Frequently a seller instructs the auctioneer not to sell below a certain price. This is known as a reserve price, and the effect of such an arrangement depends primarily on whether the sale is *notified* as being subject to a reserve price. If it is so notified, and the price is not reached, the auctioneer can withdraw the goods from the auction. In *MacManus* v. *Fortescue* (1907) the auctioneer by mistake knocked the goods down to a buyer before the reserve had been reached. When he realized his mistake he refused to proceed and it was held that, since the sale was notified to be subject to reserve, the auctioneer was under no liability to the buyer. If, on the other hand, the reserve is not notified, the auctioneer still has full power to withdraw the goods at any time before the hammer falls. If, however, the facts of *MacManus* v. *Fortescue* were to arise in such a case, it seems likely that the buyer would have a claim either against the auctioneer (for wrongly warranting his authority), or against the principal who might well be bound by the auctioneer's apparent authority. Finally, if the auctioneer advertises the auction as being 'without reserve', there were suggestions in *Warlow* v. *Harrison* (1859) that this might imply a promise by the auctioneer to sell to the highest bidder. The point, however, is not free from doubt.

Seller's right to bid

A seller may be anxious to bid himself (personally or through one or more 'puffers') to push up the price. The Act, however, restricts his right to do this. By section 58(3):

Where a sale by auction is not subject to a right to bid on behalf of the seller, it shall not be lawful for the seller to bid himself or to employ any person to bid at such a sale, or for the auctioneer knowingly to take any bid from the seller or any such person: Any sale contravening this rule may be treated as fraudulent by the buyer.

This means that the buyer, having paid an unlawfully inflated price, can treat the contract as having been induced by a fraudulent misrepresentation. He can therefore avoid the contract, or presumably he could claim damages.

The section goes on to state that if the right to bid is reserved, the seller or *one* person on his behalf may bid at the auction. In practice, the conditions of sale frequently state that the auctioneer himself is authorized to bid on the seller's behalf.

Position of auctioneer

The auctioneer is essentially an agent for the seller and, as against the seller, he has a lien over the goods for his commission and the expenses of the sale. He also has the right to sue the buyer in his own name for the price. In *Benton* v. *Campbell Parker & Co.* (1925), Salter J. examined the warranties given by an auctioneer. He held that an auctioneer impliedly warrants:

1. His authority.
2. That he knows of no defect in his principal's title.
3. That he will deliver possession to the buyer in return for the price.
4. That the buyer's possession will not be disturbed by himself or by his principal.

Normally, however, the auctioneer does not warrant that he has a right to sell, although such a term may be inferred if the auctioneer failed to disclose that he was acting for a principal.

Unlawful auctions

If goods are being offered for auction, dealers might be tempted to strike a bargain whereby one or more of them agrees, in return for a money payment, not to make a bid, the object being to acquire the article cheaply and then re-auction it amongst themselves. Such agreements are rendered illegal by the Auction (Bidding Agreements) Acts 1927–69. There is no record of a single prosecution in the forty-four years since the 1927 Act was passed, although it is common knowledge that such 'rings' do exist. The difficulty, of course, is to track them down.

The Mock Auction Act 1961, makes unlawful an auction of certain types of personal effects, if during the course of the sale (1) any lot is sold at a price below the highest bid or (2) the right to bid is restricted to persons who have bought one or more articles or (3) any articles are given away or offered by way of gift. The promotion of such a mock auction is a criminal offence.

10 Export Sales

The law relating to export sales has developed rapidly over the past fifty or sixty years, and it has done so quite independently of the Sale of Goods Act. A number of special types of contract have been brought into use, but the terms used in these contracts are not necessarily interpreted in the same way in different countries. Accordingly, much work has been done to avoid conflicts of interpretation. There is, for example, a standardized set of terms, called Incoterms, of the International Chamber of Commerce. There is also a convention on the Uniform Laws on International Sales which was signed at The Hague in 1964, and which has been incorporated into English law by the Uniform Laws on International Sales Act 1967, which will come into force on a day to be appointed. In this chapter it is proposed to examine the obligations under some of the more important types of export contract, and then to have a brief look at the Uniform Laws Convention.

Particular types of contract
F.O.B. (*Free on board*)

Under an f.o.b. contract it is the duty of the buyer to nominate an effective ship and it is the duty of the seller to load the goods, at his own expense, onto that ship. Any loading charges, therefore, will have to be borne by the seller. We have already seen that the buyer will be liable to pay damages for non-acceptance if he fails to nominate an effective ship (*Colley* v. *Overseas Exporters*, p. 111).

In the absence of contrary agreement the risk will pass to the buyer when the goods have passed over the ship's rail at the port of shipment (they are then legally 'on board' even though they are not yet on deck). Damage before this will be the seller's responsibility (*Pyrene Co. Ltd* v. *Scindia Navigation Co. Ltd* (1954)), but damage after this will be the buyer's responsibility and he should therefore make sure that the goods are adequately insured. We have already seen that the normal risk rules are modified if the seller fails to give particulars to the buyer to enable the buyer to insure (section 32(3), p. 97).

With regard to the passing of property, the basic principles considered earlier (sections 16–19, pp. 24–33) will apply. If the contract goods form part of a larger consignment, section 16 will apply and no property will pass until the contract goods are in some way set aside and earmarked to the contract. (This is an example of a case where the risk passes before the property.) If the goods are already ascertained when they are shipped, the general rule is that the property will pass at the same time as the risk, i.e. when the goods have been lifted over the ship's rail at the port of shipment (cf. section 18 rule 5(2), p. 30). Sometimes, however, the normal duties of the f.o.b. seller are extended by agreement. The seller may agree, for example, that he will make the shipping arrangements on the buyer's behalf (usually in return for a commission). In this extended type of f.o.b. contract the bill of lading will clearly play a vital part, and it may well be that property will only pass when the bill is handed, or transferred, to the buyer (cf. section 19(2)).

Very often the export of goods will require an export licence, and there is no rule of law that the duty of obtaining a licence is on the seller or on the buyer. It will be a question of construction of the documents, in the light of the surrounding circumstances. If, for example, both parties know that only the seller (or the seller's suppliers) can apply for an export licence, the courts will normally infer an agreement that this should be the seller's responsibility (*Pound & Co. Ltd* v. *Hardy & Co. Inc.* (1956)). Even this is not the end of the matter, because the courts will also have to decide whether the seller (or buyer) gave an absolute undertaking that the licence would be forthcoming, or whether he merely agreed to do his best to try to obtain a licence. In the former case he will be liable in damages if he fails to get a licence. In the latter case, he will not be liable (if, in fact, he has done his best) and the contract will be frustrated. Clearly it is most important to have an express agreement on the point.

F.A.S. (*Free alongside*)

The obligations of the parties are basically similar to those just discussed, except that the seller's duties are discharged by placing the goods alongside the ship nominated by the buyer. In this case loading, and loading charges, will be the buyer's responsibility, and the goods will be at his risk once the goods have been placed alongside. Any dues payable when the goods enter the docks will be the seller's responsibility, but port rates payable when the ship leaves port will be the buyer's responsibility in the absence of contrary agreement.

C.I.F. (*Cost, insurance, freight*)

This type of contract is immensely important because, in the words of Lord Wright, it is

a type of contract which is more widely and more frequently in use than any other contract used for purposes of sea-borne commerce.

These words were spoken in 1940 (*Bailey* v. *Ross T. Smythe Co. Ltd*), but there is no doubt that they are equally true to-day. This type of contract places additional duties on the seller, and this is reflected in the price. In other words, a price c.i.f. will almost invariably be higher than an f.o.b. price. The contract has been described as a 'sale of shipping documents' because the documents play a central role. The seller must

(a) ship the goods;
(b) make the contract of carriage;
(c) insure them for the benefit of the buyer; and
(d) tender to the buyer the shipping documents, consisting of bill of lading, insurance policy, and invoice.

The insurance policy must be on terms not less favourable than is customary in the trade, and the precise extent of the cover should be dealt with in the agreement itself. As regards the shipping documents, the modern practice is to include a clause giving the seller a right to tender a 'delivery order' in lieu of the bill of lading, and an 'insurance certificate' instead of a policy. The reason for this is that the bill of lading usually covers other goods as well as those sold to the buyer and that the policy will usually cover all goods sent out by the seller up to a specified amount. The courts must, however, examine the contract carefully to see whether it really does come within the 'sale of documents' category. If not, it may be classified as an 'ex ship' contract, even though the parties use the term 'c.i.f.' (see below).

Once the seller has performed his part of the contract, the buyer is bound to pay the price on tender of the correct documents. This is so even though, at the time of such tender, the buyer knows that the goods have already been lost, and even though he knows that the loss is not covered by the insurance policy (*Groom* v. *Barber* (1915)). It will be recalled that, by section 28, delivery and payment are concurrent conditions, and in *Clemens Horst Co.* v. *Biddell Bros.* (1912) the buyers under a c.i.f. contract stated that they would only pay when the goods themselves were delivered and examined. The House of Lords, however, held that under a c.i.f. contract 'delivery' meant 'delivery of shipping documents', and that on tender of the documents the buyers were bound to pay the price.

Under a c.i.f. contract the risk usually passes at the same time as under an f.o.b. contract, i.e. when the goods have passed over the ship's rail in the course of shipment. As regards the property, this normally passes when the bill of lading is transferred to the buyer, but in *Chao* v. *British Traders and Shippers* (1954) Devlin J. (as he then was) made it clear that what passed was conditional property only. It was conditional on the buyer having the right to examine the goods on arrival and to reject them if they did not conform with the contract. The practical importance of this is that a pledge or other dealing with the conditional property represented by the documents is not an act of 'acceptance' of the goods themselves so as to destroy the right of rejection.

Ex ship contract

Under this contract, the seller's duties are still more extensive.
He undertakes to cause delivery to be made at a named port
of destination. No property passes until this has been done,
and the goods will be at the seller's risk during the journey,
(although presumably section 33, which deals with deterioration in transit, would apply, see p. 97). The importance of
the distinction between 'c.i.f.' and 'ex ship' is that under an
'ex ship' contract the buyer is paying for the goods themselves
and not for the documents. Accordingly, even though he pays
the price in return for some shipping documents, he can
recover his price if the goods do not arrive (*Comptoir D'Achat*
v. *Luis de Ridder* (1949)).

Uniform laws

When the Uniform Law on International Sales Act 1967, is
brought into force, the parties to an 'international sale' will
be able to stipulate in their contract that the Uniform Law
shall govern the contract in whole or in part. Questions of
formation will then be governed by another Uniform Law –
the Uniform Law on the Formation of Contracts for the
International Sales of Goods. The scope of the Laws is, however, limited by a provision in the Act which defines an international sale as a sale between two parties carrying on business in different 'contracting states', i.e. states which were
parties to the convention.

The main Law deals with matters of performance and
remedies, and it does so in considerable detail (there are 95
Articles in all). It is only possible here to mention some of the
more interesting provisions.

Fundamental breach

The Law draws a distinction between a fundamental breach
and a breach which is not fundamental. Article 10 provides
that a breach shall be regarded as fundamental wherever the
party in breach knew, or ought to have known, at the time of
conclusion of the contract, that a reasonable person in the

same situation as the other party would not have entered into the contract if he had foreseen the breach and its effects. The distinction is similar to (but by no means identical with) the distinction between condition and warranty (p. 59).

Delivery

The Law contains rules as to the time and place of delivery which are similar in many ways to those in the Sale of Goods Act. There is, however, an interesting new provision which states that if there is a fundamental breach as to time or place of delivery, the buyer can either avoid the contract or require performance, but he must communicate his decision to the seller within a reasonable time, and if he fails to do this, the contract is avoided (Arts. 26 and 30).

Lack of conformity

The seller is deemed not to have performed his duty of delivery if the goods do not conform to the contract quantity or description, or if they do not correspond with sample, or if they are unfit for a particular purpose contemplated by the contract, or are unfit for their ordinary or commercial use (Art. 33). If, however, the seller has tendered the defective goods before the date fixed for delivery, he can put the matter right at any time up to that date, provided that this does not cause the buyer unreasonable inconvenience or expense (Art. 37).

Examination

The buyer must examine the goods promptly and he must usually do so at the place of destination. If, however, the goods are re-despatched and the seller knew or ought to have known this, examination can be deferred until the goods arrive at their new destination (Art. 38).

Remedies for lack of conformity

The buyer must give prompt notice of lack of conformity, and if he fails to give such notice after he discovered or ought to have discovered the defect, he will no longer be able to rely on it. If the defect occurs at any time within two years after delivery, the buyer can still exercise his rights if prompt notice is given. Once two years have passed, however, the buyer loses his right to rely on the defect unless the seller is in breach of a guarantee covering a longer period.

The precise nature of the buyer's remedies depends upon whether or not the breach is fundamental. If it is, the buyer can demand that the breach be rectified, or he can avoid the contract, or he can set up the defect in reduction of the price (Arts. 39–43).

Damages

The rules governing the assessment of damages for non-acceptance and for non-delivery are strikingly similar to those in the Sale of Goods Act.

Self-tuition test 7

1. S agrees to sell goods to B at a price of £500, delivery and payment to be made on 1 January. A week before delivery is due, B cancels his order. The market value at the date of cancellation was £350 and on 1 January it was £300. The goods are still in S's possession. What are S's rights against B?

2. S agrees to sell goods to B who re-sells them to C. S fails to deliver the goods and, as a result of this, B is unable to perform his sub-contract with C. Is S liable for B's loss of profit?

3. X, an auctioneer, conducts an auction of furniture belonging to Y. An antique desk is knocked down to Z, the highest bidder. It then transpires that the desk did not belong to Y at all and the true owner, O, recovers it from Z. Has Z any remedy against X?

4. What is the difference between an auction sale (i) which is expressed to be 'subject to reserve' and (ii) which is expressed to be 'without reserve' and (iii) which contains no reference to reserve?

5. Outline the principal obligations of the seller under (a) an f.o.b. contract (b) a c.i.f. contract (c) an ex ship contract. On whom is the risk of loss while the goods are on board?

For answers, see p. 193.

Part Two
Hire-Purchase, Conditional Sale and Credit Sale

11 Introduction:
The Growth of Hire-Purchase

The most outstanding feature of hire-purchase has been its phenomenal growth over the past fifty or sixty years. At the turn of the century it was largely unheard of by the great majority of the population; today the national hire-purchase debt is in the region of £1000 million. Before the last war, hire-purchase was used only by a limited class of persons and was frowned upon; today hire-purchase in one form or another is very widely used and has become respectable.

It all started in the latter part of the nineteenth century. In the domestic sphere the Singer company let out sewing machines on hire-purchase; in the commercial field colliery companies took wagons on hire-purchase. As the manufacturers could not provide the credit themselves, wagon companies were set up to buy the wagons from the manufacturers or dealers, and then they let them out to the colliery companies on hire-purchase. The wagon companies were the forerunners of the modern hire-purchase finance company.

At the dawn of the twentieth century there was a tremendous expansion of hire-purchase as industry geared itself to mass production and as people found themselves able, by means of hire-purchase, to acquire articles which they had never been able to own before. First with furniture and domestic appliances, and later with motor vehicles, hire-purchase became a household word. Unfortunately, faced with the prospect of a large and sometimes ill-educated market, some traders abused their very strong position. As a result, hirers received shoddy goods, and the contract contained a widely drawn exemption clause depriving them of any remedy. If they wanted to put an end to the agreement they often had to pay a very high sum for the privilege of doing so; and (perhaps worst of all) there was the system of 'snatch-back' whereby the owners were free to re-take the goods if the hirer failed to pay an instalment, even though the hirer might have paid nearly the whole of the hire-purchase price. A few traders went out of their way to encourage persons to enter into hire-purchase commitments far above their means, in the expectation that the hirer would eventually default, whereupon the goods could be snatched back without giving credit for sums already paid, leaving the owners with a good profit.

Although these abuses were by no means universal, they did cause public concern. Regrettably, as in the case of the exemption clauses considered in chapter five, the courts felt themselves unable to interfere. Although the courts had for centuries granted relief to defaulting tenants and defaulting mortgagors, they held in *Cramer* v. *Giles* (1883) that relief could not be granted to a defaulting hirer. The courts merely re-affirmed that it was for the parties to make their own bargain, and they paid no attention to the inequality of bargaining power of the parties to the 'contract' nor to the fact that hirers were often ill-educated (and sometimes even illiterate) persons who were usually totally unaware of their legal rights. In 1938 Lord Justice McKinnon, a famous common-law judge, made the following remark while hearing a hire-purchase case in the Court of Appeal (*South Bedfordshire Electrical Finance Ltd* v. *Bryant* (1938)):

If anyone is so foolish as to enter into such an agreement as this I do not know that his case can be considered harsh.

Even as recently as 1961 Lord Justice Harman vigorously asserted that 'equity mends no man's bargain' (*Campbell Discount Co. Ltd* v. *Bridge* (1961)), although Lord Denning took a different view when the case went to the House of Lords.

In the light of this disappointingly negative attitude of the courts, the only remedy was for Parliament to intervene, and in 1938 Miss Ellen Wilkinson promoted a bill which became law as the Hire-Purchase Act 1938, and which effectively curbed the abuses in the cases to which it applied. It is interesting to see how sharply the value of money has fallen. In 1938 it was thought sufficient that the Act should only apply where the hire-purchase price did not exceed £50 for a motor vehicle or railway rolling stock, £500 for livestock, and £100 for other goods. Then in 1954 we find the limits raised by the Hire-Purchase Act 1954, to £1000 for livestock and £300 for all other goods. The great gap, of course, was in relation to cars; since the price of new cars (and many second-hand ones) was over £300, hirers had no protection in relation to the one article where, by reason of the amounts involved, it often mattered most. Accordingly, the Hire-Purchase Act of 1964 increased the limit for all goods (including livestock) to £2000, so that virtually all hire-purchase agreements made by individuals are now covered.

The Acts of 1938 and 1954 and most of the Act of 1964 were repealed and re-enacted in a consolidating Act, the Hire-Purchase Act of 1965. This Act, however, does not contain the whole law relating to hire-purchase, and the law must still be gleaned from five different sources, namely:

1. The common law.

2. The Act of 1965.

3. Part III of the Act of 1964 (pp. 51-2), which was not affected by the 1965 Act.

4. The Advertisements (Hire-Purchase) Act 1967, which imposes criminal liability for certain misleading advertisements relating to hire-purchase.

5. The Orders relating to hire-purchase which are made from time to time by the Department of Trade and Industry as part of government policy of controlling the economy. If a government wants to encourage or restrict consumer demand, it frequently uses hire-purchase as an instrument. It does this by specifying the maximum period for re-payment and also the minimum deposit which must be paid. This policy is often resented by industry because it makes long-term planning impossible, but it does illustrate the immensely important part which hire-purchase plays in the country's economic life. A

hire-purchase agreement that contravenes one of these Orders will generally be illegal and void (see, for example, *Snell* v. *Unity Finance Co.* (1964)). At the time of writing there are no such orders in force.

12 The Nature of Hire-Purchase

When a man goes to a local car dealer and agrees to take a new car on hire-purchase, he thinks that he is 'buying' the car on hire-purchase from the dealer. He would be very surprised to be told by his solicitor that in law he was only hiring the car (with an option to purchase it on completion of his payments), and that he was acquiring the car not from the local dealer but from a remote finance company whom he had never seen. He might well ask: Why does the law work in such an artificial way? Why does it not reflect the business realities of the situation? In this chapter we shall try to find the answer to these questions.

What is hire-purchase?

We have just seen that at common law, a hire-purchase agreement is a simple hiring, coupled with an option to purchase, and we shall see in the next chapter that the definition in the Act of 1965 is basically the same. The contract may provide that:

if the hirer shall have duly paid all the instalments he may purchase the goods on payment of a further sum of £1;

or that

if the hirer shall have duly paid all the instalments the property shall pass to him; provided that the hirer may at any time determine this agreement by giving written notice.

In either of these cases, the property will pass to the hirer only if he decides to pay the sums due under the agreement. He is not (and this is the vital point) bound to buy. Now why this rigmarole? This answer is simple; to avoid sections 9 of the Factors Act 1889, and section 25(2) of the Sale of Goods

Act 1893 (p. 50). When hire-purchase was in its infancy, the owner was clearly anxious to prevent the hirer selling the goods and passing a good title to a third party. In *Lee* v. *Butler* (1893):

A Mrs Lloyd entered into a 'hire and purchase' agreement for some furniture. She agreed to pay £1 on the signing of the agreement and £96 at a later date. On completion of the payment the property was to vest in her. She had no power of termination. Before completing the payments she wrongfully sold the furniture. It was held by the Court of Appeal that Mrs Lloyd was a person who had 'agreed to buy' and accordingly, under section 9 of the Factors Act, the buyer from her acquired a good title.

The hire-purchase traders immediately amended their forms of agreement, and in the leading case of *Helby* v. *Matthews* (1895) the revised agreement came before the House of Lords. In that case:

One Brewster had agreed to take a piano under a hire-purchase agreement. There were a specified number of instalments, and Brewster was given an option to purchase on paying the instalments. Before completing the payments, he wrongfully pledged the piano with the defendants. When the owners sued the pledgees for the return of the piano, the pledgees claimed that as Brewster had 'agreed to buy' they were protected by section 9 of the Factors Act. The House of Lords, reversing the decision of the Court of Appeal, held that, since Brewster was under no legal obligation to buy, he had not 'agreed' to buy. The result was that section 9 did not apply and the owners were entitled to the return of the piano.

Since that decision, hire-purchase agreements have always been drafted in the *Helby* v. *Matthews* form. An agreement in the *Lee* v. *Butler* form would today be classified as a conditional-sale agreement. The '*Helby* v. *Matthews*' agreement had the great advantage that the hirer could not pass title to an innocent third party, unless he sold in market overt. In the case of motor vehicles, however, this advantage has been largely removed by Part III of the Hire-Purchase Act 1964, which, as we have seen, enables the hirer to pass a title to a private purchaser (see p. 51). The combined effect of these provisions and some of the stringent provisions of the 1965 Act has been to induce some finance companies to move away from the *Helby* v. *Matthews* agreement and to switch over to credit sale.

The role of finance companies

The finance companies, as their name implies, are in business to provide money, but in the field of hire-purchase their contribution takes a highly unusual form. Instead of simply lending money upon a mortgage of the goods, they actually buy the goods from the dealer and then let them out on hire-purchase to the customer. Since they themselves do not trade in the goods, they clearly have an interest in selecting their dealers with care. It is very common for a dealer, when selling the goods to the finance company, to enter into a 'recourse agreement' whereby he agrees to indemnify the finance company against loss suffered by reason of the hirer's default. The dealer, in his turn, has an interest in making sure that the customer is an honest man who can meet his obligations. The customer will usually fill up a proposal form in the dealer's showroom or office, and the dealer will then forward this to the finance company. The form will usually contain a statement, signed by the dealer, that the information supplied by the prospective hirer is true. In one case this information turned out to be totally untrue, and the dealer (although innocent) had to indemnify the finance company in respect of their loss (*Liverpool & County Discount Co.* v. *A. B. Motors (Kilburn) Ltd* (1963)).

Why does the finance company not simply lend on mortgage? The answer is that, just as section 9 of the Factors Act has inhibited the growth of a realistic form of hire-purchase, two other statutes have inhibited the realistic provision of finance. The first of these statutes is the Bills of Sale Act 1878 (Amendment) Act 1882. This Act was designed to protect needy persons from exploitation by rapacious lenders. It provided, in effect, that where the owner of personal chattels granted a mortgage over them and remained in possession, the document by which this was done had to comply with stringent formalities and had to be registered in the Central Office of the Supreme Court. A learned writer has stated that

so technical and stringent are the provisions of these Acts that they have resulted in the virtual disappearance of the bill of sale as a commercial instrument (Professor A. G. Guest, *The Law of Hire Purchase*, p. 44).

The other main stumbling block is to be found in the Moneylenders Acts of 1900 and 1927, which impose conditions on a person or company carrying on the business of 'moneylender' as defined in the Acts. The definition does not include any person

bona fide carrying on any business not having for its primary object the lending of money, in the course of which, and for the purpose whereof, he lends money.

It is clear from the decided cases that although the commercial function of the finance company is to lend money, they are not legally 'moneylenders' because they genuinely buy goods from the dealers and then let them out on hire-purchase (*Olds Discount Co. Ltd* v. *Cohen* (1938)). Likewise, the Moneylenders Acts do not apply to what is called 'block discounting', where a dealer lets the goods out to the customer himself and then obtains finance by assigning the benefit of the hire-purchase agreements to a finance company (*Olds Discount Co. Ltd* v. *Playfair Ltd* (1938)). If, however, the finance company were to make loans to a dealer not directly connected with hire-purchase transactions, the Moneylenders Acts might well apply (*Premor Ltd* v. *Shaw Bros.* (1964)).

The foregoing paragraphs have highlighted many anomalies and artificialities in the modern hire-purchase agreement. The Crowther Committee on Consumer Credit recommended sweeping reforms to bring the law of hire-purchase and similar arrangements for purchase on credit terms into line with business reality. A brief summary of the main Crowther proposals appears in chapter 17.

Position of dealer

The finance company, then, buys the goods in order to circumvent the Bills of Sale and the Moneylenders Acts. What is the position of the dealer where a finance company is used? We have seen that the dealer may be liable to the finance company if the statements in the proposal form are untrue, or if the hirer defaults and the finance company exercise their rights against the dealer under a recourse agreement. Is the dealer also liable to the hirer if the goods turn out to be unsatisfactory? In the case of *Drury* v. *Buckland Ltd* (1941), the Court of Appeal emphasized that the hirer could not sue the dealer for breach of the conditions implied by the Sale of Goods Act, the reason being that the sale was to the finance company and not to him. If, however, the dealer gives an express undertaking to the hirer, the position may well be different. In *Andrews* v. *Hopkinson* (1957):

A dealer said to a prospective customer who was looking at a second-hand car 'She's a good little bus – I'd stake my life on it.' Encouraged by these words the customer agreed to take it, and the dealer sold it to a finance company who let it out to the customer on hire-purchase. Unfortunately the car had a serious steering defect and an accident occurred almost at once. McNair J. said that, on the facts of the case there was a separate contract (a 'collateral contract') between dealer and hirer – the dealer had said in effect 'if you will take the car on hire-purchase I warrant that it is a good little bus'. The dealer was held liable in damages for breach of the warranty.

The liability of the dealer is not affected by the fact that the finance company may also be liable (for example, because the dealer was their agent). Where the 1965 Act applies, the dealer is expressly made the agent of the owners for certain purposes, and in particular they will be bound by any representations which he makes with regard to the goods (Act of 1965, section 16, p. 154). Apart from this, the question of agency is one of fact in each case, but the realistic view would seem to be that he is their agent for most purposes, and there are a number of cases which support this view.

Quite apart from this, the dealer may also be liable to the hirer in tort for negligence if he knew or ought to have known that the goods were defective (see *Donoghue* v. *Stevenson*, p. 86). In *Andrews* v. *Hopkinson* the dealer was also liable on this ground.

13 Hire-Purchase at Common Law

It is now time to examine the substantive law governing modern hire-purchase agreements. Most of this is to be found in the Act of 1965, which is considered in the next chapter. It may, however, be useful to start by taking a brief look at the common law rules, because some matters of general interest are not dealt with in the Act at all, and because some agreements (e.g. those made by a limited company) are outside the Act altogether.

Formation of the contract

We saw in the last chapter how the contract was usually negotiated by the dealer, and how it usually took the form of a sale by dealer to finance company and a hire-purchase agreement made between the finance company and the hirer.

Whether a valid contract has come into existence depends on the usual rules governing this matter and these were dealt with briefly in chapter two. The following cases illustrate the problems which can arise:

1. *Financings Ltd* v. *Stimson* (1962)
In this case the hirer signed an offer to take a car on hire-purchase and the dealer allowed him to take it away while he posted off the offer to the finance company for acceptance. The hirer decided that he did not like the car and returned it to the dealer. Shortly afterwards the finance company, who were unaware of this, accepted the offer and sent the hirer a copy of the 'hire-purchase agreement'. He refused to pay. *Held*: (1) the dealer was the agent of the finance company for the purpose of receiving notice of revocation; (2) the hirer's offer had been effectively revoked before accept-

ance; (3) accordingly there was no contract between the
parties.

2. *Campbell Discount Co.* v. *Gall* (1961)

The hirer signed a form which did not contain all the details,
and paid the dealer a deposit. The dealer filled in a price which
was higher than that which the hirer had agreed to pay, and
sent off the form to the finance company who accepted the
proposal and sent the hirer a copy of the agreement. The hirer
refused to pay and was sued for instalments. It was held that:
(1) the hirer was not bound by what the dealer had done because the dealer was not the agent of the hirer; (2) as between
the hirer and the finance company there was no consent as to
the price and therefore no contract; (3) accordingly the hirer
was not liable to pay instalments.

A further point arose in this case: could the hirer, who had
paid a deposit to the dealer, recover it from the finance company? The Court of Appeal held that he could not do so; but
it is now clear from the later case of *Branwhite* v. *Worcester
Works Finance Co.* (1969) that this decision was wrong. In
this later case, where the facts were similar, the House of
Lords pointed out that when the dealer sold the car to the
finance company they paid him the price *less* the deposit which
the dealer had already received from the hirer. Consequently
the finance company had, in effect, *received* the deposit and
they were liable to return it to the hirer when the hire-purchase
agreement fell through.

3. *Snell* v. *Unity Finance Co. Ltd* (1964)

The dealer and the hirer arranged the documents in such a way
as to indicate that a substantial deposit had been paid (which
was untrue), the object being to evade the relevant Control
Order which required the hirer to pay a minimum deposit.
The car was sold to the finance company, who took in good
faith. The hirer claimed damages for defects in the goods.
Held: he could not do so – the contract was illegal.

Minimum payment clauses and damages

It may often happen that the agreement will come to an end before it has run its full course, and a clause in the agreement invariably sets out the circumstances in which termination is to take place and what the owner's rights will be when it does take place. Thus the contract may provide for termination:

1. If the hirer exercises his option to terminate.
2. If the hirer defaults in payment.
3. If the hirer disposes of the goods.
4. If the hirer becomes bankrupt or (being a company) is wound up.
5. If execution is levied on the hirer's premises.
6. If the hirer dies.

A clause providing for such termination usually goes on to provide that the owner shall be entitled to recover possession of the goods. We have seen that the common law refused to grant relief in cases of hardship, and we shall see in the next chapter how the Act now gives the hirer a substantial measure of protection.

If the agreement does come to an end at an early stage, the owners may find themselves in the possession of heavily depreciated goods, and they will have lost a large part of the profit which they had hoped to make. To protect themselves, the owners (usually a finance company) insert into the contract a 'minimum payment clause', i.e. a clause which guarantees them a minimum amount, regardless of termination. The clause might provide that: 'On termination of this agreement the hirer must bring his total payments up to two-thirds of the hire-purchase price.'

Now looked at from the hirer's point of view, this could be a very serious matter, especially if the contract came to an end at a very early date. Where the Act applies, the hirer is given substantial protection, because no minimum payment clause can bring his liability beyond (a) sums accrued due and (b) such further sum (if any) as will bring his total payments up to one-half of the hire-purchase price *or* such lesser sum as the court thinks sufficient to compensate the owners (section 29). Suppose, however, that the Act does not apply. How far can the common law protect the hirer? Again, the attitude of the courts has been disappointing. Although the same minimum payment is payable on any termination, the courts have drawn a distinction between (a) termination by the hirer, (b) termination by the owner and (c) termination in other ways. The position can be summarized as follows:

(a) If the hirer exercises his option to determine the agreement, the minimum payment is the price which he must pay, and it seems that he has no defence to an action brought by the owners to recover it (*Associated Distributors* v. *Hall* (1938)). Despite criticism, it seems that this case is still good law.

(b) If it is the owners who determine the agreement by reason of the hirer's breach, the minimum payment is only recoverable if it is a genuine pre-estimate of damage and not if it is a penalty (*Cooden Engineering Co.* v. *Stanford* (1953)). Where the same sum is payable for different breaches – some large and some small – there is a presumption that it is a penalty (*ibid.*). Where the payment is referred to as 'agreed depreciation' and sums payable under the clause decrease while depreciation increases, it is clearly not a genuine pre-estimate of damage (*Campbell Discount Co.* v. *Bridge* (1961)).

Since the Bridge case, different forms of wording have been tried, but without a great deal of success. In *Anglo-Auto Finance Co. Ltd* v. *James* (1963), the hirer agreed to pay a sum which would bring his total payments up to the total hire-purchase price less the proceeds of a re-sale. The clause was struck down as a penalty.

(c) If the agreement terminates for any other reason, e.g. bankruptcy of the hirer, the position is uncertain. In *re Apex Supply Co. Ltd* (1942) Simonds J. (as he then was) considered that no question of penalty arose, but in *Cooden Engineering Co.* v. *Stanford* (1953) the Court of Appeal regarded the point as still open.

Damages

Even if a minimum payment clause is ineffective, the owners can always bring an action for damages for breach of contract if the hirer has been guilty of such a breach. Here the courts (notably Lord Denning) have sought to assist the hirer by introducing a very subtle distinction between a *repudiation* and a mere *breach*. It seems that:

(a) If the hirer's conduct shows an intention not to be bound by the contract this is repudiation, and the owners can claim:

1. All sums accrued due, and

2. the balance of the hire purchase price, less
    (i) the proceeds of a re-sale and
    (ii) the nominal sum payable for the option to purchase and
    (iii) an allowance for accelerated receipt (i.e. getting in the money earlier than they would otherwise have done).

These principles were laid down in *Yeoman Credit Ltd* v. *Waragowski* (1961) and in *Overstone Ltd* v. *Shipway* (1962).

(b) If the hirer is merely in breach of the agreement but has not repudiated it completely, it was held in *Financings Ltd* v. *Baldock* (1963) that the damages were limited to instalments in arrear and interest. In this case the owners suffered a substantial loss, but it was held that the damage flowed not from the hirer's default but from the owners' decision to terminate the agreement. Damages for failure to repair are also recoverable (*Brady* v. *St Margaret's Trust* (1963)).

Where the Act applies there is no specific provision dealing with damages, but it is highly unlikely that a hirer would be ordered to pay more than the ceiling set out in section 28.

Third-party rights

One of the risks of letting out goods on hire-purchase is that the hirer may deal with them in such a way as to prejudice the owner's rights. Thus he may:

1. Sell them.

2. Assign the benefit of the agreement.
3. Become bankrupt.
4. Create a lien for repairs.
5. Allow his landlord to levy execution.
6. Allow a sheriff to seize the goods in execution.

It is now proposed to glance very briefly at these six matters. Needless to say, the agreement should be (and usually is) very carefully drawn to protect the owner's interests as far as possible.

(a) If the hirer sells the goods before the property has passed to him, the owner can recover them from the buyer, unless the buyer acquires title under one of the exceptions to the *nemo dat* rule, e.g. sale in market overt (p. 44) or Part III of the Hire-Purchase Act 1964 (p. 51).

(b) The hirer has a special right of property by reason of his option to purchase. He can assign the benefit of the agreement and, even if the assignment takes the form of a wrongful sale, the assignee's liability to the owners is limited to the unpaid balance of the hire-purchase price (*Whiteley* v. *Hilt* (1918)). It used to be thought that the owner could protect his full ownership by inserting a clause that 'the benefit of this agreement shall not be assigned' (*United Dominions Trust (Commercial) Ltd* v. *Parkway Motors Ltd* (1955)) but it now seems that this is not so (*Wickham Motors Ltd* v. *Brooke House (Holdings) Ltd* (1967)).

(c) If the hirer becomes bankrupt, all his property passes to his trustee in bankruptcy for distribution among his creditors. By section 38 of the Bankruptcy Act 1914, the trustee will also take over any goods in the possession of the debtor in his trade or business with the consent of the owner in such circumstances that the debtor was the reputed owner thereof. The object of this rule is to compensate creditors who might have given credit believing that the debtor owned assets which were not in fact his.

(d) If goods are delivered for repairs, the general rule is that a repairer has a lien for his charges, and this lien binds the person who created it or authorized it. Since a hirer has power to use the asset, he has implied authority to have it repaired since repair is incidental to user (*Tappenden* v. *Artus* (1964)). The owners are bound in such a case. Even if the agreement forbids the creation of a lien this will not affect the repairer if he was unaware of the prohibition (*Albermarle Supply Co.* v. *Hind* (1928)). The repairer will not be able to claim a lien, however, if the hire-purchase agreement has been terminated before the order for repairs was given (*Bowmaker Ltd* v. *Wycombe Motors Ltd* (1946)).

(e) A landlord can normally levy distress (i.e. seize the goods for non-payment of rent) on all goods found on the premises, but if they do not belong to the tenant the owner can serve a declaration on the landlord to save them from distress (Law of Distress Amendment Act 1908). This power to save goods from distress is not available if the goods are comprised in a hire-purchase agreement made by the tenant, nor if they are in his possession with the owner's consent in such circumstance that he is the reputed owner thereof. Very careful drafting is required to avoid these provisions.

(f) If execution is levied on the hirer's premises by one of the hirer's judgment creditors, the owner can serve notice on the sheriff demanding the goods. If, however, the sheriff sells the goods without notice of a claim, both the sheriff and the purchaser are protected (Bankruptcy and Deeds of Arrangement Act 1913; County Courts Act 1959) but the owner can sue the judgment creditor to recover the proceeds of sale.

14 The Hire-Purchase Act 1965

Having outlined the background of the Act of 1965, it is now necessary to examine some of the main provisions of the Act (which, as we have seen, consolidated the earlier Acts). In the remainder of this book, unless otherwise stated, any reference to 'the Act' is a reference to the Hire-Purchase Act 1965, and a reference to a section is to that section of the Act. The principal provisions of the Act are set out in Appendix I.

The main object of the Act is to protect the hirer. It does this by:

1. Regulating the formation of the agreement so that the hirer is given adequate information.

2. Implying a number of conditions and warranties, with very limited powers of exclusion.

3. Regulating the hirer's right of cancellation and termination.

4. Preventing the owner from 'snatching back' the goods without county court proceedings where one-third of the hire-purchase price has been paid.

Scope of the Act

The Act applies to a hire-purchase agreement where the hire-purchase price does not exceed £2000 (section 2), but it has no application where the hirer is a body corporate (section 4).

Definition of terms

Section 1 defines a 'hire-purchase agreement' as an agreement for the bailment of goods under which the bailee may buy or under which the property in the goods will or may pass to the bailee. It also provides that, where this is the effect of two or more agreements, they are deemed to form a single hire-purchase agreement made on the date of the last one. This provision is designed to prevent an evasion of the Act by having two separate documents – a simple hiring agreement, followed later by an option to purchase.

Section 58 provides that the 'hire-purchase price' is the total sum payable by the hirer under the agreement to complete his purchase, excluding any penalty, compensation, or damages for breach of the agreement. The term includes any deposit or other initial payment, whether in cash or kind, and whether paid or credited. Where the dealer agrees to provide, for example, a Road Fund licence and insurance, and the parties agree that the cost shall be added to the price, these items will form part of the hire-purchase price, because the hirer is agreeing to take a licensed and insured car (*Mutual Finance Ltd* v. *Davidson* (1963)). If, however, the agreement as to insurance were kept separate, it would not form part of the hire-purchase price.

Formation of the agreement (sections 5–10)
Cash price

One of the abuses in the old days was that the hirer was never informed of the cash price, so that he could not work out how much he was paying for the privilege of hire-purchase. Section 6 now requires the owner to notify the hirer of the cash price *before* the agreement is made. This requirement can be complied with in three ways, namely:

1. By written notice.

2. If the hirer has selected the goods from a catalogue clearly stating the cash price.

3. If the hirer has selected goods bearing a ticket or label clearly stating the cash price.

Writing

The agreement itself must be in writing signed by the hirer personally and by or on behalf of all other parties (section 5

(1)(a)). It seems that if the hirer signs a blank form leaving the details to be filled in later, this is insufficient (*Eastern Distributors* v. *Goldring* (1957)). It will be noted that while the other parties can appoint an agent to sign the agreement, the hirer cannot do so – he must sign it himself.

Contents

The agreement must contain:

1. The hire-purchase price and cash price.

2. Details of instalments.

3. A list of the goods.

4. A notice (at least as prominent as the rest of the agreement) informing the hirer of his right of termination under section 27 and of the restrictions imposed by section 34 on the owner's rights to recover possession of the goods once one-third of the price has been paid.

Legibility, etc.

One of the criticisms levelled at hire-purchase agreements has been the smallness of the print. Accordingly, section 32 enables regulations to be made to ensure that agreements are easily legible, and the Department of Trade and Industry has made the Hire-Purchase (Documents) (Legibility and Statutory Statements) Regulations 1965. These regulations are very detailed, as the following extract shows:

> The height of the smallest letter in the document shall not be less than 0·056 of an inch and the width of any column in the document shall not exceed 4½ inches: Provided that the limit on the width of the column shall not apply to any part of the document if the height of the smallest letter in that part of the document is not less than 0·067 of an inch.

At the end of the agreement there must be a special red box. This is the place where the hirer must sign and the regulations provide that the following words must appear:

> This document contains the terms of a hire-purchase agreement. Sign it only if you want to be legally bound by them.
>
> ....
> Signature of hirer
>
>
> The goods will not become your property until you have made all the payments. You must not sell them before then.

Copies

The hirer is entitled to one (and sometimes two) copies of the agreement under sections 8 and 9. His rights depend on whether or not he signed the agreement at 'appropriate trade premises'. This term is defined in section 58 as premises where the owner normally carries on a business or where goods of the contract description or similar goods are normally offered or exposed for sale in the course of a business carried on at those premises. If the hirer signed the agreement at such premises (for example, the office of the finance company or the showroom of the dealer) the position is that:

1. If the agreement is completed by all parties there and then, he must be given a copy immediately. He is not entitled to a second copy.

2. If the document is handed to the hirer for his signature and has then to be sent off to the finance company for acceptance, the hirer must be handed one copy (in the form in which it then is) immediately after he signs it; and he is also entitled to receive a copy of the completed agreement within seven days of its completion. The object of having two copies is to nullify the device of getting the hirer to sign a form which did not show the hiring charges. If the hirer signed such a document the agreement would be unenforceable (*Eastern*

Distributors v. *Goldring*, p. 40) and it should now be easier to find out what really happened by looking at the copy which was given to the hirer when he signed.

3. If the document is sent to the hirer for signature at appropriate trade premises, a copy of the document (in the form in which it then is) must be sent at the same time, and a copy of the completed agreement must be sent to him within seven days of the completion of the agreement.

If the hirer did not sign at appropriate trade premises, the rules are slightly modified. In this case:

1. The hirer will always get two copies.

2. If the document is presented to him for signature, a copy ('first statutory copy'), in the form in which it then is, must be handed to him immediately after he signs.

3. If the document is sent to him for signature, the first statutory copy must be sent at the same time.

4. In each of these cases the hirer is entitled to a copy of the completed agreement ('second statutory copy') within seven days of completion of the agreement, and this must be sent *by post*.

5. Both the first and the second statutory copy must inform the hirer of his right of cancellation and such information must comply with the regulations as to legibility, etc.

Effect of non-compliance

If the owner fails to comply with any of the above matters, the agreement is still a valid one, but the owner is placed under severe disabilities, in that he cannot enforce

1. The agreement.
2. Any security (for example, a cheque).
3. Any guarantee.
4. Any right to recover the goods from the hirer.

If, however, the hirer has wrongfully disposed of the goods to a third party, the Act does not prevent the owner recovering them from that third party (*Eastern Distributors* v. *Gold-*

ring, p. 40), although the owner might find that the third party has acquired a good title to the goods under one of the exceptions to the *nemo dat* rule (for example, Part III of the Act of 1964, p. 51).

The severity of the owner's disabilities is greatly modified by section 10, which gives the court a discretion to waive various formalities, if the court is satisfied that non-compliance has not prejudiced the hirer and that it would be just and equitable to grant relief. There are, however, three exceptional cases where no relief can be granted, namely:

1. If the agreement is not signed by the hirer personally and by or on behalf of all other parties.

2. If the agreement was not signed at appropriate trade premises, and the second statutory copy was not sent by post or at all.

3. If the agreement was not signed at appropriate trade premises and either the first or the second statutory copy failed to contain the information relating to the hirer's right of cancellation.

Guarantees

Frequently a finance company will require the hirer to provide some other person to guarantee that he will duly perform his obligations. Section 22 provides that within seven days of the making of the hire-purchase agreement or guarantee, whichever is the later, the owner must supply the guarantor with a copy (complying with the legibility regulations) of:

(a) the hire-purchase agreement and
(b) a note or memorandum of the contract of guarantee signed by the guarantor or by his duly authorized agent.

If the owner fails to do this, he cannot enforce the contract of guarantee or any security, but the court has the usual power to grant relief.

Additional information

A hire-purchase agreement may run for two or three years and it is quite likely that the hirer may lose his copy of the agreement or he may be uncertain as to how much he has paid. To meet this possibility, section 21 provides that at any time before the final payment has been made, the hirer can make a written request for information together with a payment of 12½p for expenses. He is then entitled to receive a copy of the agreement complying with the legibility regulations and also a statement giving details of sums paid, sums due, and future instalments. If the owner, without reasonable cause, fails to comply with the request within four days, he is subject to the usual disabilities while the default continues. The section also provides that if the default continues for one month the party in default is liable, on summary conviction, to a fine not exceeding £25.

Section 23 contains provisions giving almost identical rights to a guarantor.

There may also be cases where the owner is anxious to know where the goods are. Section 24 deals with this situation by providing that where the hirer has agreed to keep the goods under his possession or control, the hirer must, on receiving a written request from the owner, inform him where the goods are at the time when the information is given. If the hirer fails to comply, without reasonable cause, for fourteen days he is liable, on summary conviction, to a fine not exceeding £25.

Agency provisions

We have seen that at common law the question of whether the dealer can be regarded as the agent of the finance company is one of fact in each case. The Act, however, is more specific. Perhaps the most important provision is that contained in section 16, which states that representations with respect to the goods made by a person conducting antecedent negotiations in the course of a business (i.e. the dealer) shall be deemed to have been made by him as agent of the owners (i.e.

the finance company), although this does not affect his own personal liability. It follows that in cases like *Andrews* v. *Hopkinson* (p. 139) the hirer would now have an action not only against the dealer but also against the finance company, because they would be bound by the representation made by the dealer as their agent.

Apart from this, the dealer is also deemed to be the agent of the owners for the purpose of receiving certain notices, namely:

1. A notice of cancellation under section 11 (section 12(3)).
2. A notice revoking an offer to take the goods on hire-purchase (section 31(1)); This would cover a case like *Financings Ltd* v. *Stimson* (p. 141).
3. A notice rescinding the agreement – for example, for misrepresentation – (section 31(2)).

Finally, section 29 makes void a clause in the agreement whereby the owner excludes his liability for the acts or defaults of his agent on the formation of the agreement, or a clause which provides that such agent shall be deemed to be the agent of the hirer. This section does not, of course, answer the basic question of whether the dealer was in fact the owner's agent at the time of the formation of the agreement, although it seems pretty clear that this is what the draftsman had in mind.

Implied terms

To protect the hirer against receipt of shoddy goods, the Act (by sections 17–19) implies a number of conditions and warranties, and severely restricts the power of exclusion.

Title

By section 17 there is implied:

1. A condition that the owner shall have the right to sell.
2. A warranty for quiet possession.
3. A warranty for freedom from encumbrances when the property is to pass.

It may be mentioned in passing that *at common law* the condition of 'right to sell' runs from the date of delivery to the hirer (*Karflex* v. *Poole* (1933)) and breach of that condition entitles the hirer to the return of all his payments (*Warman* v. *Southern Counties Car Finance Corporation* (1949). The hirer under the Act can, of course, take advantage of this wider common law condition.

Description

Section 19(2) provides that where the goods are let by description there is an implied condition that they correspond with the description, and if they are let by reference to a sample as well as by description, they must correspond both with the sample and with the description. This subsection is virtually identical with section 13 of the Sale of Goods Act (p. 69).

Sample

Section 19(1) provides that where the goods are let by sample there is an implied condition that the bulk will correspond with the sample, and also that the hirer will have a reasonable opportunity of comparing the bulk with the sample (compare Sale of Goods Act Section 15(2), p. 80).

None of the above conditions and warranties can be excluded.

Merchantable quality

Section 17(2) provides that a condition of merchantable quality is implied in every hire-purchase agreement, except that where the hirer has examined the goods or a sample there is no implied condition as regards defects which the examination ought to have revealed (section 17(3)). This condition is similar to the one in section 14(2) of the Sale of Goods Act, although it is somewhat wider in that the goods need not be let by description, and the owner need not deal in goods of that description. Section 18 provides that the condition of merchantable quality can be excluded in two cases, namely:

1. Where the goods are second-hand, and the agreement con-

tains a statement to that effect as well as a statement that the condition is excluded.

2. Where the goods are let subject to specified defects (for example, 'shopsoiled') and the agreement states that the condition is excluded in respect of these defects.

In both cases, however, the exemption clause is useless unless the owner proves that the defects and the clause were brought to the hirer's notice before the agreement was made, and the effect of the clause made clear to him.

Fitness

Section 17(4) implies a condition that the goods are reasonably fit for the hirer's purpose, where the purpose has been made known expressly or by implication to the owner or his servants or agents, or to a person conducting antecedent negotiations (i.e. the dealer) or his servants or agents. Here again exclusion is possible, but only if the owner proves that the exemption clause was brought to the hirer's notice before the agreement was made and its effect made clear to him.

An attempt to exclude the condition of fitness was considered by the court in *Lowe* v. *Lombank Ltd* (1960). In that case:

A lady took a second-hand car on hire-purchase. She signed the agreement which contained an 'acknowledgement' by her that she had not made known the purpose for which the car was required, and that the car was fit for the purpose for which it was in fact required. She also signed a delivery receipt stating that the goods were satisfactory in every respect. In fact, the car was seriously defective and dangerously unroadworthy. In an action for damages for breach of the implied condition of fitness, the Court of Appeal held that (1) the 'acknowledgement' was totally ineffective, because by asking for a car she had impliedly made it clear that she wanted it for its normal purpose, and she could not be compelled to 'acknowledge' a fact which was not true; (2) in so far as the clause constituted an attempt to exclude the statutory condition, it was also wholly ineffective, because no attempt had been made to explain its effect to the hirer; (3) the delivery receipt did not give rise to an estoppel because it had not induced the finance company to alter their position; (4) the hirer was entitled to damages.

Even after this case, it is still the practice of many finance companies to include in the agreement a declaration signed by the hirer acknowledging that (*inter alia*):

1. He has signed the agreement at appropriate trade premises.

2. The cash price was notified to him before the making of the agreement.

3. The goods have been examined and are satisfactory.

4. The exemption clause relating to fitness (and, where appropriate, merchantable quality) has been brought to his attention and explained.

The precise effect of such a clause is unsettled, but it is quite clear from *Lowe* v. *Lombank Ltd* that it cannot destroy the hirer's rights under the Act if he can show that, despite his signature, the statements were untrue.

Revocation, cancellation and termination

A hirer receiving goods on hire-purchase may wish for some reason to bring the agreement to an end. Leaving aside any question of rejection for breach of condition, there are three possibilities:

1. If he has only signed an offer to take the goods on hire-purchase and if the offer has not yet been turned into a contract by acceptance, he can revoke the offer at any time before acceptance.

2. He may have a right of cancellation under sections 11–15.

3. If the last instalment has not yet fallen due, he has a right of termination under section 27.

Revocation

The revocation of an offer to take the goods on hire-purchase is governed by the general law of contract, and it must be communicated to the offeree or his duly authorized agent before acceptance. Where the Act applies, a person conducting the antecedent negotiations (for example, the dealer) is expressly made the agent of the owners for the purpose of receiving notice of revocation (section 31), and even where the Act does not apply, such agency will frequently be found to exist (*Financings Ltd* v. *Stimson*, p. 141).

Cancellation (sections 11–15)

The Molony Committee on Consumer Protection heard many lurid tales of doorstep salesmen inducing housewives to take goods which they did not really want. To deal with such a situation, the Act gives a hirer a four-day 'cooling-off' period, but only if he signed the agreement at a place other than 'appropriate trade premises'. He can exercise his right of cancellation at any time after signing the agreement until the expiration of four days beginning with the day on which he *receives* the second statutory copy. If therefore the form is signed by him on 1 January, and the second statutory copy arrives on 15 January, his cooling-off period is the period from 1 January to 18 January. The word 'receives' suggests that if the second copy is lost in the post and does not reach the hirer, his right of cancellation remains open.

If a hirer has the right to cancel the agreement, he can do so by serving a notice of cancellation on the owner or his agent (it will be recalled that the dealer is expressly made the owner's agent for the purpose of receiving this notice). Apart from other methods of service, section 12(1) provides that a notice of cancellation shall be treated as duly served on the owner if it is sent by prepaid post to a person specified in either the first or second statutory copy, and in such a case the service takes effect as from the date of posting.

'Appropriate trade premises' are defined by section 58 as premises where the owner carries on a business (e.g. the office of a finance company) or where goods of the contract description or similar goods are exposed for sale in the course of a business carried on there (e.g. the dealer's showroom).

Effect of service of notice. If a hirer lawfully serves a notice of cancellation, the agreement is rescinded, and he can recover any sums paid by him under it (for example, a deposit). If the owner comes to collect the goods the hirer can refuse to hand them over until his payments have been refunded (i.e. he has a lien).

Re-delivery. The hirer is only bound to re-deliver the goods, at his own premises, on receiving a written request from the person entitled to possession (section 13(2)). A problem could arise if the hirer were to deliver the goods, by mistake, to someone who was not in fact entitled to possession. This problem is dealt with by section 13(3) which provides that the hirer will be safe if he delivers the goods to an 'authorized person', i.e.:

1. The owner; or
2. The person conducting antecedent negotiations; or
3. The person entitled to possession; or
4. A person specified in either the first or the second statutory copy.

Loss or damage. The hirer is bound to take reasonable care of the goods, and if damage results from his failure to do so he will be liable to an action for breach of statutory duty (section 13(7)). To encourage the owners to take their goods back promptly, section 13(4) provides that the duty of care shall come to an end twenty-one days after service of the notice of cancellation, unless within that time the hirer has received a request for re-delivery and has unreasonably failed to comply with it.

Part-exchange. Section 15 deals with the case where the hirer has handed goods to the dealer in part-exchange for the goods comprised in the cancelled agreement. It provides that unless the goods delivered in part-exchange are re-delivered to the hirer in substantially the same condition within ten days of service of the notice of cancellation, the hirer can recover the part exchange allowance from the dealer. During this ten-day period the hirer is not bound to surrender the goods until the part-exchange goods are returned to him, and after the ten-day period he will have a lien over the goods comprised in the cancelled agreement until the part-exchange allowance is paid to him.

Termination

Section 27 provides that a hirer can always terminate a hire-purchase agreement at any time before the last instalment falls due. He does this by serving written notice on the owner or on a person who is authorized to receive payments under the agreement. Once he has done that, his liability is governed by section 28 which provides that:

1. He must pay all sums which have accrued due.

2. He must pay such further sum (if any) as will bring his total payments up to one-half of the hire-purchase price, unless the court considers that a smaller sum is sufficient to compensate the owner.

3. If he has failed to take reasonable care of the goods, he must pay damages for such failure.

4. He must allow the owner to re-take the goods.

Section 29 provides that nothing in the agreement can take away these rights or fetter them in any way. If, however, the agreement contains a right of termination which is more favourable to the hirer, he can take advantage of it.

Restrictions on owner's rights

We have seen that perhaps the greatest evil of pre-war hire-purchase was the 'snatch-back'. The Act gives the hirer substantial protection, under three separate provisions.

Restrictions on entry

Section 29 makes void a clause in the agreement allowing the owner to enter any premises for the purpose of re-taking the goods. The hirer can, of course, consent at the time of entry, but if he does not give such a consent the owner will be a trespasser and may have to pay heavy damages.

Notice of default

The agreement may contain a clause that:

in the event of default in payment the owners may forthwith terminate this agreement.

Section 25 gives the hirer a short breathing space by providing that such a clause shall not take effect unless the owner serves on the hirer a written notice of default specifying the amount due and requiring payment in not less than seven days, and the default continues throughout that time. The section only applies to a clause providing for termination on non-payment, and not to a clause providing for termination on some other ground. The notice should clearly specify the consequences of non-compliance and the time within which payment must be made (*Eshun* v. *Moorgate Mercantile Co. Ltd* (1971)).

Protected Goods

Perhaps the most valuable protection is contained in section 34, which provides that, once goods have become 'protected goods' as defined by section 33, the owner cannot enforce any right to recover possession of the goods from the hirer otherwise than by action. Goods are 'protected' once one-third of the hire-purchase price has been paid or tendered by the hirer or by any guarantor, and the hirer has not himself terminated the agreement. If the owner contravenes section 34 by seizing the goods without a court order, the consequences are serious because:

1. The agreement comes to an end.
2. The hirer and any guarantor are no longer liable.
3. The hirer and any guarantor can recover all sums paid under the agreement in an action for money had and received.

If, therefore, the hirer has had a car on hire-purchase for eighteen months, has paid three-quarters of the hire-purchase price, and then finds that the owner has snatched it back, the hirer can sue the owner to recover back all his payments. There is no allowance for the eighteen-months user, and the court has no power to grant relief. If, however, the owner sends in a demand for possession and the hirer, in ignorance of his legal rights, voluntarily surrenders the goods, there will be no infringement of section 34 because the owner has not 'enforced' any right (*Mercantile Credit Ltd* v. *Cross* (1965)). Similarly, the section is only infringed if goods are seized 'from the hirer' and not, for example, if the owner takes back goods which the hirer has abandoned (*Bentick* v. *Cromwell Engineering Co. Ltd* (1971)).

Proceedings to recover protected goods

Such proceedings must be started in the county court for the district where the hirer resides or carries on business, or where he did so when he last made a payment. While the case is pending, the court can make orders protecting the goods against depreciation. At the hearing itself, the court can make a number of orders and the most common one is an order allowing the hirer to retain possession of the goods, on condition that he pays off the balance of the price on terms fixed by the court. These terms are often very favourable to the hirer.

Linked-on agreements

Where a hirer has paid a substantial part of the hire-purchase price, a dealer might be tempted to offer the hirer further goods on the basis that the old agreement would be cancelled and replaced by a new agreement comprising both the old goods and the new ones, with credit being given for sums already paid. The object of this device is to evade section 34 since the price credited under the new agreement would be less than one-third of the hire-purchase price. This matter is dealt with by section 47 which provides that once goods have become protected goods, and a new agreement is made comprising those same goods with or without others, all the goods in the new agreement are deemed to be protected goods.

Installation charges

Section 55 provides that where the owner agrees to install the goods and the installation charge forms part of the hire-purchase price, the fractions of one-half (for example, on termination, p. 161) or one-third (for example, for protected goods, p. 162) shall be taken to be the installation charge in full and one-half or one-third of the balance.

Example. X agrees to install a television set in Y's house. The hire-purchase price is £100, comprising £90 for the set and £10 for the installation charge. The goods become protected when Y has paid

$$£10 + \frac{£90}{3} = £40.$$

15 Conditional Sales and Credit Sales

Conditional sales

We have seen that the statutory definition of hire-purchase includes a bailment under which the property 'will or may' pass to the bailee. Apparently there was some doubt as to whether these words covered an agreement in the *Lee* v. *Butler* form (p. 136). Although it would seem clear that these words did *not* cover such an agreement, the Act of 1964 resolved the doubt by creating a new form of agreement known as 'conditional sale'. Section 1 of the 1965 Act defines a conditional sale agreement as an agreement for the sale of goods where the price is payable by instalments and where the property in the goods is not to pass to the buyer (even though the buyer is to have possession) until such conditions as to payment or otherwise as may be specified in the agreement are fulfilled. In other words, it covers an agreement in the *Lee* v. *Butler* form.

Scope of the Act

The Act of 1965 applies to a conditional sale agreement where the total purchase price does not exceed £2000 and the buyer is not a body corporate. In considering conditional sale agreements the terms 'seller', 'buyer' and 'total purchase price' should be used instead of 'owner', 'hirer' and 'hire-purchase price'.

The contract of conditional sale is largely assimilated with hire-purchase, so that virtually all the provisions discussed in the last chapter apply to conditional sale. Thus, although the buyer binds himself to pay all the instalments, he has the statutory right of termination under section 27 (p. 161) at any time before the last instalment falls due.

Scope of the Sale of Goods Act

A conditional sale agreement falling within the Hire-Purchase Act is also governed by the provisions of the Sale of Goods Act 1893, but with two major exceptions, namely:

1. Sections 12–15 (conditions and warranties) do not apply to conditional sale agreements – the reason being that the buyer has the benefit of the conditions and warranties implied in the Hire-Purchase Act.

2. Section 25(2) of the Sale of Goods Act and section 9 of the Factors Act 1889, do not apply to conditional sale agreements. A buyer under such an agreement is not deemed to be a person who has 'agreed to buy' so that if the facts of *Lee* v. *Butler* were to recur, the decision would now go the other way.

For the removal of doubt, it should be emphasized that if a conditional sale agreement falls outside the Hire-Purchase Act because the price exceeds £2000 or because the buyer is a body corporate, it will be governed by the *whole* of the Sale of Goods Act, including sections 12–15 and section 25(2).

Credit sales
Definition

Section 1 defines a credit sale as an agreement for the sale of goods where the price is payable by five or more instalments and which is not a conditional sale agreement. It follows from these last words that under a credit sale the property must pass immediately to the buyer.

Scope of the Hire-Purchase Act

The Act of 1965 applies, to a very limited extent only, to credit-sale agreements where the total price does not exceed £2000 and the buyer is not a body corporate. If the agreement comes within the Act, the following provisions apply:

1. Sections 5–10 (formalities on formation), except that the agreement need not contain the notice referring to sections

27 and 34, the reason being that neither of these sections applies to credit-sale.

2. Sections 11–15 (cancellation).

3. Section 22 (guarantees).

4. Section 21 (buyer's right to additional information).

5. Section 23 (guarantor's right to additional information).

6. The various agency provisions (sections 12(3), 29 and 31).

There is a further restriction, in that the provisions numbered (1), (2), and (3) above apply only where the total purchase price exceeds £30. In view of this, sellers of encyclopedias have been known to sell them by means of several credit-sale contracts, each of them in respect of volumes worth £29. This device would appear to destroy any 'cooling-off' period which the hirer might otherwise have had, and it would also make unnecessary the detailed formalities required by the Act.

Scope of the Sale of Goods Act

The whole of the Sale of Goods Act 1893, applies to credit-sale, although the parties are free to exclude it by agreement.

Use of credit-sale

We have seen that the main reason why traders and finance companies preferred hire-purchase to credit-sale was that, under a hire-purchase agreement, the hirer had not 'agreed to buy' the goods and could not therefore pass on a good title. Since the passing of the Act of 1964, with its protection of private purchasers of motor vehicles, the disappearance of the main advantage of hire-purchase has caused some finance companies to turn their attention to credit-sale. Under a credit-sale agreement, property passes to the buyer at once, so that the seller cannot insert a provision giving him the right to recover possession. He can, however, insert a clause stating:

should the buyer make default on payment of an instalment the whole price shall become due.

If such a clause is used and a buyer does default, the seller can sue for the price and obtain judgment for it, and if the buyer has not sold the goods the seller may be able to recover them by levying execution (i.e. sending in the sheriff to seize the buyer's goods to satisfy the judgment). In addition, all conditions and warranties can be freely excluded under the Sale of Goods Act. These attractions have led some finance companies to switch over to credit-sale, with the result that the Hire-Purchase Act of 1964, which was warmly welcomed as a major instrument of consumer protection, has in some ways left the consumer in a worse position than at any time since 1938.

Self-tuition test 8

1. How does the Hire-Purchase Act 1965, define (a) a hire-purchase agreement (b) a conditional sale agreement (c) a credit-sale agreement?

2. What is the essential difference between a hire-purchase agreement and a conditional sale agreement, and why did the modern hire-purchase agreement assume its present form?

3. What form does a hire-purchase transaction take where a finance company is involved? What is the legal position of the dealer in such a case?

4. How does the Hire-Purchase Act 1965, ensure that the hirer realizes the extra cost to him of acquiring the goods on hire-purchase?

5. John enters a local radio shop and says that he would like to have a television set on hire-purchase. The shopkeeper promises to prepare the hire-purchase forms and bring them round to John's home. When he does so John is out, and the shopkeeper persuades John's wife to sign the hire-purchase agreement on John's behalf. John, who wishes to keep the set, fails to pay the first instalment and the shopkeeper presses for payment. What is John's legal position?

6. During negotiations for the sale of a motor-cycle, the dealer, Fred, assured the prospective buyer Ron that 'she goes like a bomb'. Ron agreed to take it on hire-purchase. The hire-purchase agreement made with a finance company pro-

vided that: 'no dealer has any authority to make any statements with regard to goods comprised in this agreement, and any such dealer shall be deemed for all purposes to be the agent of the hirer'. The motor-cycle had serious mechanical defects and Ron was badly injured when he used it for the first time. Advise Ron as to his rights.

7. Ten days ago, Alice, a housewife, was persuaded at her home to take an expensive vacuum cleaner on hire-purchase. She now realizes that the amount of money involved is more than she can afford. Has she any right to cancel the agreement? Would your answer be affected if she had signed the hire-purchase agreement at her husband's butcher's shop (where she works) instead of at home?

8. Last year John entered into a hire-purchase agreement in respect of a second-hand car. He has lost the agreement, and the dealer with whom the hire-purchase agreement was made has refused to let him have another one. What are John's rights in this situation?

9. How does the Hire-Purchase Act 1965, seek to protect the hirer against (a) receiving shoddy goods, and (b) the risk of having the goods taken away after he has paid most of the price?

10. Why are some finance companies switching from hire-purchase to credit-sale?

For answers, see p. 196.

16 Advertisements

A person wishing to dispose of goods on hire-purchase terms may be tempted to publish an attractive advertisement indicating that the customer's obligations are modest and well within his means. The Advertisements (Hire-Purchase) Act 1957, was passed to curb advertisements which were misleading or incomplete. The Act was amended by the Act of 1964, and the two Acts were consolidated by the Advertisements (Hire-Purchase) Act 1967.

Application of the 1967 Act

The Act applies to any visual advertisement of any goods as being available for disposal by way of hire-purchase or credit-sale, if the advertisement contains one or more of the following elements:

1. An indication that a deposit is payable, or that the deposit is equal to a specified amount or a specified fraction.

2. Words indicating that no deposit is payable.

3. An indication of the amount of any one or more of the instalments payable.

4. A sum stated as the hire-purchase or total purchase price.

The term 'credit-sale' is defined in this Act as any sale of goods where the price is payable by instalments. In other words the definition covers both a credit-sale and a conditional sale.

Exception

The Act does not apply to an advertisement indicating that the goods can be acquired by way of credit-sale if:

1. It does not indicate that goods are available for disposal by way of hire-purchase.

2. The terms of the advertisement are such that no single article can be disposed of in accordance with those terms at a total price exceeding £5.

It should be noted that there is no £2000 limit, and it is immaterial if the goods are eventually let out or sold to a body corporate.

Contents of the Act

Perhaps the main criticism which could be levelled at a hire-purchase or credit-sale advertisement was that one figure was displayed with great prominence while the other, and less attractive, terms were tucked away in small print. The Act deals with this by providing that an advertisement must not be displayed or issued unless it includes all the information required by the Act and each part of the information is displayed clearly in the advertisement in such a way as not to give undue prominence to any part in comparison with any other part. The Act also contains a useful provision that where goods are advertised as being available for disposal by way of hire-purchase or credit-sale, or in accordance with two or more alternative schemes, the information will not be treated as displayed clearly unless it distinguishes clearly between these various alternatives.

If the advertisement specifies the amount of the deposit or of any instalments directly (i.e. in any manner except as a fraction of, or by reference to, some other amount), the advertisement must contain the following information:

1. The amount of the deposit directly expressed, or a statement that the deposit is a specified fraction of a specified amount, or a statement that no deposit is payable.

2. The amount of each instalment, directly expressed.

3. The total number of instalments payable.

4. The length of the period in respect of which each instalment is payable.

5. If any instalments are payable before delivery of the goods, the number of instalments so payable.

6. The cash price.

7. The hire-purchase price or total purchase price.

If, however, the advertisement does not mention the deposit or instalments at all, or only mentions them as a fraction of some other amount, the advertisement need only contain:

1. With regard to the deposit, either (i) a statement that no deposit is payable, or (ii) a statement that the amount of the deposit is a fraction (specified in the advertisement) of a price or sum the nature of which is clearly indicated in the advertisement.

2. The matters specified in (3), (4) and (5) above.

Penalties

If a person issues or displays an advertisement which does not comply with the Act, he is guilty of an offence punishable summarily, with a maximum fine of £50 on first conviction and £100 in any other case. Although the point does not appear to have been expressly decided, it would seem that a contract induced by such an advertisement would not be rendered illegal or void by the fact that the advertisement did not comply with the Act. If, of course, the advertisement gave false or misleading information, the hirer or buyer might be able to have the contract set aside for misrepresentation, and might, in appropriate cases, recover damages.

17 The Future of Credit Transactions

The present law

The Crowther Committee on Consumer Credit was set up in 1968 to investigate the law and practice of consumer credit and to consider what changes, if any, were desirable. In their report, published in 1971, the Committee was very critical of the present law, chiefly because it had grown up in a number of self-contained departments (Bills of Sale, Moneylenders, Hire-Purchase, etc.) and because it was largely concerned with artificial distinctions which had no relevance to commercial reality. A customer who wants credit in order to buy goods can do so in a number of different ways. From a business point of view the object is the same – both as regards the person providing the credit and the person receiving it. Nevertheless, the form chosen for the transaction may vitally affect the legal rights and duties of the parties. The following paragraphs, taken from the Crowther report, vividly illustrate the anomalies of the present law.

Yet despite the fundamental unity of purchase-money loans and dispositions on credit these two forms of transaction are at every point and in every aspect treated by the law in entirely different ways. This is true both of the general law and of consumer protection legislation. The Moneylenders Acts apply regardless of the size of the loan or the corporate nature of the borrower. The Hire-Purchase Act does not apply to transactions above a certain size or involving a body corporate as hirer or buyer. The lender cannot carry on the business of lending unless he is licensed or exempt from the Moneylenders Acts. The instalment seller (including for this purpose a party letting goods on hire-purchase) requires no licence to carry on business. The lender is subject to negative control on advertising, by stringent restrictions on the contents of advertisements. The instalment seller has no such restrictions but is under a positive obligation to provide certain information in certain conditions. A memorandum of a loan within the Moneylenders Acts is required to set out all the terms of the contract; a hire-purchase or instalment sale agreement need set out only those terms specified by the Hire-Purchase Act. A memorandum of a loan must state the rate of interest. A hire-purchase or instalment sale agreement need not state even the amount of finance charge, let alone an interest rate. A lender is entitled to recover his advance with stipulated interest, subject only to the power of the court to re-open transactions which are harsh and unconscionable. An entirely different set of principles governs the monetary liability of those taking goods on hire-purchase or conditional sale. A lender taking a security bill of sale and subsequently realizing his security is obliged to account to the borrower for any surplus. An owner or conditional seller lawfully repossessing from the hirer or buyer is under no such obligation. A lender taking purchase-money security by way of chattel mortgage must register the bill of sale under the Bills of Sale Acts or the Companies Act; a person supplying goods on hire-purchase or conditional sale need not register his reservation of title – indeed there is no machinery by which he can do so. A bona fide private purchaser of a motor car from one holding it on hire-purchase or conditional sale will usually acquire title under Part III of the Hire-Purchase Act 1964. A bona fide private purchaser from one who has granted a duly registered security bill of sale on his motor car acquires no title.

One can multiply these examples almost indefinitely. The illustrations given above should, however, suffice to show the serious anomalies arising from the division of credit transactions into legally distinct compartments and from the failure to accord a uniform treatment to a range of security devices all designed to achieve the same objective.

Suggestions for reform

The Crowther committee rejected the idea of tinkering with the existing law of consumer credit and came down instead in favour of root-and-branch reform. The underlying principles and recommendations of this stimulating, far-reaching and at times revolutionary report can be summarized as follows:

1. Where goods are sold on credit, the law should recognize the business reality of the situation, namely that there are two distinct aspects of the transaction – a sale and a loan. The form of the transaction – credit-sale, conditional-sale or hire-purchase – should not obscure this basic fact.

2. Accordingly the interest retained by the seller should be treated as what it really is – a security interest for payment of the price.

3. The Moneylenders Acts and the Bills of Sale Acts, which have hampered a logical system of mortgage on goods, should be repealed. There should, instead, be a comprehensive Lending and Security Act covering the lending of money on goods (and other property except land) and the security given for such loans. Under this statute the parties would have wide powers to make their own contracts, but some matters would be governed by law. Thus, as in the case of land, a mortgagee who enforced his security by sale would be bound to hand over any surplus to the mortgagor. At present, the owner of goods let out on hire-purchase and subsequently repossessed is under no such duty (although his right of re-possession is, of course, severely restricted where the Hire-Purchase Act 1965 applies).

4. Where the 'buyer' or 'borrower' disposes of the goods to an innocent third party, the present law relating to the third party's rights was described by the Committee as arbitrary and anomalous and as revealing no coherent strategy. The Committee, in what is perhaps its most revolutionary proposal, recommend the setting up of a Register of Security Interests where particulars of such interests can be filed. The filing system is to operate in respect of motor vehicles and all other pure personalty except consumer goods, and it is to be administered by a Consumer Credit Commissioner. If a lender decides not to file his interest, his rights over the goods will not bind a subsequent purchaser, even if the purchaser knows of the unfiled security interest at the time of the purchase. The Committee considered it to be essential that the new system should be easy to operate, fast and inexpensive.

If it is introduced, its success or failure will clearly depend upon whether or not these criteria are satisfied.

5. Side by side with the general Lending and Security Act there should be a Consumer Sale and Loan Act conferring a substantial degree of protection on the consumer without, at the same time, weighting the scales unfairly in his favour. Many of the consumer protection principles recommended in the Report are based upon the principles underlying the present Hire-Purchase Act 1965 e.g. the supply of adequate information, cancellation, non-excludable conditions and warranties and restrictions on re-possession. The differences between the various types of contract (hire-purchase, credit sale, etc.) would largely disappear and the consumer protection provisions would be identical. Only one major recommendation is based upon the Moneylenders Acts; the Report recommends a comprehensive licensing system, administered by a Consumer Credit Commissioner, for all persons and bodies supplying consumer credit.

6. In deciding what transactions should come within the Consumer Sale and Loan Act, the Committee, while adopting some of the criteria of the Hire-Purchase Act, again break new ground. It is recommended that the 'sale' aspect of a credit transaction should be within the Act if (i) the amount of the loan does not exceed £2000 and (ii) the loan is repayable by three or more instalments and (iii) the buyer is not a body corporate and (iv) the whole or part of the price is advanced by the seller himself or by a lender who is connected with the seller. Thus, at present, a finance company in close business relationships with a dealer (p. 137) would be treated as 'connected' with that dealer. If the other conditions were satisfied, the transaction would be known as a 'financed consumer sale' and the Act would apply to it.

With regard to loans, the Committee recommend that a loan made in connection with a financed consumer sale should be within the Act. Any other loan should also come within the Act unless:

(a) It is made to a body corporate *or*

(b) It exceeds £2000 *or*

(c) by the terms of the loan agreement the effective rate of interest does not exceed $2\frac{1}{2}$ per cent over bank rate.

7. The Committee decided against the imposition of fixed maximum rate of interest, but recommended that any rate of over 48 per cent should be treated as prima facie harsh and unconscionable (the present position under the Moneylenders Acts) and that details of the effective annual rate of interest should be given to the borrower.

There are, of course, a great many other matters discussed in this comprehensive and forward looking report. It is to be hoped that its proposals will be enacted without too much delay.

Appendix 1
Answers to Self-Tuition Tests

1. The law relating to the sale of goods developed as part of the 'common law', i.e. as the result of decided cases. The principal source of the modern law is the Sale of Goods Act 1893, which codified the common law. Nevertheless the common law rules continue to apply unless inconsistent with the express provisions of the Act (section 61), so that a substantial part of the modern law is still to be found in the common law (e.g. the rules relating to offer and acceptance, agency, fraud, duress, mistake, or other invalidating cause).

2. The word 'property' is used in the Sale of Goods Act 1893, to mean ownership.

3. A 'sale' takes place where the property passes to the buyer under the contract itself, and as such it must be distinguished from an 'agreement to sell', which takes place where, under a contract of sale, the transfer of property is to take place at a future time or subject to a condition thereafter to be fulfilled (section 1(3)).

4. (a) Goods are defined by section 62 as 'all chattels personal, other than things in action and money'. The reference to money is a reference to money that has passed into currency. If, therefore, money has passed into currency it ceases to be 'goods'. If it has not yet passed into currency, or if it has ceased to be currency, it will probably be 'goods' (*Moss* v. *Hancock*).

(b) A cheque is a chose in action and is not goods.

(c) The term 'goods' includes both 'emblements' and 'industrial growing crops', and these terms are clearly wide enough to include a crop of wheat. The crop therefore is 'goods'.

(d) Trees are goods if they are to be severed before or under the contract of sale.

5. Where goods are displayed in a shop window, this is not an offer to sell, but merely an 'invitation to treat'. It is the customer who makes the offer to buy. Accordingly S is not bound to sell the television set to B for £60 or at all.

6. If the buyer is a minor and the goods are 'necessaries', he is bound to pay a reasonable price for goods sold *and delivered* to him (section 2). If the goods are not necessaries, the contract is 'absolutely void' under the Infants Relief Act 1874. This means that the minor cannot be sued on the contract, but it seems that he can still sue on it.

7. Where one person states that he will supply goods at a price to be agreed, the documents and surrounding circumstances must be carefully examined to find out whether the parties have agreed to bind themselves by this arrangement. If this is so, the courts will usually imply a term that in the absence of agreement a reasonable price is to be paid (*Foley* v. *Classique Coaches Ltd*). If, however, the parties are still negotiating, there is no contract at all (*May & Butcher* v. *The King*).

8. Where the price is to be fixed by the valuation of a third party who cannot make the valuation, the contract is avoided (section 9(1)). Accordingly, on the death of Z, the parties X and Y have no rights under the contract. If X prevented Z from making the valuation, X would be liable in damages to Y (section 9(2)).

9. A contract of exchange is distinguished from a contract for the sale of goods because there is no money consideration (see section 1 of the Act).

10. After earlier doubts it seems that a contract for work and labour is distinguished from a contract for sale of goods by the fact that, in the former case the substance for the contract is the expenditure of skill, while in the latter case the substance of the contract is the production of a chattel for sale.

The distinction was formerly a very important one because section 4 of the Act imposed special formalities for contracts for sale of goods of £10 or upwards, whereas a contract for work and labour could always be in any form. With the repeal of section 4 the distinction has lost much of its importance.

Test 2

1. (a) Specific goods are goods identified and agreed upon at the time of the contract (section 62).

(b) Ascertained goods are probably goods identified and agreed upon *after* the making of the contract (*re Wait*).

(c) Unascertained goods are either purely generic goods, or goods forming part of a larger consignment or bulk otherwise identified.

(d) Future goods are goods to be manufactured or acquired by the seller after the making of the contract (section 62).

2. The passing of the property from seller to buyer is important because once it has passed (a) the seller can sue for the price (section 49), (b) the risk will be on the buyer, unless otherwise agreed (section 20), (c) the buyer can pass title to a third party, and (d) the buyer can usually claim the goods from the seller's trustee in bankruptcy if the seller should go bankrupt.

3. (a) By section 20 of the Sale of Goods Act 1893, unless otherwise agreed, the risk passes when the property passes. By section 18 rule 1, where there is an unconditional contract for the sale of specific goods in a deliverable state, the property passes when the contract is made. Accordingly, the property and risk had passed to X, and if the damage was purely accidental, the loss would fall on X. If, however, the damage was caused by Y's negligence, the loss would fall on him. The position would, of course, be different if the parties had made a contract excluding the operation of rule 1.

(b) A proviso to section 20 states that where delivery is delayed owing to the fault of one party, the goods are at the risk of that party as regards loss which might not have occurred but for such fault. In the present case, the loss might not have occurred if Y had delivered the goods in accordance with the terms of the contract. Consequently the loss will fall on Y unless he can show that the non-delivery was not due to his fault.

4. Goods are in a deliverable state when they are in such a state that the buyer would under the contract be bound to take delivery of them (section 62(4)).

5. The principles which apply in this case are those set out in answer 3(a) above. The risk and property have passed to Y who will have to pay the contract price of £250. The matter is not governed by rule 3 of section 18 (which only applies where the *seller* has to do the weighing, etc.), and in the absence of contrary intention it will be governed by section 18 rule 1.

6. By section 18 rule 4 (which applies unless a contrary intention appears) where goods are delivered on sale or return, property passes to the buyer, *inter alia*, if he adopts the transaction. It has been held that pledging the goods is an act adopting the transaction, and this will normally have the effect of passing the property (*Kirkham* v. *Attenborough*). If, however, the sale or return contract provides that no property shall pass until the seller has been paid, section 18 will not apply at all, and the pledging of the goods will not pass the property (*Weiner* v. *Gill*). In the present case, therefore, the pledge from Y to Z will pass the property unless the contract between X and Y shows a contrary intention.

7. (a) By section 16, where there is an agreement to sell unascertained goods, no property can pass until they are ascertained. By section 18 rule 5 (unless a contrary intention appears), the property passes when goods of the contract description in a deliverable state are unconditionally appropriated to the contract by one party with the assent of the other. The delivery to a carrier for transmission to the buyer is an unconditional appropriation, unless the seller reserves the right of disposal (rule 5(2)).

(b) The wording of this question suggests that no boxes have been appropriated to any particular buyer. If this is so, section 16 will apply, and no property can pass to any buyer until appropriation (*Healy* v. *Howlett*).

8. (a) Where goods are shipped and the bill of lading is made out to the order of the seller, he is prima facie deemed to have reserved the right of disposal (section 19(2)).

(b) Where the seller sends to the buyer a bill of lading and a bill of exchange, he will be treated, in effect, as having reserved the right of disposal if the buyer does not honour the bill of exchange (section 19(3)). In such a case, the buyer must return the bill of lading, and if he wrongly retains it, no property passes to him (*ibid.*).

9. Goods can be said to 'perish' if they are destroyed in a physical sense (e.g. by being burnt) or in a commercial sense (as in *Asfar* v. *Blundell* where dates which became impregnated with sewage were held to have 'perished'). It is an unsettled question whether goods can be said to 'perish' if, for example, they are stolen, but it is clear that the provisions of the Act relating to perishing have no application where the goods have never existed at all (*McRae* v. *Commonwealth Disposals Commission*).

10. The question does not make it clear whether the contract is for the sale of ten specific chickens or for any ten chickens. In the former case the matter will be governed by section 6 which provides that where, on a sale of specific goods, the goods have perished without the seller's knowledge, the contract is void. If the contract is not severable it seems that a perishing of part has the same effect as a perishing of the whole (*Barrow Lane & Ballard* v. *Phillips*). If, however, the contract merely provided for the sale of 'ten live chickens' X will have to find ten chickens to deliver to Y, or he will be liable to pay damages for non-delivery.

Test 3

1. The *nemo dat* rule is the basic rule that no person can give that which he does not have (*nemo dat quod non habet*), and it is to be found in section 21 of the Sale of Goods Act 1893. In other words, if a seller has no title or a defective title, the buyer will not normally get a better one.

2. The ten exceptions are:

(a) Estoppel.

(b) Sale under an order of the court.

(c) Agency.

(d) Disposition by a mercantile agent.

(e) Sale under a common law or statutory power.

(f) Sale in market overt.

(g) Sale under a voidable title.

(h) Disposition by a seller in possession.

(i) Disposition by a buyer in possession.

(j) Dispositions of motor vehicles held under hire-purchase or conditional-sale agreements.

3. Estoppel is a rule of evidence whereby A is precluded (or estopped) from asserting that a fact is untrue, because he previously represented to B (by words or conduct) that the fact was true and B altered his position in reliance on that representation. It is important in relation to sale of goods where, for example, X (the owner of the goods) represents to Z that another person, Y, has authority to sell certain goods. If Z acts on this representation by buying the goods from Y, X cannot at a later date assert that Y had no authority (see e.g. *Eastern Distributors Ltd* v. *Goldring* and section 21). The result is that Z will acquire title.

4. Where an agent sells his goods without his principal's authority, the buyer will not acquire title, unless (i) he bought in market overt or (ii) the agent had 'apparent authority' (i.e. if the principal clothed him with the appearance of authority and the buyer acted on this). A special form of 'apparent authority' occurs where a 'mercantile agent' obtains possession of goods or documents of title with the owner's consent for the purposes of his business as such agent. If he then disposes of the goods or documents in the ordinary course of business of a mercantile agent, a buyer taking in good faith will acquire title despite any lack of authority on the part of the agent (Factors Act 1889, section 2).

5. This question turns on the provisions of section 2 of the Factors Act 1889 (see above). In the case of a second-hand car, the owner's consent must extend to the log book as well as to

the car itself (*Pearson* v. *Rose & Young*). Accordingly, the question is: did Arthur consent to Sharp having the log book? If so, Jack may well get a good title under section 2; if not, he will not.

6. The general rule is that a person with no title cannot pass title (section 21). There are, however, various exceptions and the one which is relevant here is sale in market overt (section 22). The sale to C will not be covered by this exception, because even if the shop was market overt (see below), the market overt rules only apply on a sale *by* the shopkeeper and not on a sale *to* him. Accordingly, no title passed when A sold the camera to C. The sale to D, however, may be different. If the shop was in the *City* of London it will be treated, by long-established custom, as market overt, and D will have acquired a good title if (a) the sale was public and open and took place in the public part of the shop, (b) the shop was one where cameras are normally sold, (c) the sale took place between sunrise and sunset and (d) he took in good faith and without notice that the camera did not belong to C. If, however, any one of these conditions is not satisfied, the camera still belongs to B.

7. One of the exceptions of the *nemo dat* rule (see above) is a disposition by a person who, having sold goods, remains in possession and then sells *and delivers* them to a second buyer who take them in good faith and without notice of the previous sale (Factors Act 1889, section 8, and Sale of Goods Act 1893, section 25(1)). If, as seems likely, these conditions are satisfied in the present case, the radio will belong to Z.

8. If the sale by Fred to John took place in market overt (see 6 above), the company may very well find themselves unable to recover the scooter. If, however, the sale did not take place in market overt, the company can recover the scooter. Section 9 of the Factors Act 1889, will not protect John because Fred had not 'agreed to buy'. Nor will Part III of the Hire-Purchase Act 1964, assist him, because the contract with the company was hire and not hire-purchase.

9. If the contract between Charles and Blinkiron was void for

mistake, no title will pass to Tom unless he bought in market overt. If, however, the contract was merely *voidable* for misrepresentation, section 23 enables the buyer to pass a good title, if he re-sells *before* his title has been avoided. In the present case, however, it seems that Charles did avoid the contract when he went to the police, because avoidance is possible without notice to the fraudulent buyer (*Car and Universal Finance Co. Ltd* v. *Caldwell*). This means that section 23 will not apply, because the title of Blinkiron was avoided before the sale to Tom. Nevertheless, Tom may be protected by section 9 of the Factors Act 1889, because Blinkiron (a) bought the car and (b) obtained possession with Charles's consent and (c) sold and delivered it to Tom. If the sale by Blinkiron to Tom was in the ordinary course of business of a mercantile agent, Tom will be entitled to retain the car (*Newtons of Wembley* v. *Williams*).

10. By section 27 of the Hire-Purchase Act 1964, where a motor vehicle let under a hire-purchase agreement is disposed of by the hirer in favour of a bona fide private purchaser, the disposition takes effect as though the owner's title had been vested in the hirer at the time of the disposition. A 'private purchaser' is any purchaser who is not a 'trade or finance purchaser'. In the present case, Crash Ltd were not trade purchasers (since they did not buy motor vehicles for re-sale), nor were they 'finance purchasers'. Accordingly, they were 'private purchasers' and, as such, they acquired title under section 27 if they took in good faith and without notice of the hire-purchase agreement. When they sold the lorry to Alf, they passed their title to him. As he bought the lorry from the true owners, the fact that he was a car dealer is irrelevant.

Test 4

1. The essential distinction between a representation and a contractual term is that the former is merely a *statement*, whereas the latter is a statement (express or implied) *which the maker warrants to be true*. A representation merely induces the contract; a contractual term is part of the contract itself. An example of a representation would be a statement by a private

person, with no special knowledge, that, according to the log book, his car was a 1948 model (*Oscar Chess* v. *Williams*). An example of a contractual term is a statement by a car dealer that an engine has done 20,000 miles. As he has specialist knowledge of the matter, the courts will readily infer that the car dealer warranted the statement to be true (*Bentley* v. *Smith*).

2. If the misrepresentation was fraudulent, the innocent party can set the contract aside (subject to the restrictions set out below), and can also claim damages for the tort of deceit.

If the misrepresentation was innocent, the innocent party can claim damages, unless the maker of the statement had reasonable grounds to believe, and did believe, that the statement was true (Misrepresentation Act 1967, section 2(1)). He can also rescind the contract (i.e. set it aside) although this right will not be available if he has affirmed the contract, nor if he has been guilty of unreasonable delay, nor if third parties have acquired rights under the contract. Further, by section 2(2) of the 1967 Act, the court has a discretion to refuse rescission and award damages instead if it considers that, in all circumstances, rescission would be unjust to the party against whom it is claimed.

By section 3 of the 1967 Act a clause excluding liability, or remedies, in respect of a misrepresentation, is void unless the court considers reliance on it far and reasonable.

3. A condition is not defined in the Sale of Goods Act 1893, but clearly it is a vital term because, by section 11(1)(a), a buyer may treat the contract as repudiated if the seller breaks a condition. Alternatively, he may (and in one case – see 4 below – he must) treat the breach as a breach of warranty, i.e. affirm the contract and claim damages only.

A warranty is defined by section 62 as a term collateral to the main purpose of the contract, the breach of which gives rise to an action for damages, but not a right to treat the contract as repudiated. In other words, it is a minor term of the contract.

4. By section 11(1)(c), unless otherwise agreed, the buyer *must*

treat a breach of condition as a breach of warranty if the contract is not severable and the buyer has accepted the goods or part thereof.

5. A contract is severable if it is capable of being split, and is in fact split, into a series of smaller contracts, as for example where the contract provides for instalments which are to be separately paid for. In such a case, the acceptance of one or more instalments does not prevent a buyer from rejecting a later instalment for breach of condition. It is also necessary to consider whether a breach relating to one instalment is a repudiation of the entire contract (giving the innocent party a right to treat the contract as discharged) or merely a severable breach. By section 31(2) this is a question of construction, depending on all the circumstances of the case, and it has been held that the key factors are the size of the breach in proportion to the whole contract and the likelihood of its repetition (*Maple Flock Co. Ltd* v. *Universal Furniture (Wembley) Ltd*).

6. (a) Time for payment is not of the essence unless otherwise agreed (section 10(1)).

(b) Whether other time clauses are of the essence depends on the contract, and in commercial contracts clauses relating to the time for delivery or shipment are usually of the essence (*Bowes* v. *Shand*).

(c) Where time is not of the essence, or where breach of an essential time clause has been waived, time can be made of the essence by reasonable notice (*Rickards* v. *Oppenheim*; *Ward* v. *Bignall*).

7. By section 12(1), unless a different intention appears, there is an implied condition in the case of a sale that the seller has a right to sell. It was held in *Rowland* v. *Divall* that, where a seller is in breach of this condition so that the buyer does not acquire the property in the goods, the buyer can claim from the seller the full price paid by him, regardless of user, because there has been a 'total failure of consideration'. Further, the buyer cannot be said to have 'accepted' the goods; if no property passed to him there was nothing for him to accept. Once the buyer elects to treat the contract as at an end, nothing done

by the seller afterwards to perfect the buyer's title can affect the buyer's right to have his money back (*Butterworth* v. *Kingsway Motors*). If, however, the defect is cured *before* the buyer claims his money back, the buyer will probably be confined to an action for damages; since the property *has* passed to him, it cannot be said that there has been a total failure of consideration (*ibid.*). Apart from the above, the buyer may also claim other damages flowing from the breach (e.g. the cost of overhauling a typewriter which turns out to be stolen (*Mason* v. *Burningham*)).

8. A sale by description covers:

(a) All agreements to sell unascertained goods.

(b) A sale of specific goods which the buyer has not seen, and which are identified by description (*Varley* v. *Whipp*).

(c) A sale of specific goods which the buyer *has* seen, if sold not as specific goods but as goods answering a description (*Beale* v. *Taylor*).

9. By section 14(1), unless otherwise agreed, where the buyer makes known to the seller the purpose for which he requires the goods so as to show reliance on the seller's skill or judgment, and they are of a kind which it is in the ordinary course of the seller's business to supply, there is an implied condition of reasonable fitness for the buyer's purpose, provided that if the goods are sold under a patent or trade name there is no implied condition as to their fitness for any particular purpose.

In the present case, it would seem that the car is not fit for its purpose, but if the sale was simply a sale of a 'Screetcher' car, the 'trade name' proviso will exclude the condition. If, however, there were some preliminary discussions showing express reliance by John on Fred's skill or judgment (as, e.g. if Fred recommended a 'Screetcher' in answer to an inquiry from John), the condition of fitness will be implied and Fred will probably be liable for breach of it (*Baldry* v. *Marshall*).

Even if the sale was under a trade name, Fred may well be liable under section 14(2), which implies a condition of merchantable quality where goods are sold by description from a seller who deals in goods of that description. The term 'sale by description' includes a sale under a trade name (*Wilson* v. *Rickett, Cockerell & Co. Ltd*), and the condition appears to be broken because the car has defects rendering it unfit for its only proper use. If, however, John had examined the car, there would be no implied condition as regards defects which such examination ought to have revealed.

If Fred is in breach of condition, John can certainly claim damages. Whether he can reject the car after using it for one month depends on whether he has 'accepted' it. By section 35 (as amended), he is deemed to have done so if (a) he has intimated acceptance or (b) retained the car for a reasonable time without intimating rejection or (c) done an act inconsistent with Fred's ownership (section 34 will not apply because John examined the car before buying it). In any of these cases he cannot reject (section 11(1)(c)); otherwise he can.

10. An exemption clause in a contract for the sale of goods is prima facie effective to exclude the terms implied by the Act (section 55), but the courts have construed such clauses narrowly, especially where they appear in standard form contracts. One weapon used by the courts has been the doctrine of fundamental breach (or breach of a fundamental term). The essence of this doctrine is that, while a contract may contain conditions and warranties that can be excluded, every contract contains a 'core' or central obligation that cannot be excluded, because such exclusion would destroy the entire basis of the contract. Thus, a seller who contracts to sell a car cannot shelter behind an exemption clause if he supplies a vehicle with so many defects as to make it completely incapable of self-propulsion (*Karsales (Harrow) Ltd* v. *Wallis*; *Yeoman Credit Ltd* v. *Apps*). Similarly, a seller of peas is not protected if he delivers beans, and a seller who agrees to sell 'foreign refined rape oil' will not be protected if he delivers oil not answering that description (*Nichol* v. *Godts*).

Recently, in the *Suisse Atlantique* case, the House of Lords held that the doctrine was *not* based on any rule of law, but was merely a matter of construction, in the sense that if a term was fundamental the courts will usually infer that the parties did not intend the clause to cover it. The decision is unlikely in practice to lead to many cases being decided differently (*Farnworth Finance Co. Ltd* v. *Attryde*).

Test 5

1. By section 29, the question of whether it is for the buyer to take possession or for the seller to send the goods to the buyer depends on the terms of the contract, express or implied. Apart from this, the place of delivery is the *seller's* place of business if he has one or, if not, then the place of delivery is the seller's residence (section 29(1)). This basic rule is subject to a proviso that where specific goods are, to the knowledge of both parties, at some other place, that place is the place of delivery. The basic rule is frequently varied by agreement.

2. Attornment is an acknowledgement by a person in possession of the goods (e.g. a warehouseman) that he holds the goods on the buyer's behalf. Where, at the time of the contract, the goods are in possession of such third party, no delivery takes place until he attorns to the buyer (section 29(3)). Such attornment may also operate as an 'unconditional appropriation' passing the property and risk in unascertained goods (Section 18 rule 5(1)): *Wardar's (Import and Export) Ltd* v. *Norwood Ltd*).

3. Where the seller agrees to deliver the goods at the buyer's premises, he will not be liable for non-delivery if he acted reasonably in delivering them at those premises to a person appearing to be authorized to receive them (*Galbraith and Grant* v. *Block*). Accordingly, in the present case, it will be a question of fact as to whether or not the seller acted reasonably in handing the goods to the lady in question.

4. By section 13, unless otherwise agreed, where goods are sold by description, there is an implied condition that the goods correspond with the description. The quantity of the goods forms part of the description, and if there is any deviation (other than one which is so small that any businessman would disregard it), the buyer can reject for breach of condition, even though he has suffered no loss. Similarly, section 30 provides

that where a seller delivers more, or less, than he contracted to sell, the buyer may reject the entire consignment. To protect themselves in the case of small deviations, sellers often stipulate for a margin by using words such as 'about' or 'little more or less'. If such words are used, the court must examine them to decide whether, on their true construction, they are wide enough to cover the breach which has occurred (see, e.g. *Shipton Anderson* v. *Weil*).

5. Where a contract provides for delivery by instalments that are not to be separately paid for, the contract is not severable. Accordingly, section 11(1)(c) will apply, and where the buyer has accepted the goods *or part thereof* he must, unless otherwise agreed, treat a breach of condition as a breach of warranty, i.e. he cannot reject any of the goods but must content himself with an action for damages. If A is a dealer in grain, and if the sale was by description, there is, unless otherwise agreed, an implied condition that the goods are of merchantable quality, unless B has examined the goods and such examination ought to have revealed the defect (section 14(2)). Assuming however, that B accepted the first instalment, he is bound under section 11(1)(c) to accept the defective one and all remaining ones, subject to a claim for damages. The provisions of section 31(2) do not apply, because the instalments were not to be separately paid for.

Test 6

1. A seller will have a lien only if he is an *unpaid* seller, i.e. if the whole price has not been paid or tendered, or if a negotiable instrument (e.g. a cheque) has been taken as conditional payment and dishonoured (section 38). Where goods are sold on credit, an unpaid seller will have a lien if (a) the credit term has expired or (b) the buyer is insolvent (section 41). By section 62, a buyer is insolvent if he is unable to pay his debts as they fall due, or if he has ceased to pay them in the ordinary course of business. This lien is lost (a) by tender of the price (section 41) or (b) if the buyer or his agent lawfully obtains possession (section 43) or (c) where the seller delivers the goods to a carrier for transmission to the buyer without reserving the

right of disposal (*ibid.*) or (d) where the seller waives the lien (*ibid.*).

2. Stoppage *in transitu* is a process whereby an unpaid seller can recover goods which are in course of transit to the buyer. He can only do this if the buyer is insolvent (section 44). The unpaid seller can exercise his right of stoppage by taking possession of the goods or by giving notice to the carrier. Such a notice can be given either to the person in actual possession or to his principal, and in the latter case the notice must be given in such circumstances that the principal, by the exercise of reasonable diligence, may communicate it to his servant or agent in time to prevent a delivery to the buyer (section 46).

Stoppage *in transitu* has become much less important in recent years. This is because of the system of finance known as 'bankers' commercial credits'. Under this system, a bank in the seller's country accepts a bill of exchange drawn on it by the seller, who thereupon ceases to be an unpaid seller.

3. Where an unpaid seller claiming to exercise his right of stoppage *in transitu* finds that the carrier is claiming a lien for unpaid freight, the position is that the carrier's lien for that particular freight (i.e. the freight for the journey in question) has priority. This means that the unpaid seller must discharge the lien by paying the freight before he can get the goods back (*Booth SS. Co.* v. *Cargo Fleet Iron Co.* (1916)). Subject to this, the unpaid seller has priority over any general lien which the carrier may have against the buyer (*U.S. Steel Co.* v. *G. W. Rly* (1916)).

4. Section 47 states that the rights of an unpaid seller shall not be affected by a disposition made by the buyer, unless the seller has assented thereto. A seller 'assents' to a sub-sale if he acts in such a way as to show that he renounces his rights against the goods (*Mount Ltd* v. *Jay and Jay* (*Provisions*) *Ltd*). Accordingly, if A assented to the sub-sale to C, he (A) will lose his unpaid seller's rights. He will also lose his rights if (i) he has lawfully transferred a document of title (e.g. bill of lading) to B and (ii) B has transferred that document to C and (iii) C took in good faith and for valuable consideration (section 47,

proviso). If neither of these cases applies, A's rights will not be
affected by the sub-sale by B to C.

5. (a) Where a seller re-sells goods to a second buyer, the
second buyer will acquire the property in the goods if (i) the
seller was still the owner at the time of the re-sale or (ii) the
seller remained in possession and delivered them to a second
buyer taking in good faith and without notice of the previous
sale (section 8, Factors Act 1889; section 25(1), Sale of Goods
Act 1893) or (iii) the seller was an unpaid seller and re-sold the
goods after exercising his lien or right of stoppage (section
48(2)). Whether B will obtain the property in the goods will
depend on whether or not one of the above situations covers
the case.

(b) If an unpaid seller lawfully re-sells goods which he has sold,
the re-sale rescinds the original sale and the unpaid seller can
retain any profit which he makes on the re-sale. The re-sale will
be lawful if (i) the goods are perishable, or he gives notice of
his intention to re-sell, and the buyer does not pay or tender
the price within a reasonable time thereafter or (ii) the right of
re-sale is expressly reserved in the contract (sections 48(3) and
(4), and see *Ward* v. *Bignall*). If the re-sale was not lawful
within section 48, the seller is liable to the buyer for the tort of
conversion or for damages for non-delivery under section 51.
In either case, the profit will not be recoverable as such, although it might be recoverable indirectly, because the re-sale
price of the goods might indicate the value of the goods, and
this is usually the measure of damages in an action for conversion.

Test 7

1. Where a buyer wrongfully repudiates a contract of sale, the
seller may (a) accept the repudiation or (b) ignore it. If he
accepts the repudiation, the contract is at an end, although the
seller can still sue the buyer for damages. The damages will
normally be the difference between the contract price and the
market price prevailing at the date fixed for acceptance or
such earlier date as the seller ought to have re-sold in order
reasonably to mitigate his loss. In this case, therefore, it will be

necessary to consider whether S could have sold the goods elsewhere during the week, and what the market price was at that time. He will be able to claim from B the amount by which that price fell short of £500. If, however, the seller does not accept the repudiation, the contract continues in force, and there is no need for the seller to take steps to mitigate his loss, even though the market is falling. If, in the present case, the seller did not accept the repudiation he can either (a) sue for damages for non-acceptance under section 50 or (b) sue for the price under section 49, because it is payable on a day certain. If he wishes to sue for the price, he will have to deliver the goods to B, which he may not wish to do. If he were to claim damages for non-acceptance, the damages would prima facie be £200 (section 50(3)).

Accordingly the answer depends on whether or not S accepted B's cancellation of the contract.

2. Where a seller wrongfully refuses to deliver goods, the buyer can sue him for damages for non-delivery, and he can recover (*inter alia*) damage flowing naturally from the breach (section 51). In the case of lost sub-contracts, the general rule is that the buyer cannot recover his loss of profit from the seller, unless special circumstances were present *to the seller's knowledge* at the time of the contract, e.g., if in the present case, S not only knew of the sub-sale, but also knew that the goods could not be obtained elsewhere (*Patrick* v. *Russo-British Grain Co.*). In the absence of such special knowledge, B will be unable to recover his lost profit from S.

3. An auctioneer gives four implied warranties. He warrants (i) his authority; (ii) that he knows of no defect in his principal's title; (iii) that he will deliver possession to the buyer in return for the price and (iv) that the buyer's possession will not be disturbed by himself or his principal (*Benton, Parker & Co.* v. *Campbell*). The auctioneer does *not* normally warrant his right to sell, and the implied condition under section 12(1) will not apply, because the case will show a 'different intention'. Accordingly, unless one of the above warranties has been broken (and there is nothing to suggest that it has), it seems that Z has no claim against X.

4. (i) An auction sale 'subject to reserve' indicates that the seller had indicated a price below which the goods are not to be sold. The auctioneer will withdraw the goods from the auction if the reserve price is not reached, and even if he inadvertently knocks down the goods at a price below the reserve price, he is not liable if, on discovering his mistake, he refuses to proceed (*McManus* v. *Fortescue*).

(ii) An auction sale expressed to be 'without reserve' may contain a promise by the auctioneer to sell to the highest bidder (*dicta* in *Warlow* v. *Harrison*), but the position is unsettled.

(iii) If an auction sale contains no mention of a reserve, the seller may still fix a reserve price, and the auctioneer can still withdraw the goods if that price is not reached. If, however, he inadvertently knocks down the goods to the highest bidder at a price below the reserve price and then refuses to proceed, it may well be that the buyer will have an action against the auctioneer (for breach of warranty of authority), or against his principal (on the ground that the agent had apparent authority to sell the goods to him).

5. (a) Under an f.o.b. contract the seller must, at his own expense, load the goods onto a ship nominated by the buyer. During the journey the risk will be on the buyer, except that if the seller has failed to supply particulars of the shipment to the buyer, and if this has prevented the buyer from insuring the goods, the goods will be at the seller's risk during the transit (section 32(3)).

(b) Under a c.i.f. contract, the seller must (i) ship the goods (ii) make the contract of carriage (iii) insure them and (iv) tender to the buyer the shipping documents (usually invoice, insurance policy and bill of lading). During the journey the goods will be at the buyer's risk.

(c) Under an 'ex ship' contract the seller must cause delivery to be made at a named destination and during the journey the goods will be at the seller's risk. Presumably, however, the buyer must bear the risk of loss necessarily incidental to the transit (section 33).

Test 8

1. Section 1 of the Act of 1965 defines the various terms in the following way:

(a) Hire-Purchase Agreement – an agreement for the bailment of goods under which the bailee may buy or under which the property will or may pass to the bailee. Where this is the combined effect of two or more agreements, they are treated as a single hire-purchase agreement made on the date of the last one.

(b) Conditional Sale Agreement – an agreement for the sale of goods under which the price is payable by instalments and under which the property is not to pass to the buyer (even though he is to have possession) until such conditions as to payment of instalments or otherwise as may be specified are fulfilled.

(c) Credit-Sale Agreement – an agreement for the sale of goods under which the price is payable by five or more instalments, not being a conditional sale agreement.

2. The essential difference between a hire-purchase agreement and a conditional sale agreement is that in the former case there is merely an option to buy, while in the latter case the buyer is bound to buy. The modern form of hire-purchase agreement was drawn up in order to avoid section 9 of the Factors Act 1889. The leading case on this topic is *Helby* v. *Matthews*, where the House of Lords held that a hirer could not pass a good title under section 9 because he had not 'agreed to buy'. If however the conditional sale agreement comes within the Hire Purchase Act 1965 the rules are almost entirely the same as for hire-purchase and the 'conditional sale buyer' is not a person who has 'agreed to buy'.

3. If a finance company is involved, they usually buy the goods from the dealer and they then make the hire-purchase agreement with the hirer. In such a case, the dealer may be liable to indemnify them against the hirer's default. He may also be liable to them if he wrongly warrants that statements in the proposal form are true (*Liverpool Discount Co.* v. *A.B. Motors (Kilburn) Ltd*). Apart from this, the dealer may be liable to the hirer either for breach of an express warranty or in tort for negligence (*Andrews* v. *Hopkinson*). Finally, the dealer will

sometimes be the agent of the finance company, so that they will be bound by his acts.

4. The Hire-Purchase Act 1965, enables a hirer to compare the hire-purchase price with the cash price, because it provides that the hirer must be informed in writing of the cash price *before* the agreement is made. The owner is deemed to have complied with this requirement if (a) he gives written notice to the hirer of the cash price, or (b) the hirer has selected the goods from a catalogue clearly stating the cash price, or (c) the hirer has selected goods bearing a label clearly stating the cash price.

5. Section 5 provides that the hire-purchase agreement must be signed by the hirer *personally* and by or on behalf of all other parties. If this requirement is not complied with, the owner has no right to enforce the agreement, and this is one of the cases where the court has no power to grant relief. Accordingly, since the agreement was signed by John's wife and not by John, the position is that the shopkeeper cannot take any steps either to sue John for the instalments or to recover the set from John.

6. In this case it is necessary to consider Ron's rights against the finance company and against Fred.

(a) By section 16 of the Act of 1965 any representation with regard to the goods made by a person conducting antecedent negotiations in the course of a business is deemed to have been made by him as agent for the owner. Further, section 29 makes void a clause excluding the owner's liability for the defaults of his agent on the formation of the agreement, and a clause providing that such agent is to be treated as the agent of the hirer. Accordingly, in the present case the company is bound by Fred's statement, and Ron's rights will depend on how Fred's statement is classified. Assuming that it was more than trader's puff, it may be either a misrepresentation or a contractual term. If it was a misrepresentation, he may be able to rescind the contract although this is a discretionary remedy and might be refused if, e.g. the parties could no longer be restored to their previous position. He can also claim damages, unless Fred had reasonable grounds to believe and did believe that the statement was true (section 2(1), Misrepresentation Act 1967). If it was a term of the contract, it will probably be classified as a condition, and Ron can reject the machine or accept it; in either case he can also claim damages. Quite apart from this, the company will probably be in breach of one of the terms as to quality of fitness implied by the Act unless these had been effectively excluded. Here again, Ron has the alternative set out above.

(b) Fred may be liable to pay damages to Ron if the statement made by Fred was a warranty which induced Ron to enter into the hire-purchase agreement (*Andrews* v. *Hopkinson*), and he may also be liable to Ron in tort if he was negligent (consider *Donoghue* v. *Stevenson*) or fraudulent.

7. By section 11, a hirer has a right of cancellation if he signed the agreement at a place other than appropriate trade premises. By section 58, the term 'appropriate trade premises' is defined as premises where the owner carries on a business or where the goods of the contract description or similar goods are exposed for sale in the course of a business carried on there. The right of cancellation can be exercised at any time after signing the agreement until four days have passed from the date on which the hirer received the second statutory copy. Accordingly, if this four-day period has not yet expired, Alice can cancel the agreement.

If she had signed the agreement at her husband's butcher's shop, the answer would not be affected, because that shop would not come within the definition of 'appropriate trade premises'.

8. John should be advised that by section 21 he can make a written request for information before the last instalment has been paid. If he does this, and tenders $12\frac{1}{2}$p for expenses, the owner must within four days supply him with a copy of the agreement and a statement signed by him or his agent giving details of payments, sums due, and future instalments. The copy of the agreement must comply with DTI regulations as to legibility, etc., under section 32. If the owner fails to comply without reasonable cause, he cannot enforce the

agreement or any guarantee or security and if default continues for one month he is liable to a fine not exceeding £25.

9. (a) The Act seeks to protect the hirer against receiving shoddy goods by implying conditions as to quality and fitness with very limited powers of exclusion. Thus, section 17 implies a condition of reasonable fitness for the hirer's purpose where this has been made known, expressly or by implication, to the owner or to the dealer or their servant or agent. The condition can be excluded only if the owner proves that the exemption clause was brought to the hirer's notice before the agreement was made, and its effect made clear to him (see *Lowe* v. *Lombank Ltd*). There is also an implied condition of merchantable quality, except that, where the hirer has examined the goods or a sample, there is no implied condition as regards defects which such examination ought to have revealed. This condition, which is also imposed by section 17, can be excluded in the case of goods which are expressed to be let as second-hand goods, or which are expressed to be let subject to specified defects. Here again, however, the owner must prove that the exclusion clause was brought to the hirer's notice before the agreement was made, and its effect made clear to him.

(b) One of the great evils in the early days of hire-purchase trading was known as 'snatch-back', i.e. the seizure of the goods by the owner after the hirer had paid most of the instalments. The Act of 1965 now contains three provisions to protect the hirer. In the first place, section 29 makes void a clause authorizing the owner to enter premises to re-take the goods. Secondly, section 25 provides that if the hirer defaults in payment the owner cannot terminate the agreement or re-take the goods unless he first serves on the hirer a notice of default requiring payment within a period of not less than seven days and the default continues throughout that time. Finally, section 34 provides that once one-third of the hire-purchase price has been paid or tendered by the hirer or any guarantor, the owner cannot enforce any right to recover possession from the hirer otherwise than by action.

10. Formerly, hire-purchase was much more popular than credit-sale because a hirer was usually unable to pass a good title to a third party (see answer 2 above) whereas a buyer under a credit-sale agreement could pass a good title to a third party under section 9 of the Factors Act 1889 or because he was already the owner of the goods (see now Hire Purchase Act 1965, section 1). In the case of motor vehicles, however, this advantage of hire-purchase from the owner's point of view has been largely nullified by Part III of the Act of 1964 which enables a hirer to pass a good title to a private purchaser taking in good faith and without notice. This being so, credit sales have two major advantages over hire-purchase. In the first place, the only conditions and warranties are those implied by the Sale of Goods Act 1893, and they can be freely excluded. Secondly, the agreement can contain a clause providing that, should the hirer fail to pay an instalment, the whole credit price will become due, and if this occurs the owner should have no difficulty in obtaining judgment for that amount and the court has no power to grant relief to the buyer. If the buyer is still in possession of the goods, the owner may well be able to recover them by seizing them in order to satisfy the judgment.

Having regard to the matters set out above, some finance companies are switching over from hire-purchase to credit sale.

Appendix 2
Selected Statutes

Sale of Goods Act 1893
(Omitting sections 4, 11(2), 24, 40, 59, 60, 63, 64 and Schedule)

Part I. Formation of the contract
Contract of sale

1. (1) A contract of sale of goods is a contract whereby the seller transfers or agrees to transfer the property in goods to the buyer for a money consideration, called the price. There may be a contract of sale between one part owner and another.

(2) A contract of sale may be absolute or conditional.

(3) Where under a contract of sale the property in the goods is transferred from the seller to the buyer the contract is called a sale; but where the transfer of the property in the goods is to take place at a future time or subject to some condition thereafter to be fulfilled the contract is called an agreement to sell.

(4) An agreement to sell becomes a sale when the time elapses or the conditions are fulfilled subject to which the property in the goods is to be transferred.

2. Capacity to buy and sell is regulated by the general law concerning capacity to contract, and to transfer and acquire property:

Provided that where necessaries are sold and delivered to an infant, or minor, or to a person who by reason of mental incapacity or drunkenness is incompetent to contract, he must pay a reasonable price therefor.

Necessaries in this section mean goods suitable to the condition in life of such infant or minor or other person, and to his actual requirements at the time of the sale and delivery.

Formalities of the contract

3. Subject to the provisions of this Act and of any statute in that behalf, a contract of sale may be made in writing (either with or without seal), or by word of mouth, or partly in writing and partly by word of mouth, or may be implied from the conduct of the parties.

Provided that nothing in this section shall affect the law relating to corporations.

Subject matter of contract

5. (1) The goods which form the subject of a contract of sale may be either existing goods, owned or possessed by the seller, or goods to be manufactured or acquired by the seller after the making of the contract of sale, in this Act called 'future goods'.

(2) There may be a contract for the sale of goods, the acquisition of which by the seller depends upon a contingency which may or may not happen.

(3) Where by a contract of sale the seller purports to effect a present sale of future goods, the contract operates as an agreement to sell the goods.

6. Where there is a contract for the sale of specific goods, and the goods without the knowledge of the seller have perished at the time when the contract is made, the contract is void.

7. Where there is an agreement to sell specific goods, and subsequently the goods, without any fault on the part of the seller or buyer, perish before the risk passes to the buyer, the agreement is thereby avoided.

The price

8. (1) The price in a contract of sale may be fixed by the contract, or may be left to be fixed in manner thereby agreed, or may be determined by the course of dealing between the parties.

(2) Where the price is not determined in accordance with the foregoing provisions the buyer must pay a reasonable price.

What is a reasonable price is a question of fact dependent on the circumstances of each particular case.

9. (1) Where there is an agreement to sell goods on the terms that the price is to be fixed by the valuation of a third party, and such third party cannot or does not make such valuation, the agreement is avoided; provided that if the goods or any part thereof have been delivered to and appropriated by the buyer he must pay a reasonable price therefor.

(2) Where such third party is prevented from making the valuation by the fault of the seller or buyer, the party not in fault may maintain an action for damages against the party in fault.

Conditions and warranties

10. (1) Unless a different intention appears from the terms of the contract stipulations as to time of payment are not deemed to be of the essence of a contract of sale. Whether any other stipulation as to time is of the essence of the contract or not depends on the terms of the contract.

(2) In a contract of sale 'month' means prima facie calendar month.

11. (1) In England or Ireland –

(a) Where a contract of sale is subject to any condition to be fulfilled by the seller, the buyer may waive the condition, or may elect to treat the breach of such condition as a breach of warranty, and not as a ground for treating the contract as repudiated:

(b) Whether a stipulation in a contract of sale is a condition, the breach of which may give rise to a right to treat the contract as repudiated, or a warranty, the breach of which may give rise to a claim for damages but not to a right to reject the goods and treat the contract as repudiated, depends in each case on the construction of the contract. A stipulation may be a condition, though called a warranty in the contract:

(c) Where a contract of sale is not severable, and the buyer has accepted the goods, or part thereof, *or where the contract is for specific goods, the property in which has passed to the buyer*, the breach of any condition to be fulfilled by the seller can only be treated as a breach of warranty, and not as a ground for rejecting the goods and treating the contract as repudiated, unless there be a term of the contract, express or implied, to that effect. [Words in italics repealed by the Misrepresentation Act 1967.]

3. Nothing in this section shall affect the case of any condition or warranty, fulfilment of which is excused by law by reason of impossibility or otherwise.

12. In a contract of sale, unless the circumstances of the contract are such as to show a different intention, there is

1. An implied condition on the part of the seller that in the case of a sale he has a right to sell the goods, and that in the case of an agreement to sell he will have a right to sell the goods at the time when the property is to pass:

(2) An implied warranty that the buyer shall have and enjoy quiet possession of the goods:

(3) An implied warranty that the goods shall be free from any charge or encumbrance in favour of any third party, not declared or known to the buyer before or at the time when the contract is made.

13. Where there is a contract for the sale of goods by description, there is an implied condition that the goods shall correspond with the description; and if the sale be by sample, as well as by description, it is not sufficient that the bulk of the goods corresponds with the sample if the goods do not also correspond with the description.

14. Subject to the provisions of this Act and of any statute in that behalf, there is no implied warranty or condition as to the quality or fitness for any particular purpose of goods supplied under a contract of sale, except as follows:

(1) Where the buyer, expressly or by implication, makes known to the seller the particular purpose for which the goods are required, so as to show that the buyer relies on the seller's skill or judgment, and the goods are of a description which it is in

the course of the seller's business to supply (whether he be the manufacturer or not), there is an implied condition that the goods shall be reasonably fit for such purpose, provided that in the case of a contract for the sale of a specified article under its patent or other trade name, there is no implied condition as to its fitness for any particular purpose:

(2) Where goods are bought by description from a seller who deals in goods of that description (whether he be the manufacturer or not), there is an implied condition that the goods shall be of merchantable quality; provided that if the buyer has examined the goods, there shall be no implied condition as regards defects which such examination ought to have revealed:

(3) An implied warranty or condition as to quality or fitness for a particular purpose may be annexed by the usage of trade:

(4) An express warranty or condition does not negative a warranty or condition implied by this Act unless inconsistent therewith.

Sale by sample

15. (1) A contract of sale is a contract for sale by sample where there is a term in the contract, express or implied, to that effect.

(2) In the case of a contract for sale by sample –

(a) There is an implied condition that the bulk shall correspond with the sample in quality:

(b) There is an implied condition that the buyer shall have a reasonable opportunity of comparing the bulk with the sample:

(c) There is an implied condition that the goods shall be free from any defect, rendering them unmerchantable, which would not be apparent on reasonable examination of the sample.

Part II. Effects of the contract
Transfer of property as between seller and buyer

16. Where there is a contract for the sale of unascertained goods no property in the goods is transferred to the buyer unless and until the goods are ascertained.

17. (1) Where there is a contract for the sale of specific or ascertained goods the property in them is transferred to the buyer at such time as the parties to the contract intend it to be transferred.

(2) For the purpose of ascertaining the intention of the parties regard shall be had to the terms of the contract, the conduct of the parties, and the circumstances of the case.

18. Unless a different intention appears, the following are rules for ascertaining the intention of the parties as to the time at which the property in the goods is to pass to the buyer.

Rule 1. Where there is an unconditional contract for the sale of specific goods, in a deliverable state, the property in the goods passes to the buyer when the contract is made, and it is immaterial whether the time of payment or the time of delivery, or both, be postponed.

Rule 2. Where there is a contract for the sale of specific goods and the seller is bound to do something to the goods, for the purpose of putting them into a deliverable state, the property does not pass until such thing be done, and the buyer has notice thereof.

Rule 3. Where there is a contract for the sale of specific goods in a deliverable state, but the seller is bound to weigh, measure, test, or do some other act or thing with reference to the goods for the purpose of ascertaining the price, the property does not pass until such act or thing be done, and the buyer has notice thereof.

Rule 4. When goods are delivered to the buyer on approval or 'on sale or return' or other similar terms the property therein passes to the buyer:

(a) When he signifies his approval or acceptance to the seller or does any other act adopting the transaction:

(b) If he does not signify his approval or acceptance to the seller but retains the goods without giving notice of rejection, then, if a time has been fixed for the return of the goods, on the expiration of such time, and, if no time has been fixed, on the expiration of a reasonable time. What is a reasonable time is a question of fact.

Rule 5. (1) Where there is a contract for the sale of unascertained or future goods by description, and goods of that description and in a deliverable state are unconditionally appropriated to the contract, either by the seller with the assent of the buyer, or by the buyer with the assent of the seller, the property in the goods thereupon passes to the buyer. Such assent may be express or implied, and may be given either before or after the appropriation is made.

(2) Where, in pursuance of the contract, the seller delivers the goods to the buyer or to a carrier or other bailee or custodier (whether named by the buyer or not) for the purpose of transmission to the buyer, and does not reserve the right of disposal, he is deemed to have unconditionally appropriated the goods to the contract.

19. (1) Where there is a contract for the sale of specific goods or where goods are subsequently appropriated to the contract, the seller may, by the terms of the contract or appropriation, reserve the right of disposal of the goods until certain conditions are fulfilled. In such case, notwithstanding the delivery of the goods to the buyer, or to a carrier or other bailee or custodier for the purpose of transmission to the buyer, the property in the goods does not pass to the buyer until the conditions imposed by the seller are fulfilled.

(2) Where goods are shipped, and by the bill of lading the goods are deliverable to the order of the seller or his agent, the seller is prima facie deemed to reserve the right of disposal.

(3) Where the seller of goods draws on the buyer for the price, and transmits the bill of exchange and bill of lading to the buyer together to secure acceptance or payment of the bill of exchange, the buyer is bound to return the bill of lading if he does not honour the bill of exchange, and if he wrongfully retains the bill of lading the property in the goods does not pass to him.

20. Unless otherwise agreed, the goods remain at the seller's risk until the property therein is transferred to the buyer, but when the property therein is transferred to the buyer, the goods are at the buyer's risk, whether delivery has been made or not.

Provided that where delivery has been delayed through the fault of either buyer or seller the goods are at the risk of the party in fault as regards any loss which might not have occurred but for such fault.

Provided also that nothing in this section shall affect the duties or liabilities of either seller or buyer as a bailee or custodier of the goods of the other party.

Transfer of title

21. (1) Subject to the provisions of this Act, where goods are sold by a person who is not the owner thereof, and who does not sell them under the authority or with the consent of the owner, the buyer acquires no better title to the goods than the seller had, unless the owner of the goods is by his conduct precluded from denying the seller's authority to sell.

(2) Provided also that nothing in this Act shall affect

(a) The provisions of the Factors Acts, or any enactment enabling the apparent owner of goods to dispose of them as if he were the true owner thereof;

(b) The validity of any contract of sale under any special common law or statutory power of sale or under the order of a court of competent jurisdiction.

22. (1) Where goods are sold in market overt, according to the usage of the market, the buyer acquires a good title to the goods, provided he buys them in good faith and without notice of any defect or want of title on the part of the seller.

[Subsection (2) repealed by the Criminal Law Act 1967.]

23. When the seller of goods has a voidable title thereto, but his title has not been avoided at the time of the sale, the buyer acquires a good title to the goods, provided he buys them in good faith and without notice of the seller's defect of title.

25. (1) Where a person having sold goods continues or is in possession of the goods, or of the documents of title to the goods, the delivery or transfer by that person, or by a mercantile agent acting for him, of the goods or documents of title under any sale, pledge, or other disposition thereof, to any person receiving the same in good faith and without notice of the previous sale, shall have the same effect as if the person making the delivery or transfer were expressly authorized by the owner of the goods to make the same.

(2) Where a person having bought or agreed to buy goods obtains, with the consent of the seller, possession of the goods or the documents of title to the goods, the delivery or transfer by that person, or by a mercantile agent acting for him, of the goods or documents of title, under any sale, pledge, or other disposition thereof, to any person receiving the same in good faith and without notice of any lien or other right of the original seller in respect of the goods, shall have the same effect as if the person making the delivery or transfer were a mercantile agent in possession of the goods or documents of title with the consent of the owner.

(3) In this section the term 'mercantile agent' has the same meaning as in the Factors Acts.

26. (1) A writ of fieri facias or other writ of execution against goods shall bind the property in the goods of the execution debtor as from the time when the writ is delivered to the sheriff to be executed; and, for the better manifestation of such time, it shall be the duty of the sheriff, without fee, upon the receipt of any such writ to endorse upon the back thereof the hour, day, month, and year when he received the same.

Provided that no such writ shall prejudice the title to such goods acquired by any person in good faith and for valuable consideration, unless such person had at the time when he acquired his title notice that such writ or any other writ by virtue of which the goods of the execution debtor might be seized or attached had been delivered to and remained unexecuted in the hands of the sheriff.

(2) In this section the term 'sheriff' includes any officer charged with the enforcement of a writ of execution.

(3) The provisions of this section do not apply to Scotland.

Part III. Performance of the contract

27. It is the duty of the seller to deliver the goods, and of the buyer to accept and pay for them, in accordance with the terms of the contract of sale.

28. Unless otherwise agreed, delivery of the goods and payment of the price are concurrent conditions, that is to say, the seller must be ready and willing to give possession of the goods to the buyer in exchange for the price and the buyer must be ready and willing to pay the price in exchange for possession of the goods.

29. (1) Whether it is for the buyer to take possession of the goods or for the seller to send them to the buyer is a question depending in each case on the contract, express or implied, between the parties. Apart from any such contract, express or implied, the place of delivery is the seller's place of business, if he have one, and if not, his residence: Provided that, if the contract be for the sale of specific goods, which to the knowledge of the parties when the contract is made are in some other place, then that place is the place of delivery.

(2) Where under the contract of sale the seller is bound to send the goods to the buyer, but no time for sending them is fixed, the seller is bound to send them within a reasonable time.

(3) Where the goods at the time of sale are in the possession of a third person, there is no delivery by seller to buyer unless and until such third person acknowledges to the buyer that he holds the goods on his behalf; provided that nothing in this section shall affect the operation of the issue or transfer of any document of title to goods.

(4) Demand or tender of delivery may be treated as ineffectual unless made at a reasonable hour. What is a reasonable hour is a question of fact.

(5) Unless otherwise agreed, the expenses of and incidental

to putting the goods into a deliverable state must be borne by the seller.

30. (1) Where the seller delivers to the buyer a quantity of goods less than he contracted to sell, the buyer may reject them, but if the buyer accepts the goods so delivered he must pay for them at the contract rate.

(2) Where the seller delivers to the buyer a quantity of goods larger than he contracted to sell, the buyer may accept the goods included in the contract and reject the rest, or he may reject the whole. If the buyer accepts the whole of the goods so delivered he must pay for them at the contract rate.

(3) Where the seller delivers to the buyer the goods he contracted to sell mixed with goods of a different description not included in the contract, the buyer may accept the goods which are in accordance with the contract and reject the rest, or he may reject the whole.

(4) The provisions of this section are subject to any usage of trade, special agreement, or course of dealing between the parties.

31. (1) Unless otherwise agreed, the buyer of goods is not bound to accept delivery thereof by instalments.

(2) Where there is a contract for the sale of goods to be delivered by stated instalments, which are to be separately paid for, and the seller makes defective deliveries in respect of one or more instalments, or the buyer neglects or refuses to take delivery of or pay for one or more instalments, it is a question in each case depending on the terms of the contract and the circumstances of the case, whether the breach of contract is a repudiation of the whole contract or whether it is a severable breach giving rise to a claim for compensation but not to a right to treat the whole contract as repudiated.

32. (1) Where, in pursuance of a contract of sale, the seller is authorized or required to send the goods to the buyer, delivery of the goods to a carrier, whether named by the buyer or not, for the purpose of transmission to the buyer is prima facie deemed to be a delivery of the goods to the buyer.

(2) Unless otherwise authorized by the buyer, the seller must make such contract with the carrier on behalf of the buyer as may be reasonable having regard to the nature of the goods and the other circumstances of the case. If the seller omits so to do, and the goods are lost or damaged in course of transit, the buyer may decline to treat the delivery to the carrier as a delivery to himself, or may hold the seller responsible in damages.

(3) Unless otherwise agreed, where goods are sent by the seller to the buyer by a route involving sea transit, under circumstances in which it is usual to insure, the seller must give such notice to the buyer as may enable him to insure them during their sea transit, and, if the seller fails to do so, the goods shall be deemed to be at his risk during such sea transit.

33. Where the seller of goods agrees to deliver them at his own risk at a place other than that where they are when sold, the buyer must, nevertheless, unless otherwise agreed, take any risk of deterioration in the goods necessarily incident to the course of transit.

34. (1) Where goods are delivered to the buyer, which he has not previously examined, he is not deemed to have accepted them unless and until he has had a reasonable opportunity of examining them for the purpose of ascertaining whether they are in conformity with the contract.

(2) Unless otherwise agreed, when the seller tenders delivery of goods to the buyer, he is bound, on request, to afford the buyer a reasonable opportunity of examining the goods for the purpose of ascertaining whether they are in conformity with the contract.

35. The buyer is deemed to have accepted the goods when he intimates to the seller that he has accepted them, or (except where section 34 of this Act otherwise provides) when the goods have been delivered to him, and he does any act in relation to them which is inconsistent with the ownership of the seller, or when after the lapse of a reasonable time, he retains the goods without intimating to the seller that he has rejected them. [Words in brackets added by the Misrepresentation Act 1967.]

36. Unless otherwise agreed, where goods are delivered to the buyer, and he refuses to accept them having the right so to do, he is not bound to return them to the seller, but it is sufficient if he intimates to the seller that he refuses to accept them.

37. When the seller is ready and willing to deliver the goods, and requests the buyer to take delivery, and the buyer does not within a reasonable time after such request take delivery of the goods, he is liable to the seller for any loss occasioned by his neglect or refusal to take delivery, and also for a reasonable charge for the care and custody of the goods: Provided that nothing in this section shall affect the rights of the seller where the neglect or refusal of the buyer to take delivery amounts to a repudiation of the contract.

Part IV. Rights of unpaid seller against the goods

38. (1) The seller of goods is deemed to be an 'unpaid seller' within the meaning of this Act

   (a) When the whole of the price has not been paid or tendered;

   (b) When a bill of exchange or other negotiable instrument has been received as conditional payment, and the condition on which it was received has not been fulfilled by reason of the dishonour of the instrument or otherwise.

(2) In this Part of this Act the term 'seller' includes any person who is in the position of a seller, as, for instance, an agent of the seller to whom the bill of lading has been indorsed, or a consignor or agent who has himself paid, or is directly responsible for, the price.

39. (1) Subject to the provisions of this Act, and of any statute in that behalf, notwithstanding that the property in the goods may have passed to the buyer, the unpaid seller of goods, as such, has by implication of law

   (a) A lien on the goods or right to retain them for the price while he is in possession of them;

   (b) In case of the insolvency of the buyer, a right of stopping the goods *in transitu* after he has parted with the possession of them;

   (c) A right of re-sale as limited by this Act.

(2) Where the property in goods has not passed to the buyer, the unpaid seller has, in addition to his other remedies, a right of withholding delivery similar to and co-extensive with his rights of lien and stoppage *in transitu* where the property has passed to the buyer.

Unpaid seller's lien

41. (1) Subject to the provisions of this Act, the unpaid seller of goods who is in possession of them is entitled to retain possession of them until payment or tender of the price in the following cases, namely:

   (a) Where the goods have been sold without any stipulation as to credit;

   (b) Where the goods have been sold on credit, but the term of credit has expired;

   (c) Where the buyer becomes insolvent.

(2) The seller may exercise his right of lien notwithstanding that he is in possession of the goods as agent or bailee or custodier for the buyer.

42. Where an unpaid seller has made part delivery of the goods, he may exercise his right of lien or retention on the remainder, unless such part delivery has been made under such circumstances as to show an agreement to waive the lien or right of retention.

43. (1) The unpaid seller of goods loses his lien or right of retention thereon

   (a) When he delivers the goods to a carrier or other bailee or custodier for the purpose of transmission to the buyer without reserving the right of disposal of the goods;

   (b) When the buyer or his agent lawfully obtains possession of the goods;

   (c) By waiver thereof.

(2) The unpaid seller of goods, having a lien or right of retention thereon, does not lose his lien or right of retention by reason only that he has obtained judgment or decree for the price of the goods.

Stoppage in transitu

44. Subject to the provisions of this Act, when the buyer of goods becomes insolvent, the unpaid seller who has parted with the possession of the goods has the right of stopping them *in transitu*, that is to say, he may resume possession of the goods as long as they are in course of transit, and may retain them until payment or tender of the price.

45. (1) Goods are deemed to be in course of transit from the time when they are delivered to a carrier by land or water, or other bailee or custodier for the purpose of transmission to the buyer, until the buyer, or his agent in that behalf, takes delivery of them from such carrier or other bailee or custodier.

(2) If the buyer or his agent in that behalf obtains delivery of the goods before their arrival at the appointed destination, the transit is at an end.

(3) If, after the arrival of the goods at the appointed destination, the carrier or other bailee or custodier acknowledges to the buyer, or his agent, that he holds the goods on his behalf and continues in possession of them as bailee or custodier for the buyer, or his agent, the transit is at an end, and it is immaterial that a further destination for the goods may have been indicated by the buyer.

(4) If the goods are rejected by the buyer, and the carrier or other bailee or custodier continues in possession of them, the transit is not deemed to be at an end, even if the seller has refused to receive them back.

(5) When goods are delivered to a ship chartered by the buyer it is a question depending on the circumstances of the particular case, whether they are in the possession of the master as a carrier, or as agent to the buyer.

(6) Where the carrier or other bailee or custodier wrongfully refuses to deliver the goods to the buyer, or his agent in that behalf, the transit is deemed to be at an end.

(7) Where part delivery of the goods has been made to the buyer, or his agent in that behalf, the remainder of the goods may be stopped *in transitu*, unless such part delivery has been made under such circumstances as to show an agreement to give up possession of the whole of the goods.

46. (1) The unpaid seller may exercise his right of stoppage *in transitu* either by taking actual possession of the goods, or by giving notice of his claim to the carrier or other bailee or custodier in whose possession the goods are. Such notice may be.given either to the person in actual possession of the goods or to his principal. In the latter case the notice, to be effectual, must be given at such time and under such circumstances that the principal, by the exercise of reasonable diligence, may communicate it to his servant or agent in time to prevent a delivery to the buyer.

(2) When notice of stoppage *in transitu* is given by the seller to the carrier, or other bailee or custodier in possession of the goods, he must re-deliver the goods to, or according to the directions of, the seller. The expenses of such re-delivery must be borne by the seller.

Re-sale by buyer or seller

47. Subject to the provisions of this Act, the unpaid seller's right of lien or retention or stoppage *in transitu* is not affected by any sale, or other disposition of the goods which the buyer may have made, unless the seller has assented thereto.

Provided that where a document of title to goods has been lawfully transferred to any person as buyer or owner of the goods, and that person transfers the document to a person who takes the document in good faith and for valuable consideration, then, if such last-mentioned transfer was by way of sale the unpaid seller's right of lien or retention or stoppage *in transitu* is defeated, and if such last-mentioned transfer was made by way of pledge or other disposition for value, the unpaid seller's right of lien or retention or stoppage *in transitu* can only be exercised subject to the rights of the transferee.

48. (1) Subject to the provisions of this section, a contract of sale is not rescinded by the mere exercise by an unpaid seller of his right of lien or retention or stoppage *in transitu*.

(2) Where an unpaid seller who has exercised his right of lien or retention or stoppage *in transitu* re-sells the goods, the buyer acquires a good title thereto as against the original buyer.

(3) Where the goods are of a perishable nature, or where the unpaid seller gives notice to the buyer of his intention to re-sell, and the buyer does not within a reasonable time pay or tender the price, the unpaid seller may re-sell the goods and recover from the original buyer damages for any loss occasioned by his breach of contract.

(4) Where the seller expressly reserves the right of re-sale in case the buyer should make default, and on the buyer making default, re-sells the goods, the original contract of sale is thereby rescinded, but without prejudice to any claim the seller may have for damages.

Part V. Actions for breach of the contract
Remedies of the seller

49. (1) Where, under a contract of sale, the property in the goods has passed to the buyer, and the buyer wrongfully neglects or refuses to pay for the goods according to the terms of the contract, the seller may maintain an action against him for the price of the goods.

(2) Where, under a contract of sale, the price is payable on a day certain irrespective of delivery, and the buyer wrongfully neglects or refuses to pay such price, the seller may maintain an action for the price, although the property in the goods has not passed, and the goods have not been appropriated to the contract.

50. (1) Where the buyer wrongfully neglects or refuses to accept and pay for the goods, the seller may maintain an action against him for damages for non-acceptance.

(2) The measure of damages is the estimated loss directly and naturally resulting, in the ordinary course of events, from the buyer's breach of contract.

(3) Where there is an available market for the goods in question the measure of damages is prima facie to be ascertained by the difference between the contract price and the market or current price at the time or times when the goods ought to have been accepted or, if no time was fixed for acceptance, then at the time of the refusal to accept.

Remedies of the buyer

51. (1) Where the seller wrongfully neglects or refuses to deliver the goods to the buyer, the buyer may maintain an action against the seller for damages for non-delivery.

(2) The measure of damages is the estimated loss directly and naturally resulting, in the ordinary course of events, from the seller's breach of contract.

(3) Where there is an available market for the goods in question the measure of damages is prima facie to be ascertained by the difference between the contract price and the market or current price of the goods at the time or times when they ought to have been delivered, or, if no time was fixed, then at the time of the refusal to deliver.

52. In any action for breach of contract to deliver specific or ascertained goods the court may, if it thinks fit, on the application of the plaintiff, by its judgment or decree direct that the contract shall be performed specifically, without giving the defendant the option of retaining the goods on payment of damages. The judgment or decree may be unconditional, or upon such terms and conditions as to damages, payment of the price, and otherwise, as to the court may seem just, and the application by the plaintiff may be made at any time before judgment or decree.

The provisions of this section shall be deemed to be supplementary to, and not in derogation of, the right of specific implement in Scotland.

53. (1) Where there is a breach of warranty by the seller, or where the buyer elects, or is compelled, to treat any breach of a condition on the part of the seller as a breach of warranty, the buyer is not by reason only of such breach of warranty entitled to reject the goods; but he may

    (a) set up against the seller the breach of warranty in diminution or extinction of the price; or

    (b) maintain an action against the seller for damages for the breach of warranty.

(2) The measure of damages for breach of warranty is the estimated loss directly and naturally resulting, in the ordinary course of events, from the breach of warranty.

(3) In the case of breach of warranty of quality such loss is prima facie the difference between the value of the goods at the time of delivery to the buyer and the value they would have had if they had answered to the warranty.

(4) The fact that the buyer has set up the breach of warranty in diminution or extinction of the price does not prevent him from maintaining an action for the same breach of warranty if he has suffered further damage.

(5) Nothing in this section shall prejudice or affect the buyer's right of rejection in Scotland as declared by this Act.

54. Nothing in this Act shall affect the right of the buyer or the seller to recover interest or special damages in any case where by law interest or special damages may be recoverable, or to recover money paid where the consideration for the payment of it has failed.

Part VI. Supplementary

55. Where any right, duty, or liability would arise under a contract of sale by implication of law, it may be negatived or varied by express agreement or by the course of dealing between the parties, or by usage, if the usage be such as to bind both parties to the contract.

56. Where, by this Act, any reference is made to a reasonable time the question what is a reasonable time is a question of fact.

57. Where any right, duty, or liability is declared by this Act, it may, unless otherwise by this Act provided, be enforced by action.

58. In the case of a sale by auction

(1) Where goods are put up for sale by auction in lots, each lot is prime facie deemed to be the subject of a separate contract of sale:

(2) A sale by auction is complete when the auctioneer announces its completion by the fall of the hammer, or in other customary manner. Until such announcement is made any bidder may retract his bid:

(3) Where a sale by auction is not notified to be subject to a right to bid on behalf of the seller, it shall not be lawful for the seller to bid himself or to employ any person to bid at such sale, or for the auctioneer knowingly to take any bid from the seller or any such person: Any sale contravening this rule may be treated as fraudulent by the buyer:

(4) A sale by auction may be notified to be subject to a reserve or upset price, and a right to bid may also be reserved expressly by or on behalf of the seller.

Where a right to bid is expressly reserved, but not otherwise, the seller, or any one person on his behalf, may bid at the auction.

61. (1) The rules in bankruptcy relating to contracts of sale shall continue to apply thereto, notwithstanding anything in this Act contained.

(2) The rules in the common law, including the law merchant, save in so far as they are inconsistent with the express provisions of this Act, and in particular the rules relating to the law of principal and agent and the effect of fraud, misrepresentation, duress or coercion, mistake, or other invalidating cause, shall continue to apply to contracts for the sale of goods.

(3) Nothing in this Act or in any repeal effected thereby shall affect the enactments relating to bills of sale, or any enactment

relating to the sale of goods which is not expressly repealed by this Act.

(4) The provisions of this Act relating to contracts of sale do not apply to any transaction in the form of a contract of sale which is intended to operate by way of mortgage, pledge, charge, or other security.

(5) Nothing in this Act shall prejudice or affect the landlord's right of hypothec or sequestration for rent in Scotland.

62. (1) In this Act, unless the context or subject matter otherwise requires,

'Action' includes counterclaim and set off, and in Scotland condescendence and claim and compensation:

'Bailee' in Scotland includes custodier:

'Buyer' means a person who buys or agrees to buy goods:

'Contract of sale' includes an agreement to sell as well as a sale:

'Defendant' includes in Scotland defender, respondent, and claimant in a multiplepoinding:

'Delivery' means voluntary transfer of possession from one person to another:

'Document of title to goods' has the same meaning as it has in the Factors Acts:

'Factors Acts' mean the Factors Act 1889, the Factors (Scotland) Act 1890, and any enactment amending or substituted for the same:

'Fault' means wrongful act or default:

'Future goods' means goods to be manufactured or acquired by the seller after the making of the contract of sale:

'Goods' include all chattels personal other than things in action and money, and in Scotland all corporeal moveables except money. The term includes emblements, industrial growing crops, and things attached to or forming part of the land which are agreed to be severed before sale or under the contract of sale:

'Lien' in Scotland includes right of retention:

'Plaintiff' includes pursuer, complainer, claimant in a multiplepoinding and defendant or defender counterclaiming:

'Property' means the general property in goods, and not merely a special property:

'Quality of goods' includes their state or condition:

'Sale' includes a bargain and sale as well as a sale and delivery:

'Seller' means a person who sells or agrees to sell goods:

'Specific goods' means goods identified and agreed upon at the time a contract of sale is made:

'Warranty' as regards England and Ireland means an agreement with reference to goods which are the subject of a contract of sale, but collateral to the main purpose of such contract the breach of which gives rise to a claim for damages, but not to a right to reject the goods and treat the contract as repudiated.

As regards Scotland a breach of warranty shall be deemed to be a failure to perform a material part of the contract.

(2) A thing is deemed to be done 'in good faith' within the meaning of this Act when it is in fact done honestly, whether it be done negligently or not.

(3) A person is deemed to be insolvent within the meaning of this Act who either has ceased to pay his debts in the ordinary course of business, or cannot pay his debts as they become due, whether he has committed an act of bankruptcy or not, and whether he has become a notour bankrupt or not.

(4) Goods are in a 'deliverable state' within the meaning of this Act when they are in such a state that the buyer would under the contract be bound to take delivery of them.

Misrepresentation Act 1967

1. Where a person has entered into a contract after a misrepresentation has been made to him and

(a) the misrepresentation has become a term of the contract; or

(b) the contract has been performed;

or both, then, if otherwise he would be entitled to rescind the contract without alleging fraud, he shall be so entitled, subject to the provisions of this Act, notwithstanding the matters mentioned in paragraphs (a) and (b) above.

2. (1) Where a person has entered into a contract after a misrepresentation has been made to him by another party thereto and as a result thereof he has suffered loss, then, if the person making the representation would be liable to damages in respect thereof had the representation been made fraudulently, that person shall be so liable notwithstanding that the misrepresentation was not made fraudulently, unless he proves that he had reasonable ground to believe and did believe up to the time that the contract was made that the facts represented were true.

(2) Where a person has entered into a contract after a misrepresentation has been made to him otherwise than fraudulently, and he would be entitled, by reason of the misrepresentation, to rescind the contract, then, if it is claimed, in any proceedings arising out of the contract, that the contract ought to be or has been rescinded, the court or arbitrator may declare the contract subsisting and award damages in lieu of rescission, if of opinion that it would be equitable to do so, having regard to the nature of the misrepresentation and the loss that would be caused by it if the contract were

upheld, as well as to the loss that rescission would cause to the other party.

(3) Damages may be awarded against a person under subsection (2) of this section whether or not he is liable to damages under subsection (1) thereof but where he is so liable any award under the said subsection (2) shall be taken into account in assessing his liability under the said subsection (1).

3. If any agreement (whether made before or after the commencement of the Act) contains a provision which would exclude or restrict –

(a) any liability to which a party to a contract may be subject by reason of any misrepresentation made by him before the contract was made; or

(b) any remedy available to another party to a contract by reason of such a misrepresentation;

that provision shall be of no effect except to the extent (if any) that in any proceedings arising out of the contract, the court or arbitrator may allow reliance on it as being fair and reasonable in the circumstances of the case.

4. (1) In paragraph (c) of section 11(1) of the Sale of Goods Act 1893 (condition to be treated as warranty where the buyer has accepted the goods or where the property in specific goods has passed), the words 'or where the contract is for specific goods the property in which has passed to the buyer' shall be omitted.

(2) In section 35 of that Act (acceptance) before the words 'when the goods have been delivered to him and he does any act in relation to them which is inconsistent with the ownership of the seller' there shall be inserted the words '(except where section 34 of this Act otherwise provides)'.

Hire-Purchase Act 1965

Sections 1, 2, 4–34, 47, 54, 55, 57, 58 and Schedules 1 and 2

Part I. Agreements for which Parts II, III and IV of Act apply

1. (1) In this Act (subject to the following provisions of this Part of this Act) –

'hire-purchase agreement' means an agreement for the bailment of goods under which the bailee may buy the goods, or under which the property in the goods will or may pass to the bailee;

'credit-sale agreement' means an agreement for the sale of goods under which the purchase price is payable by five or more instalments, not being a conditional sale agreement;

'conditional sale agreement' means an agreement for the sale of goods under which the purchase price of part of it is payable by instalments, and the property in the goods is to remain in the seller (notwithstanding that the buyer is to be in possession of the goods) until such conditions as to the payment of instalments or otherwise as may be specified in the agreement are fulfilled.

(2) Where by virtue of two or more agreements, none of which by itself constitutes a hire-purchase agreement as defined by the preceding subsection, there is a bailment of goods and either the bailee may buy the goods, or the property therein will or may pass to the bailee, the agreements shall be treated for the purposes of this Act as a single agreement made at the time when the last of the agreements was made.

2. (1) Subject to the following provisions of this Part of this Act, references in Parts II, III and IV of this Act to hire-purchase agreements and to conditional sale agreements, and references in Part II of this Act to credit-sale agreements, shall be construed in accordance with the following provisions of this section.

(2) References in Parts II, III and IV of this Act to a hire-purchase agreement or a conditional sale agreement shall be construed respectively as references to a hire-purchase agreement (as defined by the preceding section) or a conditional sale agreement (as so defined) under which the hire-purchase price or total purchase price, as the case may be, does not exceed £2000.

(3) In Part II of this Act, except in any provision to which the next following subsection applies, any reference to a credit-sale agreement shall be construed as a reference to a credit-sale agreement (as defined by the preceding section) under which the total purchase price –

  (a) exceeds £30, but
  (b) does not exceed £2000.

(4) In any provision of Part II of this Act to which this subsection is expressed to apply, any reference to a credit-sale agreement shall be construed as a reference to a credit-sale agreement (as defined by the preceding section) under which the total purchase price does not exceed £2000.

4. Notwithstanding anything in section 2 of this Act, references in Parts II, III and IV of this Act to hire-purchase agreements and to conditional sale agreements, and references in Part II of this Act to credit-sale agreements, do not include any agreement which is made by or on behalf of a body corporate (whether incorporated in the United Kingdom or elsewhere) as the hirer or buyer of the goods to which the agreement relates.

Part II. General Provisions
Requirements in connection with making agreements

5. (1) Where goods are let under a hire-purchase agreement, or are sold, or agreed to be sold, under a credit-sale agreement or a conditional sale agreement, then (subject to the exercise of any power of the court under section 10 of this

Act) the owner or seller shall not be entitled to enforce the agreement unless

(a) the agreement is signed by the hirer or buyer, and by or on behalf of all other parties to the agreement, and

(b) the requirements of sections 6 and 7 of this Act, and the requirements of section 8 or (as the case may be) section 9 of this Act, are complied with.

(2) Where by virtue of the preceding subsection the owner or seller is not entitled to enforce an agreement –

(a) he shall not be entitled to enforce any contract of guarantee relating to that agreement;

(b) no security given by the hirer or buyer in respect of money payable under the agreement, or given by a guarantor in respect of money payable under a contract of guarantee relating to the agreement, shall be enforceable against the hirer or buyer, or against the guarantor, as the case may be, by the holder of such a security; and

(c) if it is a hire-purchase agreement or a conditional sale agreement, the owner or seller shall not be entitled to enforce any right to recover the goods from the hirer or buyer.

6. (1) The requirements of this section, in relation to an agreement, are that, before the agreement is made,

(a) the cash price of the goods has been stated in writing to the hirer or buyer by the owner or seller, otherwise than in the agreement, or

(b) if the hirer or buyer has inspected the goods or like goods, then, at the time of his inspection, tickets or labels were attached to or displayed with the goods clearly stating the cash price, either of the goods as a whole or of all the different articles or sets of articles comprised therein, or

(c) the hirer or buyer has selected the goods by reference to a catalogue, price list or advertisement which clearly stated the cash price, either of the goods as a whole or of all the different articles or sets of articles comprised therein.

(2) In this Part of this Act 'cash price', in relation to any goods means the price at which the goods may be purchased by the hirer or buyer for cash.

7. (1) The requirements of this section, in relation to an agreement, are that

(a) the agreement contains a statement of the hire-purchase price or total purchase price, as the case may be, and of the cash price of the goods to which the agreement relates, and of the amount of each instalment by which the hire-purchase price or total purchase price is to be paid, and of the date, or the mode of determining the date, on which each instalment is payable;

(b) the agreement contains a list of the goods to which the agreement relates sufficient to identify them;

(c) the agreement, at the time when it is signed by the hirer or buyer, complies with the requirements of any regulations made under subsection (2) of this section;

(d) the agreement complies with the requirements of any regulations made under section 32 of this Act; and

(e) if it is a hire-purchase agreement or a conditional sale agreement, it contains a notice, which is at least as prominent as the rest of the contents of the agreement, in the terms set out in Schedule 1 or (as the case may be) Schedule 2 to this Act.

(2) The Board of Trade may by regulations provide that, in any document which, on being signed as mentioned in section 5(1)(a) of this Act, constitutes a hire-purchase agreement, a credit-sale agreement or a conditional sale agreement, the signature of the hirer or buyer shall be inserted in a space marked in such manner, and accompanied in the document by such words, as may be specified in the regulations; and the regulations may include provision as to the location of those words in relation to the space in which the signature is inserted, and may prescribe such other requirements (whether as to type, size, colour or disposition of lettering or otherwise) as the Board may consider appropriate for securing that the words come to the attention of the hirer or buyer at the time when he is about to sign the document.

8. (1) The requirements of this section, in relation to an agreement which is signed by the hirer or buyer at appropriate trade premises, are that copies are delivered or sent to the hirer or buyer in accordance with the following provisions of this section.

(2) If either

(a) the agreement is signed by or on behalf of all other parties immediately after it is signed by the hirer or buyer, and a copy of the agreement is there and then delivered to him, or

(b) the agreement having been signed by or on behalf of all other parties before it is signed by the hirer or buyer, a copy of the agreement is delivered to him immediately after he signs the agreement,

and (in either case) the copy so delivered complies with the requirements of any regulations made under section 32 of this Act, the delivery of that copy shall be taken to have fulfilled the requirements of this section in relation to that agreement.

(3) If, in a case not falling within paragraph (a) or paragraph (b) of the last preceding subsection,

(a) either

(i) the relevant document was presented, and not sent, to the hirer or buyer for his signature, and immediately after he signed it there was delivered to him a copy of that document in the form in which it then was, or

(ii) the relevant document was sent to the hirer for his signature, and at the time when it was sent there was also sent to him a copy of that document in the form in which it then was, and

(b) in either case, a copy of the agreement is delivered or sent to the hirer or buyer within seven days of the making of the agreement,

then, if each copy delivered or sent to the hirer or buyer as mentioned in paragraph (a) or paragraph (b) of this subsection complies with the requirements of any regulations made under section 32 of this Act, the delivery or sending of those copies shall be taken to have fulfilled the requirements of this section in relation to that agreement.

(4) In this and the next following section 'the relevant document' means the document which, on being signed by the hirer or buyer and by or on behalf of all other parties to the agreement, became the hire-purchase agreement, credit-sale agreement or conditional sale agreement, as the case may be.

9. (1) The requirements of this section, in relation to an agreement which is signed by the hirer or buyer at a place other than appropriate trade premises, are that copies are delivered or sent to the hirer or buyer in accordance with the following provisions of this section.

(2) A copy of the relevant document (in this Part of this Act referred to as 'the first statutory copy') must be delivered or sent to the hirer or buyer as follows, that is to say

(a) if the relevant document is presented, and not sent, to the hirer or buyer for his signature, a copy of that document, in the form in which it then is, must be delivered to him immediately after he signs it;

(b) if the relevant document is sent to the hirer or buyer for his signature, a copy of that document, in the form in which it then is, must be sent to him at the time when that document is sent.

(3) Within seven days of the making of the agreement, a copy of the agreement (in this Part of this Act referred to as 'the second statutory copy') must be sent by post to the hirer or buyer.

(4) The first statutory copy and the second statutory copy must each contain such a statement of the rights of the hirer or buyer under section 11 of this Act, and of matters relating to or consequential upon the exercise of those rights, as may be prescribed by regulations made by the Board of Trade; and that statement must be so contained in such position, and must comply with such other requirements (whether as to type, size, colour or disposition of lettering or otherwise) as may be so prescribed.

(5) Any statement which, in accordance with regulations made under the last preceding subsection, is contained either in the first statutory copy or in the second statutory copy must

specify the name of a person to whom, and an address to which, notice of cancellation may be sent; and (without prejudice to any other respect in which, in accordance with section 57(3) of this Act, the regulations may make different provision as between the first statutory copy and the second statutory copy, or as between copies delivered and copies sent) different names and addresses may be so specified in the first statutory copy and the second statutory copy of the same document.

(6) The first statutory copy and the second statutory copy must each comply with the requirements of any regulations made under section 32 of this Act.

10. (1) Subject to the following provisions of this section, if in any action the court is satisfied that a failure to comply with any of the requirements specified in sections 6 to 9 of this Act has not prejudiced the hirer or buyer, and that it would be just and equitable to dispense with the requirement, the court may, subject to any conditions that it thinks fit to impose, dispense with that requirement for the purposes of the action.

(2) The power conferred by the preceding subsection shall not be exercisable in relation to the requirement specified in section 9(3) of this Act except where the second statutory copy has been sent to the hirer or buyer but not within the period of seven days of the making of the agreement.

(3) The power conferred by subsection (1) of this section shall not be exercisable in relation to the requirement imposed by section 9(4) of this Act.

(4) For the avoidance of doubt it is hereby declared that in subsection (1) of this section the reference to the requirements specified in sections 6 to 9 of this Act includes the requirements of any regulations made under section 32 of this Act, in so far as any such requirements relate to hire-purchase agreements, credit-sale agreements and conditional sale agreements, or to copies delivered or sent as mentioned in section 8 or section 9 of this Act.

Right of cancellation

11. (1) The provisions of this section shall have effect where a person (in this section referred to as 'the prospective hirer or buyer') signs a document (in this section referred to as 'the relevant document') which

(a) constitutes a hire-purchase agreement, a credit-sale agreement or a conditional sale agreement, or

(b) would constitute such an agreement if executed by or on behalf of another person as owner or seller of the goods to which it relates,

and (in either case) the relevant document is signed by the prospective hirer or buyer at a place other than appropriate trade premises.

(2) At any time after he has signed the relevant document and before the end of the period of four days beginning with the day on which he receives the second statutory copy, the prospective hirer or buyer may serve a notice under this section (in this Act referred to as a 'notice of cancellation')

(a) on the owner or seller, or

(b) on any person who (whether by virtue of section 12(3) of this Act or otherwise) is the agent of the owner or seller for the purpose of receiving such a notice.

(3) A notice of cancellation served as mentioned in the last preceding subsection shall have effect if, however expressed, it indicates the intention of the prospective hirer or buyer to withdraw from the transaction to which the relevant document relates.

(4) Where the prospective hirer or buyer serves a notice of cancellation, then

(a) if, at the time when that notice is served, the relevant document constitutes a hire-purchase agreement, a credit-sale agreement or a conditional sale agreement, the service of the notice shall operate so as to rescind that agreement;

(b) in any other case, the service of the notice shall operate as a withdrawal of any offer to enter into such an agreement which is contained in, or implied by, the relevant document, and as notice to the owner or seller that any such offer is withdrawn.

(5) In this section 'owner or seller', in relation to the relevant document, means the person who, at the time when the document is signed by the prospective hirer or buyer, is specified in the document as the person who is to let the goods on hire to him or to sell the goods to him, as the case may be:

Provided that, if no person is so specified at that time, any person by whom, or on whose behalf, the document is executed at any subsequent time, and who is then specified in the document as the person letting or selling the goods, shall for the purposes of this section be deemed to be, and at all material times to have been, the owner or seller in relation to that document.

(6) In sections 12 to 15 of this Act 'the prospective hirer or buyer', 'the relevant document' and 'owner or seller' have the same meanings as in this section.

12. (1) For the purposes of section 11 of this Act a notice of cancellation

(a) shall be deemed to be served on the owner or seller if it is sent by post addressed to a person specified in a statement contained either in the first statutory copy or in the second statutory copy of the relevant document as being a person to whom such a notice may be sent, and is addressed to that person at an address so specified, and

(b) where the preceding paragraph applies, shall be deemed to be served on the owner or seller at the time when it is posted.

(2) The preceding subsection shall have effect without prejudice to the service of a notice of cancellation (whether by post or otherwise) in any way in which the notice could be served apart from that subsection, whether the notice is served on the owner or seller or on a person who (whether by virtue of the next following subsection or otherwise) is the agent of the owner or seller for the purpose of receiving such a notice.

(3) Any person who conducted any antecedent negotiations, but is not the owner or seller, shall be deemed to be the agent

of the owner or seller for the purpose of receiving any notice of cancellation served by the prospective hirer or buyer.

(4) A notice of cancellation which is sent by post to a person at his proper address, otherwise than in accordance with subsection (1) of this section, shall be deemed to be served on him at the time when it is posted.

(5) So much of section 26 of the Interpretation Act 1889 as relates to the time when service is deemed to have been effected shall not apply to a notice of cancellation.

13. (1) The provisions of this section shall have effect where a notice of cancellation is served, and at any time, whether before or after the service of that notice, any of the goods to which the relevant document relates are in the possession of the prospective hirer or buyer, having come into his possession in consequence, or in anticipation, of his signing that document.

(2) The prospective hirer or buyer shall not be under any obligation (whether arising by contract or otherwise) to deliver the goods except at his own premises and in pursuance of a request in writing signed by or on behalf of the person entitled to possession of the goods and served on the prospective hirer or buyer either before, or at the time when, the goods are collected from his premises; and any such obligation shall be subject to any lien, or other right to retain the goods, which he may have under section 14(2) or section 15(3) of this Act.

(3) If the prospective hirer or buyer

(a) delivers the goods (whether at his own premises or elsewhere) to an authorized person, or to a person designated for the purpose by an authorized person, or

(b) sends the goods at his own expense to an authorized person,

he shall be taken to have done so with the consent of that authorised person and (if that person is not for the time being entitled to possession of the goods) with the consent of the person who is so entitled, and shall be discharged from any obligation (whether arising by contract or otherwise) to retain the goods or to deliver them to any person so entitled.

(4) Subject to the following provisions of this section, the prospective hirer or buyer shall be under an obligation to take reasonable care of the goods until the end of the period of twenty-one days beginning with the date of service of the notice of cancellation.

(5) Where the prospective hirer or buyer delivers the goods as mentioned in paragraph (a) of subsection (3) of this section, his obligation to take care of the goods shall thereupon cease; and if he sends the goods to an authorized person as mentioned in paragraph (b) of that subsection, he shall be under an obligation to take reasonable care to see that they are received by that person and are not damaged in transit to him, but in other respects his obligation to take care of the goods shall cease on his sending the goods to that person.

(6) Where, at any time during the period of twenty-one days mentioned in subsection (4) of this section, the prospective hirer or buyer receives such a request as is mentioned in subsection (2) of this section, and unreasonably refused or unreasonably fails to comply with it, his obligation to take reasonable care of the goods shall continue until he delivers or sends the goods as mentioned in paragraph (a) or paragraph (b) of subsection (3) of this section.

(7) Any obligation under subsections (4) to (6) of this section shall be owed to the person for the time being entitled to possession of the goods, and any breach of that obligation shall be actionable, at the suit of that person, as a breach of statutory duty.

(8) Except as provided by subsections (4) to (7) of this section, the prospective hirer or buyer shall not be under any obligation (whether arising by contract or otherwise) to take care of the goods by reason of their having come into his possession as mentioned in subsection (1) of this section.

(9) In this section 'authorized person' means a person falling within any one or more of the following descriptions, that is to say

(a) the person who conducted any antecedent negotiations in pursuance of which the prospective hirer or buyer signed the relevant document;

(b) the person for the time being entitled to possession of the goods;

(c) the owner or seller;

(d) any person who is specified, as mentioned in section 12(1)(a) of this Act, as a person to whom a notice of cancellation may be sent,

and any reference to the premises of the prospective hirer or buyer is a reference to the premises which in the relevant document are specified as his address.

14. (1) Where a notice of cancellation operates so as to rescind a hire-purchase agreement, a credit-sale agreement or a conditional sale agreement,

(a) that agreement, and any contract of guarantee relating thereto, shall be deemed never to have had effect, and

(b) any security given by the prospective hirer or buyer in respect of money payable under the agreement, or given by a guarantor in respect of money payable under such a contract of guarantee, shall be deemed never to have been enforceable.

(2) On the service of a notice of cancellation, any sum which

(a) has been paid by the prospective hirer or buyer in respect of the goods to which the relevant document relates, whether it has been paid before the signature of the document or in pursuance of any provision contained in that document, and

(b) is comprised (or would, if the document constituted a hire-purchase agreement, a credit-sale agreement or a conditional sale agreement, be comprised) in the hire-purchase price or total purchase price or (if it is not or would not be so comprised) has in pursuance of any antecedent negotiations been paid to, or for the benefit of, the owner or seller, or has in pursuance of any such negotiations been paid to, or for the benefit of, any person (other than the owner or seller) who conducted those negotiations,

shall be recoverable by the prospective hirer or buyer from

the person to whom it has been paid; and, if the prospective hirer or buyer is in possession of those goods, he shall have a lien on them for any sum which he is entitled to recover by virtue of this subsection.

(3) Any obligation to pay any sum which, if it had been paid before the service of a notice of cancellation, would have been recoverable by the prospective hirer or buyer under the last preceding subsection, shall be extinguished on the service of such a notice.

(4) Any sum recoverable under subsection (2) of this section shall be recoverable as a simple contract debt in any court of competent jurisdiction.

15. (1) The provisions of this section shall have effect where a notice of cancellation is served, and, in pursuance of any antecedent negotiations conducted by him, a person (in this section referred to as 'the dealer') has agreed to take goods in part-exchange and those goods have been delivered to the dealer.

(2) Unless, before the end of the period of ten days beginning with the date of service of the notice of cancellation, the goods in question are delivered to the prospective hirer or buyer, and are then in a condition which is substantially as good as when they were delivered to the dealer, the prospective hirer or buyer shall be entitled to recover from the dealer a sum equal to the part-exchange allowance.

(3) During the period of ten days referred to in the last preceding subsection the prospective hirer or buyer, if he is in possession of the goods to which the relevant document relates, shall be entitled to retain possession of them until either

    (a) the goods agreed to be taken in part-exchange are delivered to him in such a condition as is mentioned in that subsection, or

    (b) a sum equal to the part-exchange allowance is paid to him;

and if, immediately before the end of that period, he continues by virtue of this subsection to be entitled to retain possession of the goods to which the relevant document relates, he shall have a lien on those goods for any sum which he is entitled to recover by virtue of the last preceding subsection.

(4) Any sum recoverable under subsection (2) of this section shall be recoverable as a simple contract debt in any court of competent jurisdiction.

(5) Where the prospective hirer or buyer recovers from the dealer a sum equal to the part-exchange allowance, then, if the title of the prospective hirer or buyer to the goods agreed to be taken in part-exchange has not vested in the dealer, that title shall so vest on the recovery of that sum.

(6) For the purposes of this section

(a) the dealer shall be taken to have agreed to take goods in part-exchange if, in pursuance of the antecedent negotiations, he has either purchased or agreed to purchase those goods or has accepted or agreed to accept them as part of the consideration for the transaction to which the relevant document relates, and

(b) the part-exchange allowance shall be taken to be the sum which, in the antecedent negotiations, was agreed to be allowed in respect of the goods referred to in the preceding paragraph, or, if no such sum was agreed, the part-exchange allowance shall be taken to be such sums as in all the circumstances it would have been reasonable to allow in respect of those goods if no notice of cancellation had been served.

Representations, conditions and warranties

16. (1) Where a person (in this section referred to as 'the owner or seller') lets goods under a hire-purchase agreement, or sells or agrees to sell goods under a credit-sale agreement or a conditional sale agreement, any representations with respect to the goods to which the agreement relates which were made, either orally or in writing, to the hirer or buyer by a person other than the owner or seller in the course of any antecedent negotiations conducted by that other person shall be deemed to have been made by him as agent of the owner or seller.

(2) Nothing in this section shall exonerate any person from any liability (whether criminal or civil) to which he would be subject apart from this section.

(3) Section 2(4) of this Act applies to this section.

(4) In this section 'representations' includes any statement or undertaking, whether constituting a condition or a warranty or not, and references to making representations shall be construed accordingly.

17. (1) In every hire-purchase agreement and in every conditional sale agreement there shall be implied

   (a) a condition on the part of the owner or seller that he will have a right to sell the goods at the time when the property is to pass;

   (b) a warranty that the hirer or buyer shall have and enjoy quiet possession of the goods;

   (c) a warranty that the goods shall be free from any charge or encumbrance in favour of any third party at the time when the property is to pass.

(2) Subject to the next following subsection, and to section 18 of this Act, in every hire-purchase agreement and in every conditional sale agreement there shall be implied a condition that the goods will be of merchantable quality.

(3) Where the hirer or buyer has examined the goods or a sample of them, the condition referred to in subsection (2) of this section shall not be implied by virtue of that subsection in respect of defects which the examination ought to have revealed.

(4) Where the hirer under a hire-purchase agreement, or the buyer under a conditional sale agreement, whether expressly or by implication

   (a) has made known to the owner or seller, or to a servant or agent of the owner or seller, the particular purpose for which the goods are required, or

   (b) in the course of any antecedent negotiations has made that purpose known to any other person by whom those negotiations were conducted, or to a servant or agent of such a person, there shall, subject to the provisions of section 18 of this Act, be implied a condition that the goods will be reasonably fit for that purpose.

(5) Nothing in this or the next following section shall prejudice the operation of any other enactment or rule of law whereby any condition or warranty is to be implied in any hire-purchase agreement or conditional sale agreement.

18. (1) Where under a hire-purchase agreement or a conditional sale agreement goods are let or agreed to be sold as second-hand goods, and

(a) the agreement contains a statement to that effect, and a provision that the condition referred to in section 17(2) of this Act is excluded in relation to those goods, and

(b) it is proved that before the agreement was made the provision in the agreement so excluding that condition was brought to the notice of the hirer or buyer and its effect made clear to him,

that condition shall not be implied in the agreement in relation to those goods.

(2) Where under a hire-purchase agreement or a conditional sale agreement goods are let or agreed to be sold as being subject to defects specified in the agreement (where referred to in the agreement as defects or by any other description to the like effect), and

(a) the agreement contains a provision that the condition referred to in section 17(2) of this Act is excluded in relation to those goods in respect of those defects, and

(b) it is proved that before the agreement was made those defects, and the provision in the agreement so excluding that condition, were brought to the notice of the hirer or buyer and the effect of that provision was made clear to him,

that condition shall not be implied in the agreement in respect of those defects.

(3) The condition and warranties specified in subsection (1) of section 17 of this Act, and, except as provided by subsection (3) of that section and by subsections (1) and (2) of this section, the condition specified in subsection (2) of that

section, shall be implied notwithstanding any agreement to the contrary.

(4) The owner or seller shall not be entitled to rely on any provision in a hire-purchase agreement or conditional sale agreement excluding or modifying the condition referred to in section 17(4) of this Act unless he proves that before the agreement was made that provision was brought to the notice of the hirer or buyer and its effect was made clear to him.

19. (1) Where goods are let under a hire-purchase agreement, or are agreed to be sold under a conditional sale agreement, and the goods are so let or agreed to be sold by reference to a sample, there shall be implied in the agreement.

  (a) a condition that the bulk will correspond with the sample in quality, and

  (b) a condition that the hirer or buyer will have a reasonable opportunity of comparing the bulk with the sample.

(2) Where goods are let under a hire-purchase agreement, or are agreed to be sold under a conditional sale agreement, and are so let or agreed to be sold by description, there shall be implied in the agreement a condition that the goods will correspond with the description; and if the goods are let or agreed to be sold under the agreement by reference to a sample, as well as by description, it shall not be sufficient that the bulk of the goods corresponds with the sample if the goods do not also correspond with the description.

20. (1) Section 11(1)(c) of the Sale of Goods Act 1893 (whereby in certain circumstances a breach of a condition in a contract of sale is to be treated only as a breach of warranty) shall not apply to conditional sale agreements.

(2) A breach of a condition (whether express or implied) to be fulfilled by the seller under a conditional sale agreement shall be treated as a breach of warranty, and not as grounds for rejecting the goods and treating the agreement as repudiated, if (but only if) it would have fallen to be so treated had the condition been contained or implied in a corresponding

hire-purchase agreement as a condition to be fulfilled by the owner.

(3) A conditional sale agreement shall be treated as not being a contract of sale for the purposes of sections 12 to 15 of the Sale of Goods Act 1893 (which imply certain conditions and warranties in contracts of sale).

(4) In this section 'corresponding hire-purchase agreement' means a hire-purchase agreement relating to the same goods as the conditional sale agreement and made between the same parties and at the same time and in the same circumstances and, as nearly as may be, in the same terms as the conditional sale agreement.

Duties to supply information and documents

21. (1) At any time before the final payment has been made under a hire-purchase agreement, a credit-sale agreement or a conditional sale agreement, any person entitled to enforce the agreement against the hirer or buyer shall, within four days after he has received a request in writing from the hirer or buyer, and the hirer or buyer has tendered to him the sum of [12½p] for expenses, supply to the hirer or buyer a copy of the agreement, together with a statement signed by that person or his agent showing

(a) the amount paid by or on behalf of the hirer or buyer;

(b) the amount which has become due under the agreement but remains unpaid, and the date on which each unpaid instalment became due, and the amount of each such instalment; and

(c) the amount which is to become payable under the agreement, and the date, or the mode of determining the date, on which each future instalment is to become payable, and the amount of each such instalment.

(2) In the event of a failure without reasonable cause to comply with the preceding subsection, then, while the default continues

(a) no person shall be entitled to enforce the agreement against the hirer or buyer or to enforce any contract of guarantee relating to the agreement, and, in the case of a hire-purchase agreement or a conditional sale agreement, the owner or seller shall not be entitled to enforce any right to recover the goods from the hirer or buyer, and

(b) no security given by the hirer or buyer in respect of money payable under the agreement, or given by a guarantor in respect of money payable under a contract of guarantee relating to the agreement, shall be enforceable against the hirer or buyer or the guarantor by any holder thereof, and, if the default continues for a period of one month, the person in default shall be liable on summary conviction to a fine not exceeding £25.

(3) If a copy supplied to a hirer or buyer in pursuance of a request made by him under this section does not comply with such requirements of any regulations made under section 32 of this Act as relate thereto, the last preceding subsection shall apply as if that copy had not been supplied to him.

(4) In relation to a credit-sale agreement under which the total purchase price does not exceed £30, subsection (1) of this section shall apply with the substitution, for the words 'a copy of the agreement', of the words, 'a copy of any note or memorandum of the agreement'.

(5) Section 2(4) of this Act applies to this section.

22. (1) A contract of guarantee relating to a hire-purchase agreement, a credit-sale agreement or a conditional sale agreement, and any security given by a guarantor in respect of money payable under such a contract, shall (subject to the following provisions of this section) not be enforceable unless, within seven days of the making of the contract of guarantee or the making of the hire-purchase agreement, credit-sale agreement or conditional sale agreement, whichever is the later, there is delivered or sent to the guarantor

(a) a copy of the hire-purchase agreement, credit-sale agreement or conditional sale agreement, and

(b) a copy of a note or memorandum of the contract of guarantee, being a note or memorandum signed by the guarantor or by a person authorized by him to sign it on his behalf.

(2) Subject to the next following subsection, such a contract of guarantee, and any such security, shall also not be enforceable unless

  (a) each copy delivered or sent as mentioned in the preceding subsection, and

  (b) the note or memorandum of the contract of guarantee, complies with the requirements of any regulations made under section 32 of this Act, in so far as any such requirements relate thereto.

(3) If in any action the court is satisfied that a failure to comply with any requirement imposed by subsection (1) of this section, or with any such requirement as is mentioned in the last preceding subsection, has not prejudiced the guarantor, and that it would be just and equitable to dispense with that requirement, the court may, subject to any conditions that it thinks fit to impose, dispense with that requirement for the purposes of the action.

23. (1) Where a contract of guarantee relating to a hire-purchase agreement, a credit-sale agreement or a conditional sale agreement is for the time being in force, and the final payment under that agreement has not been made, any person entitled to enforce the contract of guarantee against the guarantor shall, within four days after he has received a request in writing from the guarantor, and the guarantor has tendered to him the sum of [12½p] for expenses, supply to the guarantor the documents specified in the next following subsection.

(2) The documents referred to in the preceding subsection are

  (a) a copy of the hire-purchase agreement, credit-sale agreement or conditional sale agreement, or, in the case of a credit-sale agreement under which the total purchase price does not exceed £30, a copy of any note or memorandum of the agreement; and

  (b) a copy of a note or memorandum of the contract of guarantee; and

(c) a statement signed by, or by the agent of, the person to whom the request in writing referred to in the preceding subsection is made, showing the matters specified in paragraphs (a) to (c) of section 21(1) of this Act.

(3) In the event of a failure without reasonable cause to comply with subsection (1) of this section, then, while the default continues,

(a) no person shall be entitled to enforce the contract of guarantee against the guarantor, and

(b) no security given by the guarantor in respect of money payable under that contract shall be enforceable against the guarantor by any holder of that security, and, if the default continues for a period of one month, the person in default shall be liable on summary conviction to a fine not exceeding £25.

(4) If a copy supplied to a guarantor in pursuance of a request made by him under this section does not comply with such requirements of any regulations made under section 32 of this Act as relate thereto, the last preceding subsection shall apply as if that copy had not been supplied to him.

(5) Section 2(4) of this Act applies to this section.

24. (1) Where by virtue of a hire-purchase agreement or a conditional sale agreement a hirer or buyer is under a duty to keep the goods comprised in the agreement in his possession or control, the hirer or buyer shall, on receipt of a request in writing from the owner or seller, inform the owner or seller where the goods are at the time when the information is given, or, if it is sent by post, at the time of posting.

(2) If a hirer or buyer fails without reasonable cause to give that information within fourteen days of the receipt of the notice, he shall be liable on summary conviction to a fine not exceeding £25.

Notice of default

25. (1) The provisions of this section shall have effect where goods are let under a hire-purchase agreement, or are agreed to be sold under a conditional sale agreement, and that agreement, or any other agreement, contains a provision (however expressed, and whether limited to defaults in payment or not) whereby, apart from this section, on the occurrence of, or at a time to be ascertained by reference to, a default in the payment of one or more instalments or other sums payable by the hirer or buyer, such of the consequences mentioned in the next following subsection as are specified in that provision (in this section referred to as 'the specified consequences') would follow.

(2) The consequences referred to in the preceding subsection are that the hire-purchase agreement or conditional sale agreement, or (in the case of a hire-purchase agreement) the bailment of the goods, shall terminate, or shall be terminable, or that the owner or seller shall have a right to recover possession of the goods.

(3) If default is made in the payment of one or more sums to which that provision (in this subsection referred to as 'the relevant provision') applies, the specified consequences shall not follow by reason of that default unless the owner or seller serves on the hirer or buyer, by post or otherwise, a notice (in this Act referred to as a 'notice of default') stating the amount which has become due, but remains unpaid, in respect of sums to which the relevant provision applies, and requiring the amount so stated to be paid within such period (not being less than seven days beginning with the date of service of the notice) as may be specified in the notice.

(4) Where a notice of default is served, the specified consequences shall not follow before the end of the period specified in the notice by reason of any default to which the notice relates; and, if before the end of that period the amount specified in the notice is paid or tendered by or on behalf of the hirer or buyer or any guarantor, the specified consequences shall not follow thereafter by reason of any such default.

(5) In a case where the specified consequences are that the hire-purchase agreement or conditional sale agreement, or (in

the case of a hire-purchase agreement) the bailment of the goods, may be terminated by notice given by the owner or seller, a notice of default may include a notice terminating the hire-purchase agreement or conditional sale agreement, or the bailment, as the case may be, at or after the end of the period specified therein in accordance with subsection (3) of this section, subject to a condition that the termination is not to take effect if before the end of that period the amount specified in the notice of default is paid or tendered as mentioned in the last preceding subsection.

26. (1) Without prejudice to the service of a notice of default in any way in which such a notice could be served apart from this subsection, a notice of default shall be deemed to be served on the hirer under a hire-purchase agreement, or on the buyer under a conditional sale agreement, if

(a) it is addressed to the person last known to the owner or seller as the hirer or buyer under the agreement, and is delivered at, or sent by post to, the last known address of that person, or

(b) in a case where that person has died, the notice (if not served in accordance with the preceding paragraph) is addressed to that person's personal representative (whether by that or any similar description, and whether for the time being there is any personal representative of his or not) and is delivered at, or sent by post to, the address which was the last known address of the deceased person.

(2) Where the person who, immediately before his death, was the hirer under a hire-purchase agreement, or the buyer under a conditional sale agreement, has died, and his rights under the agreement have not yet passed to a personal representative

(a) section 9 of the Administration of Estates Act 1925 (vesting of estate of intestate between death and grant of administration) shall not be construed as enabling a notice of default to be served on the Probate Judge (as defined by that Act) as being the hirer or buyer under that agreement, and

(b) the last preceding section shall have effect as if the

deceased person had not died, and any reference in that section to default in the payment of a sum payable by the hirer or buyer shall be construed accordingly.

Right of hirer or buyer to terminate agreement

27. (1) At any time before the final payment under a hire-purchase agreement or conditional sale agreement falls due, the hirer or buyer shall (subject to the next following sub-section) be entitled to terminate the agreement by giving notice of termination in writing to any person entitled or authorised to receive the sums payable under the agreement.

(2) In the case of a conditional sale agreement, where the property in the goods, having become vested in the buyer, is transferred to a person who does not become the buyer under the agreement, the buyer shall not thereafter be entitled to terminate the agreement under this section.

(3) Subject to the last preceding subsection, where a buyer under a conditional sale agreement terminates the agreement under this section after the property in the goods has become vested in him, the property in the goods shall thereupon vest in the person (in this subsection referred to as 'the previous owner') in whom it was vested immediately before it became vested in the buyer:

Provided that if the previous owner has died, or any other event has occurred whereby that property, if vested in him immediately before that event, would thereupon have vested in some other person, the property shall be treated as having devolved as if it had been vested in the previous owner immediately before his death or immediately before that event, as the case may be.

(4) Nothing in this section shall prejudice any right of a hirer or buyer to terminate a hire-purchase agreement or conditional sale agreement otherwise than by virtue of this section.

28. (1) Where the hirer under a hire-purchase agreement, or the buyer under a conditional sale agreement, terminates the agreement by virtue of the last preceding section, then, subject to the following provisions of this section, and without prejudice to any liability which has accrued before the termination, he shall be liable.

(a) in the case of a hire-purchase agreement, to pay the amount (if any) by which one-half of the hire-purchase price exceeds the total of the sums paid and the sums due in respect of the hire-purchase price immediately before the termination, or

(b) in the case of a conditional sale agreement, to pay the amount (if any) by which one-half of the total purchase price exceeds the total of the sums paid and the sums due in respect of the total purchase price immediately before the termination, or if (in either case) the agreement specifies a lesser amount, he shall be liable to pay the amount so specified.

(2) If in any action the court is satisfied that a sum less than the amount specified in paragraph (a) or paragraph (b) of the preceding subsection (as the case may be) would be equal to the loss sustained by the owner or seller in consequence of the termination of the agreement by the hirer or buyer, the court may make an order for the payment of that sum in lieu of that amount.

(3) Where a hire-purchase agreement or conditional sale agreement has been terminated under the last preceding section, the hirer or buyer, if he has failed to take reasonable care of the goods, shall be liable to pay damages for the failure.

(4) Where a hirer or buyer, having terminated a hire-purchase agreement or conditional sale agreement under the last preceding section, wrongfully retains possession of the goods, then, in any action brought by the owner or seller to recover possession of the goods from the hirer or buyer, the court, unless it is satisfied that having regard to the circumstances it would not be just and equitable to do so, shall order the goods to be delivered to the owner or seller without giving the hirer or buyer an option to pay the value of the goods.

(5) The preceding provisions of this section shall have effect subject to the provisions of section 55 of this Act.

Avoidance of certain provisions and contracts

29. (1) Any provision to which this subsection applies shall be void.

(2) The preceding subsection applies to any provision in any agreement (whether a hire-purchase agreement, credit-sale agreement or conditional sale agreement or not)

(a) whereby an owner or seller, or any person acting on his behalf, is authorized to enter upon any premises for the purpose of taking possession of goods which have been let under a hire-purchase agreement or agreed to be sold under a conditional sale agreement, or is relieved from liability for any such entry, or

(b) whereby the right conferred by section 27 of this Act to terminate a hire-purchase agreement or a conditional sale agreement is excluded or restricted, or whereby any liability, in addition to the liability imposed by section 28 of this Act, is imposed on a hirer or buyer by reason of the termination of a hire-purchase agreement or conditional sale agreement under the said section 27, or

(c) whereby a hirer or buyer, after the termination in any manner whatsoever of a hire-purchase agreement or conditional sale agreement or (in the case of a hire-purchase agreement) of the bailment, is (apart from any liability which has accrued before the termination) subject to a liability to pay an amount which exceeds whichever is the lesser of the two following amounts, that is to say

(i) the amount mentioned in paragraph (a) or (as the case may be) in paragraph (b) of section 28(1) of this Act, and

(ii) an amount equal to the loss sustained by the owner or seller in consequence of the termination of the agreement or bailment, or

(d) whereby any person acting on behalf of an owner or seller in connection with the formation or conclusion of a hire-purchase agreement, credit-sale agreement or conditional sale agreement is treated as, or deemed to be, the agent of the hirer or buyer, or

(e) whereby an owner or seller is relieved from liability for the acts or defaults of any person acting on his behalf in connection with the formation or conclusion of a hire-purchase agreement, credit-sale agreement or conditional sale agreement.

(3) There shall also be void any provision in any agreement (whether a hire-purchase agreement, credit-sale agreement or conditional sale agreement or not)

(a) excluding or restricting the operation of any enactment contained in sections 11 to 15 of this Act or the exercise of any right conferred by such an enactment or imposing any liability in consequence of the exercise of such a right, other than or in addition to any liability imposed by such an enactment, or

(b) excluding or restricting the operation of any enactment contained in section 16 or section 31 of this Act, or

(c) excluding or modifying any condition implied by virtue of section 19 of this Act.

(4) Any contract, whether oral or in writing, which apart from this subsection would have effect as a contract to enter into a hire-purchase agreement, a credit-sale agreement or a conditional sale agreement (as distinct from a contract constituting such an agreement) shall be void.

(5) Section 2(4) of this Act applies to subsections (2) and (3) of this section.

30. (1) The provisions of subsection (2) or (as the case may be) subsection (3) of this section shall have effect where goods are let under a hire-purchase agreement, or are agreed to be sold under a conditional sale agreement, and that agreement, or any other agreement, provides that, on the occurrence of, or at a time to be ascertained by reference to, one or more events referred to in the provision in question.

(a) the hire-purchase agreement or conditional sale agreement, or (in the case of a hire-purchase agreement) the bailment of the goods, shall terminate, or shall be terminable, or the owner or seller shall have a right to recover possession of the goods to which the hire-purchase agreement or conditional sale agreement relates, or

(b) any sum shall become payable by the hirer or buyer or any guarantor, or any liability of the hirer or buyer or any guarantor shall be increased or accelerated, or

(c) any right of the hirer under the hire-purchase agreement or of the buyer under the conditional sale agreement shall cease to be exercisable, or shall be, or shall become liable to be, restricted or postponed.

(2) If the only event specified as mentioned in the preceding subsection is the death of the hirer or buyer, so much of the agreement as makes any such provision as is mentioned in that subsection shall be void.

(3) If two or more events are so specified, and one of them is the death of the hirer or buyer, so much of the agreement as makes any such provision shall have effect as if any reference to the death of the hirer or buyer were omitted.

(4) Without prejudice to the preceding provisions of this section, where

(a) goods are let under a hire-purchase agreement, or are agreed to be sold under a conditional sale agreement, and

(b) that agreement, or any other agreement, contains any provision (whether expressed as a provision that the hire-purchase agreement or conditional sale agreement shall be personal to the hirer or buyer or otherwise) which, if the hire-purchase agreement or conditional sale agreement is in force immediately before the death of the hirer or buyer, would apart from this subsection have the effect of terminating the last-mentioned agreement on the death of the hirer or buyer or otherwise preventing the benefit of that agreement from being transmitted on his death,

that provision shall be void in so far as it would have that effect.

Supplementary provisions

31. (1) Where a person has made an offer to enter into a hire-purchase agreement, a credit-sale agreement or a conditional sale agreement, in a case not falling within section 11(1) of this Act, and wishes to withdraw that offer before it is accepted, any person who conducted any antecedent negotiations shall be deemed to be the agent of any other person concerned for the purpose of receiving notice that the offer is withdrawn.

(2) Where the hirer or buyer under a hire-purchase agreement, a credit-sale agreement or a conditional sale agreement claims to have a right to rescind the agreement, any person who conducted any antecedent negotiations shall be deemed to be the agent of the owner or seller for the purpose of receiving any notice rescinding the agreement which is served by the hirer or buyer.

(3) In subsection (1) of this section 'other person concerned', in relation to an offer, means any person who would be in a position to accept the offer if it were not withdrawn; and in the last preceding subsection 'rescind' does not include

    (a) the service of a notice of cancellation, or

    (b) the termination of an agreement under section 27 of this Act, or by the exercise of a right or power in that behalf expressly conferred by the agreement.

(4) The preceding provisions of this section shall have effect without prejudice to the operation of section 12(3) of this Act.

(5) Section 2(4) of this Act applies to this section.

32. (1) The Board of Trade may make regulations prescribing such requirements (whether as to type, size, colour or disposition of lettering, quality or colour of paper, or otherwise) as the Board may consider appropriate for securing that documents to which this section applies are easily legible.

(2) Subject to the next following subsection, the documents to which this section applies are documents of any of the following descriptions, that is to say

    (a) any hire-purchase agreement, credit-sale agreement or conditional sale agreement;

    (b) any such copy as is mentioned in subsection (2) or subsection (3) of section 8 or in subsection (2) or subsection (3) of section 9 of this Act;

    (c) any copy supplied to a hirer or buyer in pursuance of a request made by him under section 21 of this Act;

(d) any note or memorandum of a contract of guarantee relating to a hire-purchase agreement, credit-sale agreement or conditional sale agreement, and any such copy as is mentioned in paragraph (a) or paragraph (b) of section 22(1) of this Act;

(e) any such copy as is mentioned in paragraph (a) or paragraph (b) of subsection (2) of section 23 of this Act which is supplied to a guarantor in pursuance of a request made by him under subsection (1) of that section.

(3) Without prejudice to the operation of section 57(3) of this Act in relation to any regulations made under this section, any such regulations

(a) may specify which parts of the contents of a document to which the regulations apply are permitted to consist of handwriting or a reproduction of handwriting, and may prescribe different requirements in relation to so much of the contents of such a document as is permitted to consist, and consists, of handwriting or a reproduction of handwriting and in relation to the remainder of the contents of such a document; and

(b) may except from any of the requirements of the regulations any marginal notes or other subsidiary parts of a document.

(4) In relation to so much of any document falling within paragraph (a) or paragraph (b) of subsection (2) of this section as consists of

(a) words or other matters prescribed by regulations made under section 7(2) of this Act, or

(b) a statement required to be contained therein as prescribed by regulations made under section 9(4) of this Act, any regulations made under this section shall have effect subject to the provisions of the regulations referred to in paragraph (a) or paragraph (b) of this subsection, as the case may be.

Part III. Recovery of possession and other remedies
Protected goods

33. (1) For the purposes of this Part of this Act goods are 'protected goods' if for the time being the following conditions are fulfilled, that is to say

(a) that the goods have been let under a hire-purchase agreement, or agreed to be sold under a conditional sale agreement;

(b) that one-third of the hire-purchase price or total purchase price has been paid (whether in pursuance of a judgment or otherwise) or tendered by or on behalf of the hirer or buyer or a guarantor; and

(c) that the hirer or buyer has not terminated the hire-purchase agreement or conditional sale agreement, or (in the case of a hire-purchase agreement) the bailment, by virtue of any right vested in him.

(2) In this Part of this Act 'the agreement', in relation to any protected goods, means the hire-purchase agreement or conditional sale agreement in respect of which those conditions are fulfilled.

34. (1) The owner (where the agreement is a hire-purchase agreement) or the seller (where it is a conditional sale agreement) shall not enforce any right to recover possession of protected goods from the hirer or buyer otherwise than by action.

(2) If the owner or seller recovers possession of protected goods in contravention of the preceding subsection, the agreement, if not previously terminated, shall terminate, and

(a) the hirer or buyer shall be released from all liability under the agreement, and shall be entitled to recover from the owner or seller, in an action for money had and received, all sums paid by the hirer or buyer under the agreement or under the security given by him in respect thereof, and

(b) any guarantor shall be entitled to recover from the owner or seller, in an action for money had and received, all sums paid by him under the contract of guarantee or under any security given by him in respect thereof.

47. (1) The provisions of this section shall have effect where

(a) goods have been let under a hire-purchase agreement, and, at any time after one-third of the hire-purchase price has been paid or tendered, the owner makes a further hire-purchase agreement with the hirer, or, as seller, makes a conditional sale agreement with the hirer as buyer, or

(b) goods have been agreed to be sold under a conditional sale agreement, and, at any time after one-third of the total purchase price has been paid or tendered, the seller makes a further conditional sale agreement with the buyer, or, as owner, makes a hire-purchase agreement with the buyer as hirer,

and (in either case) the subsequent agreement relates to the whole or any part of those goods, with or without other goods.

(2) In any case falling within the preceding subsection, section 33 of this Act shall have effect in relation to the subsequent agreement as if paragraph (b) of subsection (1) of that section were omitted.

54. For the purposes of section 9 of the Factors Act 1889 and of section 25(2) of the Sale of Goods Act 1893 (under which, notwithstanding that the property in the goods has not been transferred to him, a person who has bought or agreed to buy goods and is in possession of them can confer a good title to the goods) the buyer under a conditional sale agreement shall be deemed not to be a person who has bought or agreed to buy goods.

55. (1) Where under a hire-purchase agreement or a conditional sale agreement the owner or seller is required to carry out any installation, and the agreement specifies, as part of the hire-purchase price or total purchase price, the amount to be paid in respect of the installation (in this section referred to as 'the installation charge')

(a) any reference in section 28(1) of this Act to one-half of the hire-purchase price or one-half of the total purchase price shall be construed as a reference to the aggregate of the installation charge and one-half of the remainder of the hire-purchase price or total purchase price, as the case may be, and

(b) any reference in Part III of this Act to one-third of the hire-purchase price or one-third of the total purchase price shall be construed as a reference to the aggregate of the installation charge and one-third of the remainder of the hire-purchase price or total purchase price as the case may be.

(2) In this section 'installation' means

(a) the installing of any electric line (as defined by the Electric Lighting Act 1882) or any gas or water pipe;

(b) the fixing of goods to which the agreement relates to the premises where they are to be used, and the alteration of premises to enable any such goods to be used on them; and

(c) where it is reasonably necessary that any such goods should be constructed or erected on the premises where they are to be used, any work carried out for the purpose of constructing or erecting them on those premises.

Part V. Supplementary provisions

57. (1) Any power of the Board of Trade to make regulations under this Act shall be exercisable by statutory instrument.

(2) Anything required or authorized by or under this Act to be done by, to or before the Board of Trade may be done by, to or before the President of the Board, any Minister of State with duties concerning the affairs of the Board, any secretary, under-secretary or assistant secretary of the Board or any person authorized in that behalf by the President.

(3) Where a power to make regulations is exercisable by virtue of this Act, regulations made in the exercise of that power may make different provision in relation to different classes of cases.

(4) Any power (exercisable in accordance with section 61(2) of this Act) to make regulations under this Act before the date of the commencement of this Act shall include power,

by any regulations so made, to revoke any regulations made under any of the enactments which, as from that date, are repealed by this Act.

58. (1) In this Act, except in so far as the context otherwise requires, the following expressions have the meaning hereby assigned to them respectively, that is to say

'action', 'buyer' (except in relation to a conditional sale agreement), 'delivery', 'goods', 'property', 'sale', 'seller' (except in relation to a conditional sale agreement) and 'warranty' have the meanings assigned to them respectively by the Sale of Goods Act 1893;

'appropriate trade premises', in relation to a document means premises at which either the owner or seller (as defined by section 11(5) of this Act) normally carries on a business, or goods of the description to which the document relates, or goods of a similar description, are normally offered or exposed for sale in the course of a business carried on at those premises; 'buyer', in relation to a conditional sale agreement, means the person who agrees to purchase goods under the agreement and includes a person to whom the rights or liabilities of that person under the agreement have passed by assignment or by operation of law;

'conditional sale agreement', 'credit-sale agreement' and 'hire-purchase agreement' have the meanings assigned to them by Part I of this Act;

'contract of guarantee', in relation to a hire-purchase agreement, credit-sale agreement or conditional sale agreement, means a contract, made at the request (express or implied) of the hirer or buyer, either to guarantee the performance of the hirer's or buyer's obligations under the hire-purchase agreement, credit-sale agreement or conditional sale agreement, or to indemnify the owner or seller against any loss which he may incur in respect of that agreement, and 'guarantor' shall be construed accordingly;

'hire-purchase price' (subject to subsection (2) of this section) means the total sum payable by the hirer under a hire-purchase agreement in order to complete the purchase of goods to which the agreement relates, exclusive of any sum payable as a penalty or as compensation or damages for a breach of the agreement;

'hirer' means the person who takes or has taken goods from an owner under a hire-purchase agreement and includes a person to whom the hirer's rights or liabilities under the agreement have passed by assignment or by operation of law;

'notice of cancellation' has the meaning assigned to it by section 11(2) of this Act;

'owner' means the person who lets or has let goods to a hirer under a hire-purchase agreement and includes a person to whom the owner's property in the goods or any of the owner's rights or liabilities under the agreement has passed by assignment or by operation of law;

'seller', in relation to a conditional sale agreement, means the person who agrees to sell goods under the agreement and includes a person (other than the buyer) to whom that person's property in the goods or any of that person's rights or liabilities under the agreement has passed by assignment or by operation of law;

'total purchase price' (subject to subsection (2) of this section) means the total sum payable by the buyer under a credit-sale agreement or a conditional sale agreement, exclusive of any sum payable as a penalty or as compensation or damages for a breach of the agreement.

(2) For the purposes of this Act, any sum payable by the hirer under a hire-purchase agreement, or by the buyer under a conditional sale agreement, by way of a deposit or other initial payment, or credited or to be credited to him under the agreement on account of any such deposit or payment, whether that sum is to be or has been paid to the owner or seller or to any other person or is to be or has been discharged by a payment of money or by the transfer or delivery of goods or by any other means, shall form part of the hire-purchase price or total purchase price, as the case may be.

(3) In this Act 'antecedent negotiations', in relation to a hire-purchase agreement, credit-sale agreement or conditional sale agreement, means any negotiations or arrangements with the hirer or buyer whereby he was induced to make the agreement or which otherwise promoted the transaction to which the agreement relates; and any reference in this Act to the person by whom any antecedent negotiations were conducted is a reference to the person by whom the negotiations or arrangements in question were conducted or made in the course of a business carried on by him.

(4) The last preceding subsection

(a) shall have effect in relation to a document to which section 11 of this Act applies, but which does not constitute a hire-purchase agreement, a credit-sale agreement or a conditional sale agreement, as if reference to the agreement and to making the agreement were references respectively to the document and to signing the document and any reference to the hirer or buyer were a reference to the prospective hirer or buyer (within the meaning of that section), and

(b) for the purposes of section 31(1) of this Act, shall have effect in relation to any offer to enter into a hire-purchase agreement, credit-sale agreement or conditional sale agreement as if any reference to the agreement were a reference to the offer and any reference to the hirer or buyer were a reference to the person making the offer.

(5) For the purposes of this Act any negotiations conducted, or arrangements or representations made, by a servant or agent, if conducted or made by him in the course of his employment or agency, shall be treated as conducted or made by his employer or principal; and anything received by a servant or agent, if received by him in the course of his employment or agency, shall be treated as received by his employer or principal.

In this subsection 'representations' has the same meaning as in section 16 of this Act, and references to making representations shall be construed accordingly.

(6) Without prejudice to the operation of section 1(2) of this

Act, any reference in this Act to a document which constitutes a hire-purchase agreement, credit-sale agreement or conditional sale agreement shall be construed as including a reference to a document which together with one or more other documents constitutes such an agreement, and any reference to a document which, if executed by or on behalf of another person, would constitute such an agreement shall be construed accordingly.

(7) Except in so far as the context otherwise requires, any reference in this Act to an enactment shall be construed as a reference to that enactment as amended or extended by or under any other enactment, including this Act.

Schedule 1
Notice to be included in Hire-Purchase Agreement Notice
Right of hirer to terminate agreement

1. The hirer may put an end to this agreement by giving notice of termination in writing to any person who is entitled to collect or receive the hire-rent.

2. He must then pay any instalments which are in arrear at the time when he gives notice. If, when he has paid those instalments, the total amount which he has paid under the agreement is less than (*here insert the minimum amount which the hirer is required to pay in accordance with the provisions of sections* 28 (1) *and* 55 *of this Act*) he must also pay enough to make up that sum, unless the court determines that a smaller sum would be equal to the owner's loss.

3. If the goods have been damaged owing to the hirer having failed to take reasonable care of them, the owner may sue him for the amount of the damage unless that amount can be agreed between the hirer and the owner.

4. The hirer should see whether this agreement contains provisions allowing him to put an end to the agreement on terms more favourable to him than those just mentioned. If it does, he may put an end to the agreement on those terms.

Restriction of owner's right to recover goods

5. **[After (*here insert an amount calculated in accordance with the provisions of sections 33 and 55 of this Act*) has been paid, then,]* unless the hirer has himself put an end to the agreement, the owner of the goods cannot take them back from the hirer without the hirer's consent unless the owner obtains an order of the court.

6. If the owner applies to the court for such an order, the court may, if the court thinks it just to do so, allow the hirer to keep either –

(a) the whole of the goods, on condition that the hirer pays the balance of the price in the manner ordered by the court; or

(b) a fair proportion of the goods having regard to what the hirer has already paid.

Schedule 2
Notice to be included in Conditional Sale Agreement Notice
Right of buyer to terminate agreement

1. The buyer may put an end to this agreement by giving notice of termination in writing to any person who is entitled to collect or receive the instalments of the purchase price.

2. He must then pay any instalments which are in arrear at the time when he gives notice. If, when he has paid those instalments, the total amount which he has paid under the agreement is less than (*here insert the minimum amount which the buyer is required to pay in accordance with the provisions of sections 28(1) and 55 of this Act*) he must also pay enough to make up that sum, unless the court determines that a smaller sum would be equal to the seller's loss.

3. If the goods have been damaged owing to the buyer having failed to take reasonable care of them, the seller may sue

* If the agreement is a subsequent agreement to which section 47 of this Act applies, the words in square brackets should be omitted.

him for the amount of the damage unless that amount can be agreed between the buyer and the seller.

4. The buyer should see whether this agreement contains provisions allowing him to put an end to the agreement on terms more favourable to him than those just mentioned. If it does, he may put an end to the agreement on those terms.

Restriction of seller's right to recover goods

5. *[After (*here insert an amount calculated in accordance with the provisions of sections 33 and 55 of this Act*) has been paid, then,] unless the buyer has himself put an end to the agreement, the seller of the goods cannot take them back from the buyer without the buyer's consent unless the seller obtains an order of the court.

6. If the seller applies to the court for such an order, the court may, if the court thinks it just to do so, allow the buyer to keep either

(a) the whole of the goods, on condition that the buyer pays the balance of the price in the manner ordered by the court; or

(b) a fair proportion of the goods having regard to what the buyer has already paid.

* If the agreement is a subsequent agreement to which section 47 of this Act applies, the words in square brackets should be omitted.

Table of Cases

Table of Statutes

Sections quoted in Appendix 2 are indicated by an asterisk

Index